SECOND EDITION

LEADERSHIP
for
RESILIENT SCHOOLS
and
COMMUNITIES

We would like to dedicate this book to our family members, who have helped us to be resilient with their love and care—Angella, Chris, Dave, John, Kelly Nicole, Kurt, Robin, Tema, and Terrae.

SECOND EDITION

LEADERSHIP
for
RESILIENT SCHOOLS
and
COMMUNITIES

MIKE M. MILSTEIN
DORIS ANNIE HENRY
Foreword by Richard A. Schmuck

CORWIN PRESS
A SAGE Company
Thousand Oaks, CA 91320

For information:

Corwin Press
A SAGE Company
2455 Teller Road
Thousand Oaks, California 91320
www.corwinpress.com

SAGE India Pvt. Ltd.
B 1/I 1 Mohan Cooperative
   Industrial Area
Mathura Road, New Delhi 110 044
India

SAGE Ltd.
1 Oliver's Yard
55 City Road
London, EC1Y 1SP
United Kingdom

SAGE Asia-Pacific Pte. Ltd.
33 Pekin Street #02-01
Far East Square
Singapore 048763

Printed in the United States of America

Library of Congress Cataloging-in-Publication Data

Milstein, Mike M.
Leadership for resilient schools and communities / Mike M. Milstein,
Doris Annie Henry. — 2nd ed.
    p. cm.
Rev. ed. of: Spreading resiliency.
Includes bibliographical references and index.
ISBN 978-1-4129-5593-5 (cloth)
ISBN 978-1-4129-5594-2 (pbk.)
    1. Community and school—United States. 2. Educational
leadership—United States. 3. Educational change—United States. I.
Henry, Doris Annie. II. Milstein, Mike M. Spreading resiliency. III.
Title.

LC221.M554 2008
370.15'8—dc22

2007040307

This book is printed on acid-free paper.

08 09 10 11 12 10 9 8 7 6 5 4 3 2 1

Acquisition Editor:	Elizabeth Brenkus
Managing Editor:	Arnis Burvikovs
Editorial Assistants:	Ena Rosen, Desireé Enayati
Production:	Appingo Publishing Services
Cover Designer:	Michael Dubowe
Graphic Designer:	Karine Hovsepian

Contents

Tables and Figures

Foreword

As I read and considered Mike and Annie's richly practical workbook on making resiliency happen I was reminded of long discussions that Mike and I had forty years ago when Phil Runkel and I were training the Highland Park Junior-High faculty to specify and solve its own educational problems. Mike and I wondered, then, if Phil's and my organization-development design and methods in suburban Beaverton, Oregon, could be spread to the much more urban schools in Buffalo, New York. The complicated answer, considerably simplified, was *yes*. Now, two generations later, the simple answer *yes* can be given to the question of whether resiliency concepts and resources can be disseminated from Albuquerque, New Mexico, to Ashland, Oregon, to down under in Nelson, New Zealand. But, let me present a bit of intellectual history first.

Throughout my long professional career as an applied Lewinean social psychologist (Kurt Lewin, University of Iowa, mentored Ron Lippitt, University of Michigan, who mentored me), I learned and taught that one's nagging frustrations must be converted into clearly defined problems for constructive change to occur. I used the word *problem* to mean a discrepancy between a current state of affairs and a more preferred state of affairs, sufficiently more preferred that one is ready and willing to spend energy to get there. I professed, as Lewin and Lippitt did with different language before me, that without the two parts, the current situation and the more desirable target, a problem has not been pinpointed.

Although irritation, anger, confusion, and tension frequently are features of frustration and therefore part of the situation, they are not in themselves problems. An early step in problem solving, therefore, must be to ascertain with some precision the images that the people concerned have of their situation and target. In other words, a frustration is turned into a problem once a target state can be imagined that satisfies one's values more than does the present state.

In applying that sort of thinking to planned improvement in schools, Phil Runkel and I argued that the proper starting point for school change is the students', educators', and parents' own educational problems as they view them, not those problems that may be conceived by outsiders. Constructive and successful action, we thought, can spring only from the reality perceived by the participants in the specific school themselves, who also would be carrying forward the change process. Thus, present constructive action can start only from the participants' present images of their reality. We saw it as essential that the school participants' own frustrations serve as the launching pads for the specification, analysis, and solving of their problems.

Moreover, along with the participants' awareness of a discrepancy between situation and target, "having a problem," we argued, also meant optimistically contemplating change and together taking action. In other words, school participants with a problem specified are energized to move collaboratively from the current situation to a more satisfying target. Thus, Phil and I taught that a problem has three basic aspects: the present situation, the more valued target, and the paths or proposals that might be planfully taken to reduce the discrepancy between situation and target. That problem-solving paradigm we labeled, STP.

Unfortunately, any of the three aspects may be unclear when the school participants first experience frustration. A problem begins to take shape and become clear when the school participants collaboratively conceptualize situations and targets and explain to one another their images of them. Indeed, school participants often do become energized when they can conceive alternative proposals to bring the situation closer to the target. A school's achieving clarity about the three aspects of problem solving, we argued, is necessary for effective action and for true school improvement to occur.

Part of the reason, I think, that Mike and Annie's concepts and resources on resiliency will continue to disseminate internationally resides in their implicit adaptation of the STP paradigm in organizing their invigorating book. With clear, straightforward, no-nonsense prose, not only have they been guided by STP thinking, but they have contributed well beyond it by deftly pinpointing positive targets of contemporary importance and by creating practical proposals or paths for moving beyond the situation of low resiliency.

Mike and Annie start their workbook by defining, as highly desirable targets for everyone, the basic concepts of resiliency. Their Part I is appropriately titled, "Basic Concepts." In Chapter 1, they warn readers about the pitfalls of approaching problems by dwelling on deficits, deficiencies, and pathologies. Instead of thinking pessimistically, Mike and Annie propose that we accentuate the positive targets of resiliency: prosocial bonding, clear and consistent boundaries, life skills, caring and support, high expectations, and meaningful participation. With an attitude of optimism, they show readers how to apply each sub-target of resiliency to themselves. Mike and Annie go on in Chapter 2 to elaborate on what resilient communities are like nowadays, how to visualize resilient communities precisely, and why schools can serve as strategic cultures for building and spreading community resiliency. Part I, thus, defines the primary targets of micro- and macro-resiliency.

Part II accentuates the highly practical nature of this guide to planned change. Here, Mike and Annie offer concrete proposals for promoting resiliency in students (Chapter 3), educators (Chapter 4), school cultures (Chapter 5), and communities (Chapter 6). In each of those four chapters, they present creative exercises and useful strategies for enhancing resiliency. Part III gathers all ingredients of the foregoing six chapters by proposing an overarching meta-strategy for administering and measuring the change process (Chapter 7) and by offering illuminating case studies of actual community resiliency projects (Chapter 8).

With this achievement of a book, Mike and Annie offer, both, a clear rationale for advocating resiliency as a target and a practical guide for acting to progress on the path toward resiliency. In a way this important book has been forty years in gestation; the answer to our shared dissemination question way back then applied to today is a resounding *yes*.

—Richard A. Schmuck
Professor Emeritus
University of Oregon and Visiting Professor
Arizona State University

Foreword to First Edition

Someone recently sent me a quote that reminded me, "A man of character finds a special attractiveness in difficulty, since it is only by coming to grips with difficulty that he can realize his potentials." I have no idea who said that, but I know the author understood the core of what resiliency is and should be. *Merriam Webster's Collegiate Dictionary* (2003) tells us that resilience is "the ability to recover from or adjust easily to misfortune or change." Since we live in a world of constant change and too much misfortune, the need for teaching resilience makes it as basic as the other R's in education. Education is, after all centered on helping children reach their potential and learning how to overcome difficulty.

It has always interested me why some people bend while others break. I suppose I am interested because, like many others, my own story is one of resilience. My academic career marked my movement from being a nonreader, to slow learner, to underachiever, to honor student. I have always credited my progress to the support of parents and teachers and to an incredibly strong streak of stubbornness, which has served me well. Understanding why I am stubborn and resist failure at this point in my life becomes a moot question. To put a twist on the old philosophic statement, "I am stubborn, therefore I am successful."

The exercise of will throughout my life has allowed me to forge through the unknown, to stand strong in the winds of change and to exhibit a sense of self-worth even when external circumstances would question my self-confidence. Yet will, by itself, can merely be aggravating to others or even self-destructive. It has to be balanced by flexibility. I once called this paradox "confident humility." Confident humility is the ability to believe in yourself while leaving room for the possibility that someone else has a better idea. I think the sense of balance implied by this paradox is a key to unlocking our understanding of resiliency. The healthiest place is between the extremes. If you lean too far in one direction, it is easy to be pushed over. A sense of balance allows you to recover and to adjust.

How can schools build the strong, healthy ego implied by that sense of balance? In the wake of the Columbine tragedy, that question becomes even more pertinent and powerful. How can we help our children grow up unscarred and unscathed in a changing and disconnected world where images of violence permeate? How can we give children a sense of purpose, a sense of confidence, and a sense of balance when everything around them seems to question purpose, to destroy confidence, and to knock them down before they even get started?

The power of teaching resilience is the power of giving children the strength to handle change and to recover easily from misfortune. Sadly, for many of our children, misfortune is a way of life. How can we, as adults, prepare students for what they need to be resilient people? That is what this book is all about.

Hillary Rodham Clinton wrote a book a few years ago and took the title from an African proverb: "It takes a village to raise a child." This recognizes that the creation of resilient children is not something that is done only in a home or in isolation. It requires a team. Sadly, in today's world we must ask, if it takes a village to raise a child, what does it take to raise a village? Far too many of our children are growing up in a world where there is no village—no safety net of support to catch them when they fall. They are growing up isolated and emotionally neglected. Their emotional care and feeding is being left up to the schools. And far too often, the schools are not up to it. Schools cannot be parent, friend, mentor, guide, doctor, nurse, social worker, and minister. The task is too overwhelming. It does take the village.

A national movement is needed to bind school, family, and community together. The movement toward "schools of promise," which grew out of the America's Promise initiative led by General Colin Powell, is one way of connecting schools to communities. The initiative is rooted in the reality that schools exist at the physical and psychological centers of what can become the village. By helping schools reach out to the community, and the community to reach in to the schools, we can begin building villages around our children.

This effort must be done with a sense of respect and mutuality. There is another proverb—less well known but just as appropriate. It reminds us that "when elephants fight, the grass gets trampled." When adults fight, children suffer. Resilience in children starts with adults acting responsibly and respectfully toward each other. Resiliency does not just happen; it is created by caring adults. If we expect children to show respect, they must be shown respect, and they must witness it in the adults they observe. That, too, is what this book is about.

Researchers at the University of Minnesota have recently established that a strong connection to schools reduces the risk-taking behaviors that lead to failure. School connection also enhances those behaviors that lead to success. This provides clues to what we must do to create resilient young people. We must find ways to get them connected to school. Caring adults must create a web of support around children for them to grow with a sense of efficacy, which becomes the foundation for resilient behavior. Schools are there to elevate a child's chances for success. The key is the child's ability to stay balanced and to adjust to life's challenges. This can be taught.

Mike Milstein and Annie Henry have given us a blueprint to create schools and communities that will spread resiliency in young people. The book is a guide for making schools and communities healthier places, and it shows how to create an environment that will produce healthier adults and children. Much has been written lately about the school reform movement. I think the movement breaks down because it is, at its core, mechanistic. Even the language of reform uses mechanistic phrases, with much talk of "fixing" and "leveraging." Schools and their communities are essentially organic. They cannot be broken into parts; they must be treated systemically. They do not need fixing, they need healing. This is what the authors contend, and the bulk of the book is about how this can be done. It is not merely a call to action, but a primer for making it happen.

Spreading Resiliency: Making It Happen for Schools and Communities can help school and community leaders create caring places where families and children can move from coping to thriving. Rubber bands are resilient. But their resiliency is more than just snapping back into place once they are pulled. They store and release kinetic energy. As any teacher knows, rubber bands are good at propelling small objects. If we are to give our children the gift of success, we must find ways of helping them prosper in an uncertain, and too often unfriendly, environment. We want children to snap back, to recover, and to adjust. We also want them to move forward, to propel themselves with the confident humility that will lead to their success. Through their success, we want them to blaze a trail for all of us. Ultimately, this is what the book is about.

—Paul D. Houston
Executive Director for the American Association of School Administrators

Preface

"I am because we are" (a saying of the Xhosa people, South Africa).

The second edition of *Spreading Resiliency* is dedicated to helping readers respond to school and community problems in ways that promote the well-being of all community members, regardless of age, ethnicity, or socioeconomic status. We believe that it is urgent to focus attention and energy on this purpose. In fact, many community development initiatives being conducted around the world are focusing on this purpose. These efforts, some of which are described within the book, provide assurance that there is growing awareness of the need to come to grips with issues and develop responses that can improve the health of our schools and communities.

> The only thing we have to fear is fear itself.
>
> —*Franklin Delano Roosevelt*

There are no pat answers when it comes to responding to the complex and significant challenges that confront those who are ready and dedicated to improving the wellness of their schools and communities. But there is enough evidence from efforts currently being conducted to show that schools and communities, working together, *can* begin to shift the emphasis from pathology and fatalism to wellness and support *for everyone*. What is needed is recognition that, with belief, will, and effort, we *can* make a positive difference in the well-being and effectiveness of our schools and communities. Where there is widespread concern and understanding and where there is vision that like-minded people share, anything is possible.

Leading Resilient Schools and Communities is intended to be of help to anyone who is concerned about the well-being of schools and communities. This includes teachers, administrators, counselors, and other educators; parents and other community members; as well as leaders of voluntary organizations, higher education institutions, businesses, organizations, and local government agencies. It is presented in workbook style so readers can use it to serve their particular needs and interests. Because every school-community situation is unique, our responses must also be unique.

One thing is certain: moving schools and communities toward resiliency, or better states of wellness and effectiveness, requires that everyone's involvement needs to be encouraged! In fact, involvement is the key to the process. As the ancient Chinese proverb reminds us,

I hear and I forget.
I see and I remember.
I do and I understand.

Organization of the Book

Leadership for Resilient Schools and Communities is intended to help everyone become more resilient, but it is not enough to say to individuals, "Learn to be tougher, be more capable, cope better," if the environments in which they exist deplete their resiliency capabilities. For this reason, *Leadership for Resilient Schools and Communities* is dedicated to helping you learn how to modify environments—classrooms, schools, and communities—in ways that move away from resiliency depletion and toward resiliency building.

> All our knowledge has its origins in our perceptions.
>
> —*Leonardo da Vinci*

In the process, you will be challenged to examine your biases, perceptions, attitudes, and beliefs, all of which directly affect how you see your environment and how you react to it. During the process, you may find it demanding to reconceptualize how you view your school and community, but we think you will find it to be worthwhile.

Leadership for Resilient Schools and Communities is organized in three parts. Part I, which includes the first two chapters, explores the meaning of resiliency and why it is so important for school and community well-being. Chapter 1 presents basic information about resiliency and provides necessary definitions and language systems that will be used throughout the book. Chapter 2 explores the concept of community, which is illusive, partly because of our tendency to frequently and widely move about and partly because of the rapidly changing demographic composition in many of our communities. We believe that the meaning of community may be undergoing a significant change. Physical proximity is becoming less relevant as the defining basis for community. In fact, community can be defined as an attitude as well as a location.

> Change your thoughts and you change your world.
>
> —*Norman Vincent Peale*

Part II, which includes four chapters, focuses on strategies that promote resiliency for students, educators, schools, and communities. Chapter 3 centers on students, their strengths, and their needs and on how schools can help build their resiliency capacities. We emphasize how schools tend to limit their role in building student resiliency and what they can do to change this situation. Chapter 4 examines the resiliency of educators, their capabilities and difficulties, and how the schools' environments in which they work affect them. Ways that schools can help educators enhance their own resiliency, and, in the process, help them to be better role models for their students are examined. Chapter 5 explores how schools and their leaders can support or detract from the resiliency needs of students, educators, and community members. With some forethought, there are ways that schools can be organized, structured, and operated in supportive ways. Chapter 6 focuses on communities, which are vitally important to the support and maintenance of our schools. Schools need to learn how to partner better with their communities so they can provide the most effective education for students. Because we also believe that schools need to take responsibility for supporting and sustaining their surrounding communities, the chapter also examines ways that they can become more proactive as partners with their communities.

Part III consists of two chapters. Chapter 7 presents ideas that can to help schools and communities move toward resiliency. The chapter offers strategies for school leaders who are responsible for facilitating the introduction of resiliency in schools and communities. The emphasis is on concepts and skills required to manage and assess change.

Chapter 8 provides a summary of efforts under way in communities that, in one way or another, are aimed at the development of resilient schools and communities. Learning about these efforts can be quite helpful to those who want to improve resiliency in their schools and communities. For those who may be interested, basic information, including ways of making contact, is provided for these and other community resiliency initiatives. Resources that can be used to guide school and community resiliency efforts are also catalogued.

In addition, there is a set of handouts that relate to the book's exercises. These can be freely copied for use in your school and community setting.

Leadership for Resilient Schools and Communities is a highly interactive book. There are activities throughout the first six chapters that can help you develop a better understanding of the concepts and strategies presented. Included are ways of diagnosing current situations and implementing strategies for change, as well as questions, exercises, surveys, quotations, and other stimuli that are intended to help you and other members of your school and community dialogue and, hopefully, engage in activities that can spread resiliency. We strongly encourage you to pursue the activities that are suggested in the book to promote this purpose.

We have not suggested any sequencing or timeframes for the exercises because each situation is different (e.g., current dynamics, number of individuals involved, time available, and readiness to engage, which can vary from low interest, to concern, to commitment to take whatever steps are necessary to promote resiliency in the school and the community). Depending on the situation, the exercises can be used for a variety of purposes, ranging from awareness raising at short meetings to an in-depth focus at retreats dedicated to goal setting and action planning. If people are ready to engage, the more time that is committed the more comprehensive the discussion will be and the more likely it is that shared understandings and commitments will be developed. The intent is not to complete all the exercises but to select the ones that meet the needs of your school and community. Furthermore, to the extent that you are able to engage others, it can turn out to be the start of a journey toward the development of a healthier, more resilient school and community.

This second edition incorporates what we have learned as a result of resiliency efforts we have facilitated over the eight years since the first edition, titled *Spreading Resiliency: Making It Happen for Schools and Communities*, was published, in national settings as diverse as the United States, the United Kingdom, Israel, and New Zealand. Modifications in our thinking have also been affected by feedback we have received on our presentations at educator conferences and numerous workshops we have conducted in schools as well as the feedback we have received from educators who have used the book to improve their schools. We believe the incorporated changes will improve the usefulness of the book for readers. For example, definitions and language used in the resiliency model have been clarified so they are clearer and easier to understand and many exercises have been updated. In addition, we have put greater focus on the role of educational leaders, including specific tips at the end of relevant chapters, in the initiation, development, and institutionalization of resiliency efforts. We have also included a brief rating exercise at the end of the chapters for leaders to assess their own readiness to facilitate resiliency initiatives.

We would like to thank the many educators and community members whose input has helped us advance our thinking about resilient schools and communities. The collaboration between Nan Henderson and Mike Milstein (1996, 2002), which resulted in the publication of *Resiliency in Schools: Making It Happen for Students and Educators*, provided the basic framework for the understanding and further development of our work on resiliency. Our work with the Ashland, Oregon, community in pursuing community-wide resiliency, which is summarized in the Chapter 8, provided the initial stimulus for the development of the book. In particular, Dr. John Daggett, retired Superintendent of the Ashland Public Schools, provided the vision and leadership required to make the Ashland dream a reality and encouraged us to continue our efforts regarding community resiliency. To all the wonderful people who have shared thoughts and efforts with us so openly and freely, we give our heartfelt thanks. The contributions of the following reviewers are also gratefully acknowledged.

Corwin Press gratefully acknowledges the contributions of the following individuals:

- Brenda Dean, Assistant Superintendent, Curriculum and Instruction, Hamblen County Department of Education, Morristown, Tennessee
- Gwen Gross, Superintendent, Irvine Unified School District, Irvine, California
- Peter Hilts, High School Principal, The Classical Academy, Colorado Springs, Colorado
- Steve Hutton, Educational Consultant, Villa Hills, Kentucky
- Mary Johnstone, Principal, Rabbit Creek Elementary School, Anchorage, Alaska
- Rocky Killion, Superintendent, West Lafayette Community School Corporation, West Lafayette, Indiana
- Paul Young, Past President, National Association of Elementary, School Principals, Executive Director, West After School Center, Inc., Lancaster, Ohio

We hope that you find resiliency as an approach to school and community improvement as exciting and important as we do. If you engage in efforts aimed at supporting the resiliency of your community and its members, we would appreciate hearing about your efforts.

Mike M. Milstein (agewell@ihug.com.nz)
D. Annie Henry (annie58@ihug.com.nz)
The Resiliency Group, Ltd.
8 Ngapua Place
Nelson
New Zealand

About the Authors

Mike M. Milstein is a partner in The Resiliency Group, Ltd., and Professor Emeritus of Educational Leadership at the University of New Mexico. His professional career also includes being Professor of Educational Leadership at the University of Buffalo and a classroom teacher. His teaching, research, and writing interests are in the areas of resiliency and organizational change and development. He has been actively engaged in school and community resiliency-development efforts in such places as Nelson, New Zealand; Ashland, Oregon; Battle Creek, Michigan; and Shelby County, Tennessee. The resiliency initiatives he has facilitated include classroom instruction and curriculum improvement efforts, school-wide activities that enhance the resiliency of educators, and school-community partnerships that support resiliency development for both children and adults. He has written eleven books, including coauthoring *Resiliency in Schools* (1996, 2002).

Doris "Annie" Henry is a partner in The Resiliency Group, Ltd., and retired Professor of Educational Leadership. Her research and writing interests focus on resiliency, restructuring, change, organization development, and school improvement. Her work with developing resiliency efforts includes Nelson, New Zealand; Ashland, Oregon; Tennessee State Department of Education; and Memphis, Tennessee. She has facilitated resiliency at the classroom, school-wide, and community-school partnership levels. Currently, she is the National President of the New Zealand Educational Administration and Leadership Society (NZEALS), and serves on eleven international, national, and local boards. Her professional career includes being Professor of Educational Leadership at New Mexico Highlands University, the University of Memphis, and at the University of Nebraska at Omaha; an elementary school principal for nearly a decade in Arizona and Oklahoma; and a classroom teacher. She has published and presented widely in her areas of interest, most notably as coauthor of the national study, *Becoming a Superintendent: Challenges of School District Leadership* (1997).

PART I

Basic Concepts

Resiliency

Promoting Everyone's Potential to Succeed

"It's a funny thing about life. If you refuse to accept anything but the best, you very often get it."
—Somerset Maugham

We believe that it is urgent for schools, families, and communities to come together to provide mutual support and improve the potential for *everyone*—youngsters, adults, and the elderly—to lead positive, meaningful, and healthy lives. In support of this contention, this introductory chapter explores the widespread problems that confront our schools and communities and the reasons our problem-focused thinking is unable to overcome them. It also provides an introduction to resiliency, which is an important and positive shift in the way we think about and respond to our school and community challenges. Fostering resiliency in classrooms, schools, families, volunteer groups, community organizations, and formal governmental agencies can do much to move us along the path to school and community improvement.

WHY THE URGENCY?

Many schools face a rising tide of problems that include bullying, violence, gang-related activities, substance abuse, absenteeism, high dropout rates, suicides, low levels of parental support and involvement, and changing family structures.

Communities are struggling with problems such as growing numbers of its members who are unable to maintain a decent quality of life along with a growing disparity between the haves and the have-nots, a fracturing of acceptance and understanding among individuals and groups, a declining level of participation in civic affairs, and in general, a growing distrust of the intentions or abilities of those in authority positions to function equitably and effectively on behalf of all citizens.

Are these problems that are widespread in your school and community? Responding to Exercise 1.1 can help sharpen the picture of how your community is doing with these issues.

Exercise 1.1: Taking Stock of Your School and Community

An important initial step in making significant improvements is to be sure that everyone understands and agrees about the current state of affairs. Invite others to explore the following questions with you. Remember to focus on perceptions about what the situation is *now*.

1. What problems do you think schools in your community are encountering that hinder their ability to provide an effective education for students?

2. What problems do you think the community is encountering that hinders its ability to provide support needed by its members?

3. Why do you think your schools and community are experiencing these problems?

4. Are these problems being addressed? If so, which ones? In what ways?

Record members' responses on a chalkboard or on a sheet of chart paper. Ask the group to review the responses and identify shared understandings. Underline agreements or rewrite those that might need to be modified so they can serve as the basis for further discussion if the group agrees to continue the conversation, as well as to guide actions if the group decides to pursue ways of promoting resiliency.

Living in stressful times creates the need to develop skills and the knowledge required to cope effectively. This has probably always been a reality, but it has become especially true during the closing decades of the twentieth century and the beginning years of the twenty-first century because of the increasing pace of change that we are experiencing. Accompanying the rapidity of change are breakdowns of institutions such as the church and the family, which have traditionally acted as sources of shared understanding, support, and authority for communities, nations, and the world. With these breakdowns have come endless arrays of problems that appear to be intractable. Some of these problems are listed below. You are encouraged to add others that may be relevant in your setting. Being clear about what is at issue is the first step to remediation and improvement.

> We live in the midst of alarms; anxiety beclouds the future; we expect some new disaster with each newspaper read.
>
> —Abraham Lincoln

For Children and Adolescents

We are all too familiar with the many negative manifestations that are exhibited by children and adolescents in these trying times. These include

- various forms of antisocial behavior such as vandalism, truancy, and bullying;
- negative peer influence including pressure to join antisocial gangs;
- violence and crime;
- broken families;
- child abuse;
- drug abuse;
- high unemployment rates among teens;
- academic failures and school dropouts;
- premarital teen births; and
- hopelessness and suicide attempts.

Add other factors you think are important for children in your community:

- _____
  _____
- _____
  _____
- _____
  _____

For Schools

Schools, whether rural, small-town, suburban, or urban, are confronted with problems that test their abilities to create effective responses, including

- fear and violence;
- changing student enrollments and, often, large class sizes;
- employment agreement stresses;
- an aging workforce;
- dilapidated and outdated buildings;
- increasing reliance on expensive and complex technologies; and
- increasing criticism and decreasing parental and community involvement.

Add other factors that are important in your situation:

- _____
  _____
- _____
  _____
- _____
  _____

For Families

A major factor in the increasing incidence of youth problems is the breakdown occurring in traditional family structures. For example, there are widespread occurrences of

- marital problems and high divorce rates;
- single-parent families;
- dispersal of extended families across distant locations;
- families with no adult members available during the day, which has exacerbated the growing problems associated with children returning to an empty home after school hours (latchkey children);
- negative adult role modeling regarding addictive behaviors associated with tobacco, alcohol, and other drugs and sexual promiscuity;
- lack of clarity and agreement about family roles and responsibilities;
- lack of close family and friendship ties; and
- lack of home-based motivation for achievement.

Add other factors that you think are important in your situation:

- _____
  _____
- _____
  _____
- _____
  _____

For Communities

Communities provide the frame of reference and the basic orientation that guides behaviors of children, adolescents, and adults. This becomes more difficult to achieve in times of rapid change. We may no longer agree about what we even mean by community. For many it is still defined by geographical space—neighborhoods, towns, and cities—but for others it may be around commonalities such as ethnicity, religion, work connections, or personal interests. However they are defined, communities will be hard pressed to provide the positive guidance that is necessary, unless adequate responses are developed regarding problems such as the following:

- the high rate of mobility which affects people's attachments to communities;
- inequities in earning and housing opportunities;
- lack of meaningful employment opportunities;
- fragmentation of values and norms;
- fear and violence; and
- lack of opportunities to gather, interact, and celebrate together.

Add other factors that you think are important for your community:

- _____
  _____
- _____
  _____

The problems listed are just the tip of the iceberg. The old Chinese curse, "You should live in interesting times," certainly applies to the current reality in most of our communities. One perspective is that we are witnessing community structures that are coming apart at the seams. Another perspective, which is less pessimistic, is that we are living through a major transition that may be confusing, disorienting, and erratic but one that is also natural, necessary, and responsive to changing times.

In either case, many problems do appear to be intractable. These are indeed interesting times. In part, this is because we focus on issues narrowly as student, school, family, or community problems. In reality, they are interconnected and affect each other, sometimes positively and sometimes negatively. Figure 1.1 illustrates this basic interconnection.

As Figure 1.1 denotes, each subsystem overlaps with the other subsystems. Sometimes, the connections are unilateral such as when schools deal with student-related issues. Sometimes, the connections are multifaceted such as when communities and families interact with schools and students in the process of education. Narrowly focusing on one subsystem does not account for the potential impacts, positive and negative, that can be caused by the other subsystems.

Figure 1.1 The Linkages Between Students, Schools, Families, and Communities

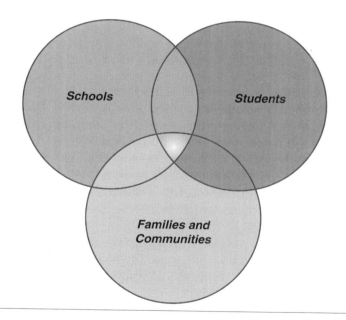

The important thing to realize is that because they are interconnected and affect each other, it is not likely that working to change any one of them without making parallel efforts to change the others will have a lasting impact. We need to develop supportive partnerships across the three subsystems. They are interconnected and problems are frequently shared. Some examples include drug abuse in the schools and in the community, segregated housing and segregated schools, youth who commit suicide, broken homes, and children who exhibit antisocial behaviors in school and in the community. Such problems are not likely to be solved unless our responses take the improvement of all three subsystems into account.

Issues that seem to be unique and limited to any one of the subsystems such as student learning difficulties, educator stress, negative school environment, lack of family support for children's growth and development, or challenges to the well-being of the community itself are, in reality, related and interconnected. Initiating a

> What is the use of a house if you haven't got a tolerable planet to put it on?
>
> —Henry David Thoreau

program here or a project there is not likely to make much of a dent in the problems we ponder. To be effective, we need to create comprehensive responses to complex problems, responses that cut across the different subsystems identified in Figure 1.1. Furthermore, these responses should focus on prevention where possible and on early intervention when it is too late for prevention. The absolute worst option is to wait until problems have become full-blown crises. While a crisis may get everyone's attention, it is likely to be adversarial and polarized, which is neither a reasonable nor an effective way of responding to complex problems.

We are witnessing a major shift toward understanding the connections between schools, families, and communities. We can no longer drift along and hope for the best while preparing for the worst. Certainly, we need to work at understanding our problems, but then we need to formulate positive and effective community-wide structures and processes to respond to them. We need approaches that hold promise of doing this effectively. The fact that you have chosen to read this book indicates that you are exploring these connections and disconnections.

AN INTRODUCTION TO RESILIENCY

Given the many issues that schools and communities are confronted with, it is seductively easy to become obsessed with ways to *solve* them. This thinking can easily become pathological, placing emphasis on behavioral difficulties such as teen pregnancy, bullying, school dropouts, drug abuse, suicides, and criminal behavior. Emphasis is put on patterns such as broken homes, dysfunctional neighborhoods, and poverty in the attempt to be able to predict behaviors. It is only a short step in logic to conclude that anyone, child or adult, whose demographics reflect those of individuals who exhibit such problem behaviors, is highly likely to exhibit similar behaviors at some point in time.

The resiliency approach is a powerful paradigm shift away from the way of thinking that focuses on maladaptation, deficits, illness, and problems. The resiliency perspective focuses on wellness, adaptation, protective factors, capacity building, and improvement. It is a mind map that emphasizes the possible and the belief that things can and will work. It is, in fact, a major psychological reorientation. As Blum's (1998) seminal review in *Psychology Today* pointed out, resiliency represents a way of thinking that is a major change from the victim-and-damage focus that has been promoted by psychology from the 1940s until quite recently.

Throughout life, each of us has many opportunities to become more resilient. From prenatal experience until our dying days, endless challenges foster resiliency, including

- growing from initial inception and an embryo to a full birth delivery;
- mastering basic human survival skills such as walking and communicating;
- expanding connectedness and relationships beyond the family of origin;
- establishing one's own place in the world;
- gaining the knowledge and skills required to be self-supporting;

- taking responsibility for others including caring for spouses and children and assuming formal leadership roles;
- coping with physical and emotional manifestations of aging;
- reflecting on the meaning of life, giving back to our environment, and leaving a legacy; and
- bringing closure to life.

Each of us can expand on this bare-bones list of life's challenges from our own experiences, all of which have the potential to promote and enhance resiliency. For some, the road through life is paved with endless challenges that are environmentally related such as poverty, broken homes, drug and other addictions, or the lack of adequate support systems. Some do not travel such bumpy roads but, for most of us, there are likely to be more than sufficient opportunities to test our resiliency.

> No individual can arrive even at the threshold of his potentialities without a culture in which he participates.
> —*Ruth Benedict*

For those with too many safeguards (e.g., wealth, overprotective parents, and being buffered from daily risks) and promises of privileged positions in the future, there may not be sufficient opportunities to develop necessary coping skills and resiliency capabilities. In fact, there may be more danger for those who have too much protection than there is for those who are viewed as being at risk.

> Adversity reveals genius, prosperity conceals it.
> —*Horace*

There are many definitions and models of resiliency, but they are quite similar. Four good examples follow:

- "The process of coping with disruptive, stressful, or challenging life events in a way that provides the individual with additional protective and coping skills than prior to the disruption that results from the event" (Richardson, Neiger, Jensen, & Krumpfer, 1990, p. 34)
- "The process of self-righting and growth" (Higgins, 1994, p. 1)
- "The capacity to bounce back, to withstand hardship, and to repair yourself" (Wolin & Wolin, 1993, p. 5)
- "The ability to cope well with high levels of ongoing disruptive change; sustain good health and energy when under constant pressure; bounce back easily from setbacks; overcome adversities; change to a new way of working and living when an old way is no longer possible; and do all this without acting in dysfunctional or harmful ways" (Siebert, 2005, p. 5)

These definitions have several things in common—gaining additional protective factors, self-righting, and bouncing back because of life's experiences. All have to do with the capacity to deal with difficulties and become more capable of coping positively in the future. Difficulties are easy to find in our rapidly changing world. Either we respond effectively to these changes or we become victims of them. Some people collapse or barely survive adversity. Some struggle on and learn to cope adequately. Others are more resilient.

We define resiliency as the ability to bounce back from adversity, learn new skills, develop creative ways of coping, and become stronger. Resilient people meet life's challenges, overcome them, and use experiences to improve their ability to deal with the problems that will inevitably come their way in the future.

Exercise 1.2 can help you get a quick sense of your own resiliency. (This exercise is also available in the Resource section as Handout 1.)

Exercise 1.2: How Resilient Are You?

How resilient are you? Here's a little test to help you get a sense of your own resiliency. Circle the choice that is *most true* or *most typical* of you for each of the following questions:

1. When I have difficulties I am more likely to
   a. confront them by taking the initiative.
   b. avoid them in hopes they will pass.

2. Regarding leisure time,
   a. I enjoy reading, learning, and exploring.
   b. I fill the time by pondering my situation and worrying about my future.

3. When faced with challenges,
   a. I enjoy figuring out how to respond to them.
   b. I let others take the lead.

4. My work and home environments are
   a. supportive and energizing.
   b. stressful and exhausting.

5. I believe that
   a. good things are most likely to happen to me.
   b. bad things are most likely to happen to me.

6. I believe that the best years of my life are
   a. yet to come.
   b. behind me.

7. I
   a. have a sense of purpose about life.
   b. find myself drifting from year to year without goals.

8. I am
   a. proud of my accomplishments and my abilities.
   b. not as capable as I could be when coping with challenging situations.

9. When going through life's inevitable transitions, I
   a. feel at ease with them.
   b. feel unsettled and need time to adjust.

10. I believe that I
    a. must earn whatever I get.
    b. am entitled to rewards that I want.

The more *a* responses you selected, the more likely it is that you exhibit resilient behaviors. These responses indicate that you probably feel good about yourself most of the time. You also probably view challenges that come your way as a part of life and try to respond to them effectively.

If you chose *b* responses more often than you chose *a* responses, you might want to consider making some changes:

continued

- Focus on your attitudes and behaviors. Practice more positive self-talk, especially if you tend to be self-critical.

- Observe and talk with people who you think are highly resilient. See what you can learn from them.

- Read and think about resiliency-related areas such as self-esteem, career development, life stages, and dealing with transitions.

- In whatever ways possible, try to learn about and practice qualities and skills that promote resiliency.

What can we learn from resilient people to increase our own resiliency? Higgins (1994) concluded that resilient individuals have three qualities in common. First, they maintain a positive attitude. Second, they confront issues and take charge of their lives. Third, and above all else, they have a deep and abiding faith that creates meaning in their lives. These qualities are regularly found among resilient individuals, no matter how rocky or smooth their lives have been.

Internal and Environmental Protective Factors

Like most important things in life, resiliency does not just happen. It requires effort and the courage to change beliefs and habits because of life's experiences. It is a combination of what is out there and what is in you. In fact, one way of thinking about what affects our resiliency is to separate things that are either *internal* to us or from our *environments*. Table 1.1 identifies key internal and environmental protective factors that are needed for the development and maintenance of resiliency. (It is also Handout 2 in the Resource section.)

Table 1.1   Internal and Environmental Protective Factors

Internal Protective Factors
Characteristics of Individuals That Promote Resiliency

1. Gives of self in service to others or a cause or both
2. Uses life skills, including good decision making, assertiveness, impulse control, and problem solving
3. Is sociable and has ability to be a friend and form positive relationships
4. Has a sense of humor
5. Exhibits internal locus of control (i.e., belief in ability to influence one's environment)
6. Is autonomous, independent
7. Has positive view of personal future
8. Is flexible
9. Has spirituality (i.e., belief in a greater power)
10. Has capacity for connection to learning
11. Is self-motivated
12. Is "good at something," has personal competence
13. Has feelings of self-worth and self-confidence
14. Other:

continued

Environmental Protective Factors

Characteristics of Families, Schools, Communities, and Peer Groups That Promote Resiliency

1. Promotes close bonds
2. Values and encourages education
3. Uses high warmth, low criticism style of interaction
4. Sets and enforces clear boundaries (rules, norms, and laws)
5. Encourages supportive relationships with many caring others
6. Promotes sharing of responsibilities, service to others, "required helpfulness"
7. Provides access to resources for meeting basic needs of housing, employment, health care, and recreation
8. Expresses high and realistic expectations for success
9. Encourages goal setting and mastery
10. Encourages prosocial development of values (such as altruism) and life skills (such as cooperation)
11. Provides leadership and opportunities for meaningful participation and decision making
12. Appreciates the unique talents of each individual
13. Other:

SOURCE: Adapted from Henderson and Milstein (1996).

How much we are able to exhibit resiliency is directly related to the extent to which these internal and environmental protective factors exist in our lives. We differ in our abilities to manifest resiliency based on how we respond to life, to our personalities and genetics, and to our homes, neighborhoods, and community environments. As the ideas and strategies presented herein illustrate, we can do much to promote these factors for ourselves as well as for others, both children and adults, in our schools and communities.

Exercise 1.3, which follows, is intended to help you gain a better sense of the extent of your own internal and environmental protective factors.

Exercise 1.3: Your Resiliency Story

Exercise 1.3 is intended to give you and other members of your group a chance to become more familiar with the internal and environmental protective factors listed in Table 1.1. As you become more aware of these factors, you will find it easier to observe and assess the extent to which you and others in your school and community, both children and adults, exhibit them.

1. Think about a time in your life that was especially challenging or difficult (e.g., death of a loved one, divorce, a financial crisis, or major physical problems).

2. Review the list of internal protective factors in Table 1.1 (or Handout 2). Which of these were you able to draw on to help you through this difficult situation? Include other internal protective factors that are not listed but that you think are important.

3. Review the list of environmental protective factors. Which of these were you able to draw on? Include are other environmental protective factors that are not listed but that you think are important.

4. What other internal and environmental factors listed in Table 1.1 do you think would have also been helpful to get you through the situation?

5. Share your life situation and your internal and environmental protective factors assessment with others and ask them to share theirs with you.

Resiliency Elements

The internal and environmental protective factors framework provides a good starting point for understanding and, one hopes, inventorying individual and environmental strengths as well as areas that may be in need of attention. They help us become more aware that our resiliency status is rooted both in the resources and abilities we possess and in what is available to us within our environments to meet life's challenges.

For several reasons, however, it is somewhat limited as a foundation for the development of comprehensive resiliency improvement efforts in schools and communities. First, the internal factors are aspects of our own personalities and life histories, neither of which is easily changed. Second, the number of factors involved and others you might choose to include make it an unwieldy tool for planning and development. Finally, it does not serve as a framework that is holistic, which is what is required if resiliency efforts are to be effective and lasting.

A different way of structuring thinking about resiliency is to summarize the key findings of the at-risk literature (e.g., Hawkins, Catalano, & Miller, 1992) and the resiliency literature (e.g., Benard, 2004; Werner & Smith, 1992) into a limited but inclusive number of elements.

As the Resiliency Wheel depicted in Figure 1.2 (adapted from Henderson & Milstein, 1996; Henry & Milstein, 2004; Milstein & Henry, 2000) portrays, six key elements make up resiliency. Whether referring to children or adults or to schools or communities, these elements are the basic building blocks of resiliency. The definitions have been modified as follows:

1. *Positive connections.* When we are connected in profound ways with people, activities, programs, institutions, communities, and society, as well as the core values that underlie them, we know who we are, that we are part of something bigger than ourselves, and how we fit in with those around us. Positive

   > He who has a why to live can bear almost any how.
   >
   > —*Friedrich Nietzsche*

   connections that are healthy and supportive provide meaning and value for our lives. We need to seek out, maintain, and nurture positive connections that support our sense of belonging and meaning.

2. *Clear, consistent, and appropriate boundaries.* Our boundaries, or our senses of self and place, include expectations that are formal and communicated in writing such as laws, policies, and procedures, as well as expectations that are informal but powerful such as norms and cultural preferences. Our behav-

   > To enjoy freedom we have to control ourselves.
   >
   > —*Virginia Woolf*

   iors are greatly affected by the formal and informal expectations of others. If they are clear and consistently enforced and appropriate to our needs and abilities they can serve as a safety net, providing guidance for appropriate behaviors. They are also important for growth and development, which are more feasible if we feel safe and secure.

3. *Life-guiding skills.* Life-guiding skills that are required to navigate life's twists and turns include goal setting, planning, problem solving, decision making, communications, conflict management and resolution, and the ability to be reflective. It is important that these skills be developed, honed through experience, and applied flexibly as conditions change and life progresses.

   > The supreme end of education is expert discernment in all things—the power to tell the good from the bad, the genuine from the counterfeit.
   >
   > —*Samuel Johnson*

Figure 1.2 The Resiliency Wheel

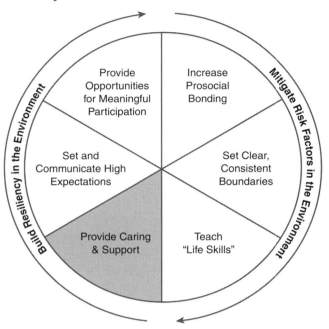

4. *Nurture and support.* We thrive when we are cared for and supported by relatives, friends, and others around us. Our lives are more worth living when we matter to others. We feel more fully alive when we experience unconditional regard from others. All people, from newborns to centenarians, thrive more if they are loved and cared for. Learning how to ask for and receive such nurturance and support is important. It is equally important to be able and willing to give nurturance and support to others for our own sense of well-being.

> The deepest principle of Human Nature is the craving to be appreciated.
>
> —*William James*

5. *Purposes and expectations.* With clear goals and priorities and the motivation to achieve them, we are more likely to respond positively to life's challenges. Purposes and expectations motivate us to grow and develop. In fact, meaning is the driving energy in life. Without purposes and expectations, we are likely to become alienated and adrift, with little drive beyond mere survival. Our purposes and expectations may be suggested by teachers, parents, and others, but ultimately, we must choose and prioritize our own expectations—for example, to become independent, become financially secure, find a mate, raise a family, and do well in our chosen line of work.

> Lord, grant that I may always desire more than I can accomplish.
>
> —*Michelangelo*

6. *Meaningful participation.* We are social beings. When we participate meaningfully with our family, friends, and the community we live in, we realize that we are not alone, that we have skills and worthwhile inputs to offer, and that we have a responsibility to give back to the environments that have nurtured us. It is important to note that people may have the time, life experiences, and knowledge to participate meaningfully, but they also need to be invited to participate appropriately.

> Few things help an individual more than to place responsibility on him, and to let him know that you trust him.
>
> —*Booker T. Washington*

While it is easier to visualize the resiliency elements just mentioned as the six pieces of a pie that are depicted in Figure 1.2, in reality they are tightly interrelated. That is, the strengthening, or depletion, of one of the elements will have a direct and significant impact on the other five. Figure 1.3 is a more accurate depiction of the dynamic interplay of the six resiliency elements.

Figure 1.3 Resiliency Elements Wheel

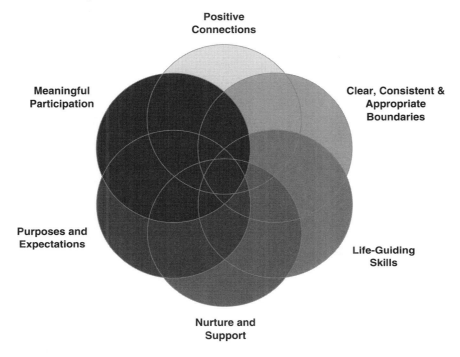

THE RESILIENCY ELEMENTS WHEEL: DYNAMIC INTERPLAY OF THE SIX ELEMENTS

To deepen your understanding of these six resiliency elements we encourage you and others in your group to respond to Exercise 1.4.

Exercise 1.4: You and the Resiliency Wheel

This exercise is intended to help you become more acquainted and comfortable with the six resiliency elements. It should also help you establish a sense of your current resiliency status and the ways that you may be contributing to the resiliency of others.

1. Review the definitions for each of the six resiliency elements. Identify and record the extent to which they actually exist and promote resiliency in your own life situation.

- Positive Connections:

   _____

- Clear, Consistent, and Appropriate Boundaries:

   _____

continued

- Life-Guiding Skills:

_____

- Nurture and Support:

_____

- Purposes and Expectations:

_____

- Meaningful Participation:

_____

2. Share your thoughts about the extent to which each element exists in your life with other individuals, and ask them to do the same with you.

3. Now think about ways you promote the resiliency of others you know and care about, particularly your friends and family members. Describe how you try to provide support for each of the six resiliency elements for these individuals.

- Positive Connections:

_____

- Clear, Consistent, and Appropriate Boundaries:

_____

- Life-Guiding Skills:

_____

- Nurture and Support:

_____

- Purposes and Expectations:

_____

- Meaningful Participation:

_____

4. Share your list with others and ask them to do the same with you.

5. Finally, discuss responses to the following questions with others.

- What were some of the key things you identified that you do to support your resiliency?

_____

- What were some of the key things you identified that you do to support the resiliency of others you care about?

_____

continued

- Was your list similar to those of other participants?

  _____

- Did you find it easier to list thoughts for some of the six elements than you did for others regarding yourself? Regarding others?

  _____

- If so, why do you think this is the situation?

  _____

Putting It All Together

Our lives play out differently depending on our capacity to develop and exhibit resiliency. Figure 1.4 depicts four levels of responses that we might make to adversity (adapted and modified from Richardson et al., 1990). At the lowest level, if we do not have much access to the six elements of the Resiliency Wheel and the internal and environmental protective factors, we can feel overwhelmed and withdraw from the situation, which is a *dysfunctional response*. An example is teachers who leave the profession after a short time because they find that they are not able to respond well to student discipline issues or because they have not figured out how to relate effectively with colleagues or deal successfully with the educational bureaucracy. At the second level, we learn how to *survive*, scrape by, and develop response mechanisms that are at least minimally successful. Using the same situation, teachers who are unable to master good classroom management techniques may minimize interactions with students and require them to do lots of busy work, like regularly requiring them to respond to the questions at the end of the textbook's chapters. They stay in the profession, but they are not likely to remain motivated or to motivate their students.

> With a good heredity, nature deals you a fine hand at cards; and with a good environment, you learn to play the hand well.
> —*Walter C. Alvarez*

At the third level, we may persist and develop more adequate responses until we reach a *comfort zone* and we no longer feel threatened by the situation. Teachers who reach this level of competency are like the thermostats in our homes, which are engineered to keep the temperature at a comfort level.

At the fourth level, we continue our journey in dealing with the initial adversity until we have developed new insights and skills, a higher degree of confidence and increased self-esteem, and we have gained support from our environment. This is a *resilient response*. These teachers continue to learn, develop, and be motivated and positive about teaching throughout their careers. They are usually viewed by their colleagues as exemplary teachers and faculty leaders.

By now, it should be apparent that although resiliency may be a relatively new term to you, the basic elements are deeply embedded in your own life. We all give daily attention to coping and succeeding, and as we do so, we enhance our potential to be resilient. The more we do so the more we seek situations that provide opportunities for us to charge our resiliency batteries as well as opportunities to help others charge theirs. In like manner, we instinctively shield ourselves from situations that are negative and can drain our resiliency batteries.

Figure 1.4 Levels of Responding to Adversity

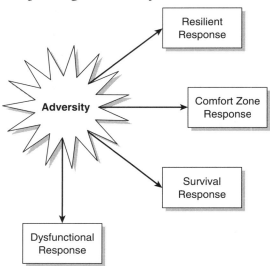

Resiliency is not just about developing our individual capabilities. It is also about developing resiliency-supporting environments. There is a direct relationship between how supportive our environments are and how resilient we feel and behave.

> Experience is not what happens to a man; it is what a man does with what happens to him.
>
> —Aldous Huxley

Very few of those who survived the Holocaust during World War II emerged from that experience as whole, healthy individuals. The Holocaust is an extreme case of an environment that purposefully and comprehensively depleted the resiliency of those who were caught up in it. Fortunately, few of us have been put to such a severe test. Still, we do live in a world marked by rapidly changing societal conditions. We need to be able to respond effectively to these conditions as individuals, groups, and communities. Our willingness and competence to do so will dictate how effective we are in positively affecting the resiliency of ourselves, those we are responsible for and care about, our schools and communities, and ultimately, the long-term well-being of the world.

> The world breaks everyone and afterward many are strong at the broken places.
>
> —Ernest Hemingway

How do we pursue the path to resiliency? How do we come to an agreed-on understanding of the situation we find ourselves in and what needs to be done to improve it? These are daunting questions but our experiences as well as those of others engaged with resiliency initiatives in schools and communities in diverse national settings lead us to believe that it is within your ability to institute meaningful and effective improvements. In fact, this book is dedicated to helping you help yourself and others to a more resilient future.

THE PROBLEM WITH PROBLEM SOLVERS

> The essence of belief is the establishment of a habit.
>
> —Charles S. Pearce

We need to understand that how we currently think about children, schools, families, and communities must be reconsidered before we can start down the path to resiliency. The dominant belief system is that we can improve things by identifying problems and figuring out ways to solve them.

It is seductively easy to focus on problems, deficits, and at-risk behavior. After all, they are all around us and easy enough to find. Furthermore, most of us pride ourselves on being problem solvers, and we all know what problem solvers do— they look for problems to solve. In other words, most of us have *mind maps* that emphasize shortcomings, risk behaviors, and difficulties. We tend to focus on the reasons that things *do not, cannot,* or *will not work.* Exercise 1.5 sheds some light on how this mind map can affect our thinking.

Exercise 1.5: What You See Is What You Get

This exercise can be done individually, but it will have a greater impact if it is done in a group and someone is asked to facilitate the activity.

1. Think about a situation at your school or in your community that seems to be highly resistant to improvement. Examples might include ineffective discipline policies and procedures, poor academic achievement, low morale among faculty members, low parental involvement, high crime rates, or community apathy. Be sure to select a situation that has meaning for you.

2. List all the reasons why things don't or can't work regarding the situation you selected. Put them on a chalkboard or chart paper. You probably can list many reasons why things don't or can't work. In fact, the list probably looks quite imposing.

3. Now regarding the same situation, think of all the reasons why things have worked as well as they have up until the present time. In other words, things could probably be worse. Why aren't they? What positive things are going on? Record these reasons on a chalkboard or chart paper.

4. What can be done to improve the situation? Record these suggestions.

5. Review the responses to questions 3 and 4. Do you think that the situation still seems intractable? Or, does the situation seem less difficult or negative now that you have given some thought to the positive side of it?

If you found it difficult to see the positive side of the situation and the potential for its improvement, you may be exhibiting the approach of the "dreaded problem solver" who finds it easier to focus on the "can'ts" and "won'ts" than the "cans" and "wills." Even if you found many positives, are you surrounded by others who zero in on the negatives? Problem solvers readily identify deficits, but this focus can also leave them less sensitive to the identification of assets, potentials, and possibilities.

> Is the unspoken worldview that underlies the assumptions from which I practice my profession perhaps, unwittingly, contributing to the very problem that I am committed to solve?
>
> —Anne Wilson Schaef

Equally troublesome, problem solvers often fail to see strengths and possibilities that are right in front of them because they are so busy focusing on problems. Worst of all, where predispositions lead us to anticipate certain behaviors, the Pygmalion effect is likely to occur as we label individuals and groups, whether negatively or positively. That is, people will behave according to our expectations.

What is needed is nothing less than a radical shift in how we think about youngsters, schools, and communities. We need to free ourselves of the problem-focused, "can't do" orientation and move on to a wellness-focused, "can do" orientation. Ultimately, what we see is the best predictor of what we get. As Covey (1989) noted,

> The hopeful man sees success where others see failure, sunshine where others see shadows and storm.
>
> —O. S. Marden

Whether they shift us in positive or negative directions, whether they are instantaneous or developmental, paradigm shifts move us from one way of seeing the world to another. And those shifts create powerful change. Our paradigms, correct or incorrect, are the sources of our attitudes and behaviors and ultimately our relationships with others (p. 30).

> . . . Enhance the humanity of the other, because in that process, you enhance your own.
>
> —Desmond Tutu

That is what this book is about—shifting the paradigm from the negative to the positive, the reasons why schools and communities are in trouble and how schools and communities can improve and become more resilient.

Exercise 1.6: Considerations for Leaders

Leaders set the tone. Their understanding of the meaning and importance of resiliency goes a long way in shaping the ability of students, teachers, parents, and other community members to develop and exhibit resiliency. For this reason, each chapter includes a final exercise for leaders. These exercises offer leaders the opportunity to do an assessment of their current levels of understanding and abilities to lead resiliency initiatives. Concerning the content of Chapter 1, for the following items, what rating, on a scale of one (low) to five (high), would you give to your knowledge and ability to develop and maintain schools and communities that promote resiliency?

1. I have a clear understanding about local issues and difficulties regarding
   a. children and adolescents.
   b. the school.
   c. families.
   d. the community.

2. I understand what my own level of resiliency is currently.

3. Resiliency has meaning in my life. Each of the elements and the internal and environmental protective factors are reminders of how I continue to build resiliency within me, within my environment, and my influence on the environment.

4. The six resiliency elements serve as a lens for how I make decisions and are a useful guide for developing others. Rate each one.
   a. Positive connections
   b. Clear, consistent, and appropriate boundaries
   c. Life-guiding skills
   d. Nurture and support
   e. Purposes and expectations
   f. Meaningful participation

5. I have a choice as to how I respond to adversity as well as understand how others respond to it. I can provide examples of each level in the local setting and understand how to move people from one level to a more healthier one:
   a. Dysfunctional response
   b. Survival response
   c. Comfort zone response
   d. Resilient response

We continue the journey with Chapter 2, which explores the meaning and importance of resilient communities.

2

Building Resilient Communities

"We don't accomplish anything in this world alone . . . and whatever happens is the result of the whole tapestry of one's life and all the weavings of individual threads from one to another that creates something."

—Former Justice Sandra Day O'Connor, first woman on the U.S. Supreme Court

When we think and talk about communities, it feels as natural as breathing air. But when asked to describe them, our experiences, interactions, and perceptions bound our responses. Our schools, places of worship, workplaces, housing subdivision, shopping areas, and parks, among other things, are all part of the community portrait. So what do we mean by community? More specifically, what do we mean when we talk about communities that support the needs of their members? Sergiovanni (1995) defined such a community as a "collection of people bonded together by mutual commitments and special relationship, who together are bound to a set of shared ideas and values that they believe in, and feel compelled to follow. This bonding and binding helps them to become members of a tightly knit web of meaningful relationships and moral overtones. In communities of this kind, people belong, people care, people help each other, people make and keep commitments, people feel responsible for themselves and responsible to others" (p. 100).

Communities are about connections. Resilient communities promote positive connections. Such communities provide for the basic human need to relate and connect. We all need interactions with familiar, supportive people on a regular basis. Relationships are essential to our well-being and growth. Without healthy relationships, individuals merely survive or become dysfunctional. If we help each other we can grow, develop, and become more resilient as individuals and as a community.

The chapter explores the relationship of the ecology of the community to its members' wellness and resiliency. The intent of the chapter is to gain a clearer sense of what a resilient community looks and feels like and how to form the essential components of community building. The chapter is divided into six sections. First, it addresses understanding why community development and resiliency building are important. Second, it examines traditional ways of thinking about community. Third, it explores the three kinds of communities that schools exist in—rural, urban, and suburban. Fourth, it examines images of resilient communities. Fifth, it presents a foundation for building resilient communities. Last, it discusses strategies that leaders can use to build community resiliency.

WHY COMMUNITY DEVELOPMENT AND RESILIENCY BUILDING ARE IMPORTANT

Resilient communities meet challenges in constructive ways. They face issues and learn from them. These communities are characterized by

- members' sense of belonging;
- shared values and beliefs;
- an infrastructure that supports well-being; and
- common goals that benefit everyone.

How are the characteristics of a resilient community manifested? Can a community become more resilient? How resilient is your community? For communities to be resilient, members need to have a sense of belonging, shared values, and beliefs, common goals that benefit everyone, and an infrastructure that supports the well-being of the community. The clearer all of these are articulated, the healthier a community will become.

> I am more convinced than ever of the importance of reinventing community, both within our schools and within our neighborhoods. This sense of place, of belonging, is a crucial building block for the healthy development of children and adolescents.
>
> —James Comer

A sense of belonging for community members is promoted by conscious effort to bring people into the information and decision-making processes. Typically, at least initially, a small core of people willingly and actively give in ways that help the community. They may be small in numbers, but they are motivated to make a difference and are willing to expend the required energy. They are committed to making a positive difference, and we are thankful that they are. This small group might be the core members of the parent association that supports the school.

It is relatively simple to reach out to these early volunteers. Their skills and abilities are already known and they have proven themselves responsive. Others who have the same values and beliefs may be in the same approximate physical location and can be tapped to come together in positive, constructive ways. But do we know who they are? If we do, do we welcome them? Reaching them and others in the community takes effort, time, and planning. Without this effort, there may be perceptions of exclusion, which can fracture the community further and swell the number of members who feel disaffected.

> No individual can arrive even at the threshold of his potentialities without a culture in which he participates. Conversely, no civilization has in it any element which in the last analysis is not the contribution of an individual.
>
> —Ruth Benedict

How can leaders in the school and community promote a widespread sense of belonging? Expanding participation to include other stakeholders in the community so that they can express their values and beliefs and join in the effort to move the community in positive, constructive ways must be addressed if a sense of belonging is to exist. There has to be involvement across all segments of the population. This includes people who are on the periphery in meaningful ways. For community resiliency to be developed, these members have to have a sense of belonging.

> The history of man is a graveyard of great cultures that came to catastrophic ends because of their incapacity for planned, rational, voluntary reaction to challenge.
>
> —*Erich Fromm*

Shared values and beliefs are what attract people to take an active role in community development efforts. Those who volunteer more than likely share the values and beliefs that are being fostered. Focused activities such as community meetings can generate dialogue that is needed to promote shared values and beliefs across the

> The health of a democratic society may be measured by the quality of functions performed by private citizens.
>
> —*Alexis de Tocqueville*

community. Communicating these values and beliefs clearly and frequently is a way to increase understanding, ownership, and commitment to them.

Infrastructure is required to identify, access, and distribute resources that enhance community resiliency. Infrastructures are built through identifying information and resources desired to build a strong community. The infrastructure needs to be readily accessed. For example, in a school's effort to become the hub for community resources, they included health care, budgeting, financial assistance, and other resources that parents and other community members want located at the school.

People stay connected with groups such as communities, professional organizations, and schools if there are *common goals that benefit everyone*. Widespread ownership of goals helps people focus on them instead of on issues, problems, disagreements, and differences of opinions.

TRADITIONAL WAYS OF THINKING ABOUT COMMUNITY

Resilient communities are those that use challenges to become healthier. No two communities are alike. We need to know who the individuals and groups are within our communities, to have a collective sense of purpose, and to promote relationships that are healthy to promote well being and resiliency.

Every community must take its own path to resiliency. Take, for example, the comments of an Alaskan Native American who reflected on the problems his Arctic Circle village was having with child abuse, alcoholism, gambling, malnutrition, and violence: "They took away the people one by one for treatment, but really the disease was in the village. We could only understand what was happening by looking at the community" (Pipher, 1996, p. 15).

Everyone has stories about the community they know best—the one in which they grew up. These early images of community are firmly planted in our minds. Exercise 2.1 can help clarify the meaning of community by encouraging you to delve into yours from your youth as well as the one(s) you are in now.

Exercise 2.1: If You Don't Know Where You Are, How Can You Know Where You Are Going?

This exercise is intended to give you a better sense of your experience of community and give you and your group a clearer understanding of how the community in which you currently live is envisioned. It can also help you identify ways of moving the community to a healthier place.

This exercise works best in dyads or small groups. If you are leading the exercise, ask everyone to think about the community in which he or she grew up. How would they describe it?

1. Take 2 or 3 minutes to reflect on the community in which you grew up. Jot down the strengths of that community and the areas you would have liked to change. What were its strong points? What were the shortcomings?

2. Have each person share the strengths and shortcomings with others in your group or in a dyad for 2 or 3 minutes each.

3. After everyone is finished, make two columns on chart paper or a chalkboard: one for strengths and one for shortcomings. Record everyone's statements about both. Identify and put an asterisk by the commonalities.

4. Community has meaning for individuals as well as for groups. What are some common ways group members define their communities? Record agreements.

5. Last, ask members to compare the communities in which they grew up with the ones in which they are living or working (or both) in now:
   • How are they similar? How are they different?
   • What can you learn from the community in which you grew up that may be beneficial to the community you are in presently?
   • Challenge the group to craft a meaningful definition of community.

THREE REALITIES OF COMMUNITY: RURAL, URBAN, AND SUBURBAN

Our communities vary in location, size, wealth, and sustainability, but most all fit into the traditional typology of communities: Rural, urban, and suburban. Being aware of the differences between these three kinds of communities and the similarities within communities of each grouping is a good backdrop for understanding our own communities.

> Man shapes himself through decisions that shape his environment.
>
> —Rene Dubos

Rural Communities

The American rural heritage is perceived as one in which community members shared values and where lives were shaped by shared economic development. Geographically, communities were separated from each other, but within them, people lived close to each other. In many instances, just about everyone in the community was known. Similar to many tribal or clan cultures, communities were territorial, bounded by proximity.

The community that many of us desire is one that is captured by images of places in the past when agrarian life predominated. For the most part, images we hold are of caring and positive relationships. They also include a clear sense of geographic boundaries, widespread support for economic and community development, familiarity, and a common set of values about how we all benefit from being a part of a community.

We tend to romanticize the rural or small town setting. Certainly, it has exhibited strengths. It is a place where everyone is known, and it is small enough to promote togetherness, support, belonging, and protection. Neighbors can usually be counted on to help when you need them. There is a strong sense of being cared for and supported. The individual is perceived as being a part of a larger community. People who live in these communities for generations become keen observers of and participants in each other's lives. Starratt (1996) described this situation as one in which individuals become absorbed in a communal identity.

> There is a destiny that makes us brothers, none goes his way alone. All that we send into the lives of others comes back into our own.
>
> —*Edwin Markham*

An excellent example of this rural strength comes from the life of Marian Wright Edelman (as cited in Schorr, 1997), founder and president of the Children's Defense Fund, who grew up in Bennettsville, South Carolina: "I went everywhere with my parents and was under the watchful eye of the congregation and community who were my extended family. They kept me when my parents went out of town, they reported on me and chided me when I strayed from the straight and narrow of community expectations, and they basked in and supported my achievements when I did well" (p. 303).

Of course, rural communities also exhibit shortcomings. Probably most important is the sense of intrusiveness that comes with smallness: everyone knows your business. The balancing act of having a personal, private life and being connected in small communities can be difficult. The sense of privacy that individuals need is difficult to find in this setting, which "explains why, for millennia, the dream of rural people was to escape into the city" (Drucker, 1998, p. 3).

Urban Communities

Urban communities developed more recently. The industrial revolution of the nineteenth century drew those who were unhappy with the forced intimacy of rural life and who found the anonymity of city life to their liking. Of course, this was not a new phenomenon. The motivation to find freedom in cities dates back to medieval times and earlier—when serfs fled from the country to become free people with the privileges of citizenship that cities granted.

> Few people are capable of expressing with equanimity opinions which differ from the prejudices of their social environment.
>
> —*Albert Einstein*

Like the serfs, groups of people from many countries left behind oppressive conditions to migrate to other countries or places where they could start anew. Immigrants were clustered in the growing cities in neighborhoods in which they were identified as Smith (1943) described in *A Tree Grows in Brooklyn*. There they could preserve and practice their cultures and traditions. In these enclaves, they also found protection from other segments of society that did not understand or accept them.

Cities are multifaceted places with a variety of opportunities for income, anonymity, and individuality. This has been especially true since the twentieth century. If you are willing to work and physically able then jobs are available. People who moved from rural settings felt a new freedom to be themselves because of the diversity and anonymity that exists in the cities. They also viewed the city workplace as

> Unless justice be done to others, it will not be done to us.
>
> —*Woodrow Wilson*

compartmentalized from personal life, in contrast to rural settings where work and personal identities are melded into one. Expression of individuality in cities is accepted, whereas it was often difficult to pursue in small, rural communities.

Despite all the benefits individuals could find in cities, and more recently in the many sprawling suburbs that surround them, there was a missing element—the sense of community. Cities presented an enticing alternative to the intrusiveness of rural communities that people deserted, but this came with a high cost—the loss of the caring, support, and belonging that these smaller communities could provide.

> We won't have a society if we destroy the environment.
> —*Margaret Mead*

There are other problems unique to city life. For example, disease and epidemics shortened the lives of early city dwellers. As cities grew at an alarming rate, planning became a major consideration. Most ironic, with the influx of people from rural communities as well as immigrant groups the chances of finding and keeping jobs became more difficult in many cities.

In summary, the idyllic picture of the city was as unrealistic as that of the rural setting: it "was attractive precisely because it offered freedom from the compulsory and coercive community. But it was destructive because it did not offer any community of its own" (Drucker, 1998, p. 4).

Suburban Communities

Suburban communities are an outgrowth of sprawling cities and increased wealth. In the suburbs, people believe they can escape the hassle of city life and live in a quiet, safe, and comfortable neighborhood. They know their neighbors but maintain privacy to lead their own lives. They view the suburbs as a safe haven from the crime and difficulties of the urban centers. It is idealized as the combination of cities and rural communities—that is, being known without being too close.

One of the best known suburbs created after World War II was Levittown, a planned community where all the streets and amenities were thoughtfully arranged. Many other communities followed this lead. The result is a feeling of sameness about them. Values and beliefs are articulated in laws, rules, and policies.

Suburbs are often referred to as "bedroom communities" because they have limited commercial business and their residents work in the cities they surround. Even though many fled the big cities because of the fear of crime, within a few decades suburbs also became the target for crime. Homes in these quiet communities were burglarized while families were away at work or in school. Along with the increase of crime, there has been an increase of stress: stress commuting to work, stress with insuring the homes with expensive alarm systems, and stress of keeping up with the neighbors (Masters & Shear, 1998).

Paralleling the increase of crime is the increase of parents protecting their children. The more affluent the suburbs are the more likely the children would be protected from the harshness of the world that their parents saw commuting into the cities. The increased wealth also gave children more available cash to experiment with drugs and at-risk activities. The suburbs have not been immune to the drug trafficking that increased from the 1980s onward. "People want what you have and they'll take it in a second," said Joan Fredericks, of Falls Church, whose husband was shot and killed in a carjacking in a quiet Fairfax cul-de-sac in 1993. "Because of drugs, people's attitudes have changed. . . . It's not enough to steal anymore. They'll take your life, too" (Masters & Shear, 1998, p. A1).

The predictability and sameness of the community coupled with the high expectations of children to perform contributed to the change in values and dreams of the suburbs. Today the suburbs still have the values and beliefs of a safe environment but with the assistance of alarms and stricter laws to keep the neighborhood safe.

Some of the advantages of being a suburbanite are that they enjoy the values and culture of their neighborhoods. People know what is expected and appreciate their neighbors' standards and general respect for each other. Some of the disadvantages are the tendency to be overprotective of their children and crime that is increasing because both parents are typically working, leaving their homes vulnerable to burglars.

CHALLENGES THAT ARE COMMON TO ALL COMMUNITIES

The evolution of our society from agrarian to urban and suburban has shifted people and their realities. Furthermore, there is no end to the list of possible obstacles that exist for all of our communities. These include high mobility rates, inequities of earnings and housing, fragmentation of values and norms, fear and violence, policies and rules that conflict across government agencies within single communities, rapid advances in technology and communications, an increase in single-parent homes, large corporations that are squeezing neighborhood stores out of business, and a lack of opportunities to gather and celebrate. Just listing these potential stumbling blocks can create a sense among community members that they are insurmountable and promote a fatalistic "why bother to try to improve the situation" kind of attitude.

Without a strong community orientation, a problematic cycle of events can easily be created. No community is exempt from problems. The only difference is how communities cope with them and the frequency of them. The cycle might be described as follows. People move to cities to improve their economic well-being and to shed the intrusiveness of small communities. After an initial period of time, they seek connection through community. As a substitute for the small community, neighborhoods take form and grow. They then go through transitions. Those who were once neighborhood guardians move on. Those left behind become more fearful and isolated from each other. In time, they turn away from each other and seek any means that are available to provide for their protection and security.

> I believe that that community is already in process of dissolution where each man begins to eye his neighbor as a possible enemy, where nonconformity with the accepted creed, political as well as religious, is a mark of disaffection.
>
> —Judge Learned Hand

When all is said and done, individuals may feel more secure but at the price of feeling disconnected from neighbors and the larger community. As opportunities for positive connections shrink and boundaries become more difficult to define and maintain, individuals seek alternative forms of community. These may come in the form of gangs that provide connections between individuals, especially for those who feel most isolated and alienated. Gangs are a response to the absence of constructive means and ends, whether we are talking about "the gangs of Victorian England, or the gangs that today threaten the very social fabric of the large, American city (and, increasingly, of every large city in the world)" (Drucker, 1998, p. 5).

VISUALIZING THE RESILIENT COMMUNITY

Resilient communities are those that confront problems in ways that bring individuals and groups together to interact and provide necessary support. They are communities in which schools, other governmental agencies, higher education institutions, and voluntary and business organizations join together to plan and develop activities that promote positive, shared experiences and relationships.

> Democracy is measured not by its leaders doing extraordinary things, but by its citizens doing ordinary things extraordinarily well.
>
> —John Gardner

Our dream is to create communities that are capable of meeting the needs of their members. These may appear to be overwhelming, or perhaps not even clearly understood. Further, does the very notion of community bounded by geographic location fit with the fluidity of today's society? Does the concept of community as we have known it relate to our changing world?

A move outside the parameters of our traditional understanding of community is called for if we are going to be able to answer these questions. Getting out of our traditional ways of thinking is needed so that new ideas and new behaviors can flourish in ways that promote community resiliency. With the changing scope and size of urbanized centers and the shifting roles of society's major institutions including the home, the church, and schools as well as the globalization of economies, redefining and rebuilding communities is vitally important for the health of our own generation and the health of coming generations.

> Man must cease attributing his problems to his environment, and learn again to exercise his will— his personal responsibility in the realm of faith and morals.
>
> —Albert Schweitzer

We need to think differently about what a community is and what it looks like: to do this "will require . . . a transformation of our limited understanding of both the individual and of the community" (Starratt, 1996, p. 93). We can move toward the development of resilient communities, but in most cases not as we have known them in the past. Individuals and groups must discover new ways to work with each other and create sustainable communities that meet current realities and are fluid enough to adapt to realities as they unfold in the future.

> I know of no more encouraging fact than the unquestionable ability of man to elevate his life by a conscious endeavor.
>
> —Henry David Thoreau

KEY FACTORS IN COMMUNITY BUILDING

Leaders are in a key position to promote discussions about the strengths and challenges of the community and begin the process of moving it toward resiliency building. They can facilitate discussions about what should be changed. What are we trying to become? Why is it important for individuals, groups, and the community to pursue the discussion? Who should be involved in the discussion? Which allies and key stakeholders should collaborate in the process?

When there is understanding and commitment to recreate communities, they will grow and prosper. Key factors of community building include the following.

Knowing One Another

Getting to know each other can change community dynamics rapidly and dramatically. An example of this is when a village in Italy found itself confronted with a growing crime problem. All of the business owners and residents were asked to leave their homes fifteen minutes early before going to work each day so they could meet and talk with their neighbors. People made an effort to get to know their neighbors, which caused them to care about what happened to each other. This was a major shift from a sense of fear, isolation, and need to protect themselves from each other, to a willingness to reach out and support each other. The results of this simple outreach effort were overwhelming. Crime was cut almost in half in just six months.

> Perfect valor is to do unwitnessed what we should be capable of doing before all the world.
> —Duc de La Rochefoucauld

Positive Relationships

The relationships between community members in the preceding example promoted a healthier community. It is but one example of how neighbors responding to each other in healthy ways can promote positive relationships. Communities that promote relationships are communities that can become healthier. Positive relationships can do much to reduce the sense of isolation and improve the capacity for community building.

> Civilization is a method of living, an attitude of equal respect for all men [and women].
> —Jane Addams

Stability

Change creates instability and unfamiliarity. Schools and communities undergoing change are likely to feel tremors, much like those felt during an earthquake. Stability needs to be pursued to offset these tremors. This can be created through the development and communication of purposes, expectations, and boundaries. Knowing where we are heading, how we intend to get there, and what the boundaries are helps, as do stable structures, which provide the protection needed while experiencing change.

> I think somehow, we learn who we really are and then live with that decision.
> —Eleanor Roosevelt

Skills and Abilities to Promote Growth and Transcend Our Differences

To participate effectively as community members, individuals will need to learn new skills. Most important, learning how to negotiate and cope effectively with the apparent differences that proliferate in our complex communities between age groups, sociodemographic groups, voluntary groups, and across different governmental agencies are essential. At these boundary points, the system is most vulnerable to positive change. "Rather than being self-protective walls, boundaries become the place of meeting and exchange . . . They are the place where new relationships take form, an important place of exchange and growth as one individual chooses to respond to another. As connections proliferate and the system weaves itself into existence, it becomes difficult to interpret boundaries as defenses, or even as markers of where one individual ends" (Wheatley & Kellner-Rogers, 1998a, p. 12).

> Education has in America's whole history been the major hope for improving the individual and society.
> —Gunnar Myrdal

We need to think about community as an entity, a receptacle that can be used to bring everyone together, rather than as being composed of unique and disparate parts that have little in common.

Connectivity

All stakeholders in the community have legitimate roles to play and legitimate ends to serve. As such, participation from all stakeholders about ways to strengthen the community brings more depth to the discussions. A balance of the differing voices promotes uncovering ideas that can be explored and agreed upon by all stakeholders. In fact, even one voice can be very powerful, as Rosa Parks reminded us as she moved us deeply to join together to help shape a new community image about race relations.

> The only thing necessary for the triumph of evil is for good men to do nothing.
>
> —Edmund Burke

Engaging collective voices from across the community spectrum can lead to efforts to promote community resiliency. The glue is connectivity and participation that holds us together to create the foundation for a healthy and resilient community.

Exercise 2.2: What Holds Your Community Together?

This exercise works best if it includes a representative sample of community members. This broadens appreciation of different facets within the community. The exercise can also be used with like composition of groups if that is what is required.

Each community has its strengths and areas in need of improvement. Understanding what the community in which we work and/or live has makes a difference in what we see. In examining your community's strengths and shortcomings, think about the following five areas: (1) knowing one another, (2) positive relationships, (3) stability, (4) skills and abilities to promote growth and transcend boundaries, and (5) connectivity.

1. Divide into five groups. Each group will take one of the above five topical areas. Give each group chart paper and marking pens to write down their thoughts.

2. Have each group identify some of the changes in the community that have occurred regarding the area they are focusing on, e.g., "knowing one another."

3. Next, have the members in each group identify examples of how their community effectively meets that area and then generate ideas to strengthen it. How do you know that people know each other? What would you do differently?

4. Each small group shares what they have discussed with the entire group.

5. After each group has shared, ask the large group to identify the commonalities across the five areas? What do you need to do to continue to support the areas that are working well? What are the areas that need strengthening? Pick one or two areas to prioritize.

LEADERSHIP ACTIVITIES FOR BUILDING A RESILIENT COMMUNITY: WHERE DO WE START?

The diversity of life experiences and the talents and skills of all residents are often untapped. All are required to create a resilient community. When voices are heard, positive energy can be created and a sense of belonging and support can be developed throughout the community.

A good starting place for leaders is to clarify present attitudes and perceptions about the community. To what extent is it a place that cares, promotes connections, forges relationships, and supports growth? Exercise 2.2 can be used to provide the impetus for a dialogue with community members. It is important to foster these qualities for a community to be healthy and resilient.

Leaders who promote shared values and purposes tend to minimize formal mechanisms of control, focusing more on the development of normative understandings that encourage individuals and groups to come together for the well-being of all. Policies, rules, and structures can provide boundaries and promote stability. They can also be unresponsive to individual differences and needs. In fact, policies, rules, and structures can be a big part of the problem, getting in the way of the development of shared values and purposes.

> Take care of yourself.
> Take care of each other.
> Take care of this place
>
> —*Margaret Wheatley and Myron Kellner-Rogers*

Radical actions are not always required to improve the health of a community. In fact, leaders who help change the course a degree or two, over time, can make a powerful difference in moving a community away from dysfunctional behaviors and toward healthy ones.

> Act well at the moment, and you have performed a good action to all eternity.
>
> —*Johann Kaspar Lavater*

Community building does not require that everyone agree about everything that needs to be done, but they do need to agree to start. It is important that all community members believe they matter to each other. If this belief exists and it is fostered, anything is possible.

> That action alone is just that does not harm either party to a dispute.
>
> —*Mohandas Gandhi*

Leaders and Schools as the Starting Place to Build Community Resiliency

The often-used saying "think globally and act locally" is the only realistic way we will begin to move our complex communities and, thus, our nation and world toward the health and resiliency that we so clearly need. Acting locally, taking on the work that needs to be done, piece by piece, is how, over the long haul, the larger community will be positively affected.

> This is still a very wealthy country. The failure is of spirit and insight.
>
> —*Jerry Brown*

Schools are the local focus of this book not only because we believe that resiliency in schools is so desperately needed to achieve their purposes but also because resilient schools have an immediate and direct impact on the improvement of community resiliency. Schools are where community members spend their formative years. They are also likely to be one of the primary places where many community members interact.

What Can Leaders Do?

Leaders who have vision are able to move their schools and communities into a more resilient place. They create a sense of belonging, shared values and beliefs, common goals that benefit everyone and an infrastructure that supports well-being.

> The worst sin towards our fellow creatures is not to hate them, but to be indifferent to them; that's the essence of inhumanity.
>
> —*George Bernard Shaw*

Exercise 2.3: Considerations for Leaders

Leaders who focus on building and expanding the sense of community create a more resilient one. Take into consideration the following areas. What rating on a scale of one (low) to five (high) would you, your staff, your parents, and other community members give for each of the areas? How would you answer each of the questions?

1. Sense of belonging
   - What tells you that your school and community have a sense of belonging?
   - How do you access people who are not currently participating?
   - Do you have representation from all facets of your community in the formal and informal structures of the school and community?

2. Shared values and beliefs
   - How do you know you have shared values and beliefs in your school and community?
   - Have you conducted activities where you identified and embraced shared values and beliefs? How long ago did you discuss these values and beliefs? How do you continue to strengthen them?
   - Who is involved in the process?

3. Infrastructure that supports well-being
   - How do people know where they can get support when needed?
   - Who sets up and maintains the support structure?
   - How organized is the school and community?

4. Common goals that benefit everyone
   - Who created the goals? How often does the community discuss them?
   - Have you done an analysis of the shifts within your community? Are the sociodemographics still the same? What about other factors?
   - How and where are the goals displayed?

Leaders need to reflect on these community building areas. What other areas would you add to the list? What examples can you give of each one? How would your staff, parents, and other community members rate each of the areas?

Leaders can make a difference in schools and communities. Leaders who have the vision, support, determination, patience, and skills needed to reach out to a community will find a community that reaches back.

To help leaders make a positive difference, the four chapters in Part II provide focused attention on students, educators, the school, and the community. Chapter 3 starts the journey by discussing ways of promoting resiliency among students.

PART II

Resiliency for Everyone

3

Student Resiliency

Building a Base for Positive Living

"The object of education is to prepare the young to educate themselves throughout their lives."
—Robert Maynard Hutchins

Kids are at the heart of our families, schools, communities, and dreams. They are the keepers of our dreams. From birth to adulthood, the stories about kids who have overcome extraordinary odds to become productive members of society are powerful.

Consider the following documentary story, told by Susan Drury (2006) on *This American Life*, about Chauncey Julius from Columbia, Tennessee, who was following in his father's footsteps by dealing drugs to his ninth-grade classmates. His mom had a good job in a factory, but his father used up the money for drugs. After nearly getting caught for selling drugs, Chauncey decided that he did not want to end up running all the time and stopped selling drugs. He had written some goals that he kept with him. His goals were to graduate from high school and go to college. He was entering tenth grade with only half of a credit from ninth grade. He knew he needed help and asked for it at school. He worked with a guidance counselor, Mary Lynn, who believed in his goals to graduate from high school and enter college. She, as well as other teachers, worked with him, and he started bringing his grades up. He attended summer school, joined the football team, and later became captain. He was selected to go to Boys State as a delegate, where he was elected to the highest position, governor. That was a turning point for him. He became an ordained minister and continued turning his life around. He became one of the most popular kids in school with lots of support and attention. People saw him as a kid who would go far. But he did not graduate from high school, lacking one credit and, thus, his dream to go to college. He was disappointed and thought his dream ended until he decided to take the GED, and was admitted to college with a scholarship. He felt the momentum he gained in high school was lost in college and dropped out after the first term. He did not want people to know that he had failed, so he joined the military where he received promotions because he was seen to have the leadership ability and the attitude to be successful. When he got out of the service, he married and decided to return to college. This time he was successful and graduated.

A story is told by Eric Butterworth (as cited in Canfield & Hansen, 1993) about a professor who asked his students to study 200 young boys from a Baltimore slum and predict what their future lives would be like. The basic conclusion they came to was that these boys would probably not lead very successful lives. A quarter of a century later, another professor asked his students to do a follow-up study and see how things actually turned out for them. Of the 180 men who were in their thirties that they could find, 176 had defied the odds to live productive lives. Many had become doctors, lawyers, and businessmen. Wondering how the earlier predictions could be so wrong, the professor asked some of these men to identify the sources of their success. The frequent reply was, "There was a teacher." More specifically, most of them mentioned the same teacher. He searched for and found the long since retired fourth-grade teacher, and he asked her what she did to help them become successful. Her straightforward answer was, "It's really very simple, I loved those boys."

A documentary movie, *Hoop Dreams*, spans the teen years of two African American youths who struggle to overcome the effects of poverty and living in communities replete with antisocial elements. Counterbalancing these negative factors are understanding and supportive home environments, as well as a special talent that they possess—the ability to play basketball extremely well. The movie illustrates the extraordinary difficulties they confront and how, inch by inch, they cope with and overcome many of these difficulties.

> In every child who is born, under no matter what circumstances, and of no matter what parents, the potentiality of the human race is born again.
>
> —James Agee

We tend to think of such stories as exceptions to the rule. In reality, there are many similar stories that we can all recall from our own experiences. What stories come to mind when you think about youngsters you have known who have overcome significant odds and succeeded? Probably, with very little thought, you can identify many such youngsters, maybe even yourself.

The intriguing question to explore is what is it about them that accounts for their successes, whereas others in similar situations have not succeeded? In this chapter, we focus on problems that many youth are coping with and why, too often, we seem to be unable to respond to their problems effectively. We then examine how our unconscious problem solver mind maps contribute to the situation and how we can shift this approach to a more positive and effective approach—resiliency. We discuss various ways to affect students' resiliency positively, focusing on the six resiliency elements introduced in Chapter 1. We also explore ways of restructuring our schools as well as our attitudes and beliefs so we can relate more effectively with our students. Last, strategies for leaders for building resilient youth are given.

WHAT ARE THE PROBLEMS THAT YOUTH FACE?

We often ignore problems that youth face until they become crises, and then we are forced to recognize them. A sad example of this pattern of behavior is our response to the rash of killings—of students, parents, teachers, and administrators—committed by predominately young males over a little more than a decade, from 1996 through 2007. Worldwide, there have been 48 incidents and countless deaths with 75 percent, or 36 out of 48, of them occurring in the United States. Males committed all of the killings, except one that a female committed. These tragedies were sufficiently dramatic and widespread to catch our attention, particularly the most tragic of them: the mass killings at Virginia Polytechnic Institute and State University in Blacksburg, Virginia. It should be noted that this does not really represent an increase in teen homicides—only a change of venue from the inner city to suburban and rural homicides.

These highly charged negative behavioral manifestations of youngsters who are in jeopardy are neither isolated events nor a new phenomenon. A few years ago, the Children's Defense Fund (2005) published *The State of America's Children*, concluding that, on any given day,

- 1 mother dies in childbirth;
- 4 children are killed by abuse or neglect;
- 5 children or teens commit suicide;
- 8 children or teens are killed by firearms;
- 77 babies die before their first birthdays;
- 177 children are arrested for violent crimes;
- 375 children are arrested for drug abuse;
- 390 babies are born to mothers who received late or no prenatal care;
- 860 babies are born at low birth weight;
- 1,186 babies are born to teen mothers;
- 1,900 public school students are corporally punished;
- 2,076 babies are born without health insurance;
- 2,341 babies are born to mothers who are not high school graduates;
- 2,385 babies are born into poverty;
- 2,482 children are confirmed abused or neglected;
- 2,756 high school students drop out;
- 3,742 babies are born to unmarried mothers;
- 4,262 children are arrested; and
- 16,964 public school students are suspended.

According to the Children's Defense Fund's (1990) Report Card, seventeen years ago, the outlook for children on any given day was that

- 6 teenagers commit suicide;
- 10 children die from guns;
- 30 children are wounded by guns;
- 211 children are arrested for drug abuse;
- 437 children are arrested for drinking or drunken driving;
- 623 teenagers get syphilis or gonorrhea;
- 1,512 teenagers drop out of school;
- 1,629 children are in adult jails;
- 1,849 children are abused or neglected;
- 2,556 children are born out of wedlock;
- 2,989 children see their parents divorced;
- 3,288 children run away from home;
- 7,742 teens become sexually active; and
- 135,000 children bring a gun to school.

In comparing the two lists, some statistics have not changed significantly (e.g., suicides and death by firearms), while others have increased dramatically (e.g., abuse, neglect, and drug abuse) and others have decreased (e.g., teen pregnancies). The focus on what is reported also has shifted. The 2005 list is more comprehensive and details more than the 1990 list does.

Many efforts have been made to deal with these stark realities, but for the most part, the problems have proved to be rather intractable. In fact, many of the negative trends regarding adolescents were actually diminishing during the 1980s, but during the 1990s and sustaining through the early years of this century, these figures moved back upward. For example, one study noted, "Teenage cigarette smoking is up by as much as 2 percent per year since 1992. Marijuana use has increased for three straight years among 8th, 10th, and 12th grade students. More teens live in poverty now than during the previous decade [and] teenage homicide has increased" (Blum & Rinehart, 1997, p. 5).

The Children's Defense Fund's report (Davis, 2006) that focused on gun violence, found,

> 2,827 children and teens died as a result of gun violence in 2003—more than the number of American fighting men and women killed in hostile action in Iraq from 2003 to April 2006. In 2003, 56 preschoolers were killed by firearms, compared to 52 law enforcement officers killed in the line of duty.
>
> More 10- to 19-year-olds die from gunshot wounds than from any other cause except motor vehicle accidents. Almost 90 percent of the children and teens killed by firearms in 2003 were boys. Boys ages 15 to 19 are nearly nine times as likely as girls of the same age to be killed by a firearm.
>
> In 2003, there were more than nine times as many suicides by guns among White children and teens as among Black children and teens. The firearm death rate for Black males ages 15 to 19 is more than four times that of White males the same age.

Another problem that children and teens face is bullying. With easy access to cell phones, instant messages, and the Internet, bullying has expanded beyond a kid who pushes another one down. Children are being hounded to the extent that one Japanese child committed suicide to get away from his perpetrators. Mozes (2007) reported Tarshi's survey results that nine out of ten elementary students were bullied either physically or psychologically. One-third of the kids who skip school in Britain are bullied (Bindel, 2006). Lelchuk (2007) reported that 40 percent of teens were bullied.

> There is no greater insight into the future than recognizing when we save our children, we save ourselves.
> —*Margaret Mead*

Given the energy expended and the minimal positive impact for the effort, most of us shake our heads and wonder how could this have happened. Exercise 3.1 offers a useful way to look at this question.

Exercise 3.1: How Could This Have Happened?

This exercise can be used to encourage people (e.g., teachers, parents, or both together) to share their concerns and discuss why we find ourselves in the difficult situations that exist in many of our communities. In the process, members can get a better picture of the many factors involved and, hopefully, start to develop a commonly held set of beliefs and a clearer set of understandings as a basis for taking action.

1. Distribute copies of the Children's Defense Fund (2005) findings (Handout 3 in the Resource section). Ask group members to review the findings and discuss which ones seem to be true of their community. Ask the group to review similarities and themes as they may relate to youngsters in their community. Which, if any, are observable among the youth? If information summaries concerning your own community, region, or state are available and are similar to the Children's Defense Fund findings, you might want to distribute them at this point. (Check with the local health department, police department, mayor's office, and the school information office for this information.) Lead a discussion and record agreements.

3. Ask the group whether they know of efforts currently under way in the community (by the school, local government, voluntary groups, or others) that are seeking to respond to these themes. Ask them to share what they know about these efforts. Record group members' thoughts.

4. If efforts are presently going on, ask the group to explore how effective each is in improving the lives of youths in the community. Where they appear to be successful, explore why this is the case. Where they fall short, explore why this appears to be the situation.

5. Last, ask the group to discuss whether there are other ways of addressing the identified shortcomings and, as a way of moving toward positive response, whether they would like to reconvene to talk about next steps.

CHANGING OUR MIND MAPS: FROM DEFICITS TO POTENTIALS

Because we spend so much time and energy talking about problems, we soon come to see everything as just that—problems. Most well meaning parents, teachers, and administrators are constantly on the watch for problems that youngsters may possess (e.g., learning disabilities, short attention spans, antisocial behaviors, and substance abuse).

There certainly are enough problems around for us to worry about. But there is a downside to focusing on problems: we soon come to view things in a myopic and negative fashion, similar to the way many police officers tend to see everyone as potential criminals.

> When I see the *Ten Most Wanted Lists*... I always have this thought: If we'd made them feel wanted earlier, they wouldn't be wanted now.
>
> —*Eddie Cantor*

This problem-oriented perspective has significant implications for how we deal with youngsters. First, coming from this perspective, we focus our energies on problems children may display. We highlight negative behaviors rather than *all* behaviors, their strengths as well as their shortcomings. Second, coming from this perspective, we tend to generalize from experiences with so-called problem kids we know to any youngsters who appear to have *the potential* to exhibit similar shortcomings. Exercise 3.2 emphasizes the impact of the way we view youngsters.

> People are always ready to admit a man's ability after he gets there.
>
> —*Bob Edwards*

Exercise 3.2: Strengths or Deficits: What Do You See?

To get the most out of the exercise, *please respond to the instructions in the order they are given.* Provide group members with a page of blank paper, and ask them to do the following:

1. Think of a *real* youngster you know who you believe possesses multiple at-risk factors. Risk factors might include environmental realities as well as personal problems, behaviors, and attitudes. Draw a stick figure of this youngster and label it "At Risk."

2. As you think of the factors this particular youngster exhibits, write them next to the stick figure.

3. Get together with another member of your group. Taking turns, share the risk factors that each of you has identified regarding both of your youngsters. Listen carefully for commonalities.

4. Ask the group to come together to share risk factors that they mentioned most frequently. List them on a chalkboard or on chart paper.

5. Provide a second sheet of blank paper for each group member and ask him or her to draw another stick figure and label it the "Resilient" youngster.

6. Next, think about *the same youngster you just identified as exhibiting multiple risk factors.* What does this youngster have going for him or her? These resiliency factors can be environmentally related or emanate from personal behaviors and attitudes. As they come to mind, write them next to the resilient stick figure.

7. Share your thoughts about this youngster's resiliency factors with the same partner you talked with in Step 3, and listen carefully for common conclusions as that person shares with you.

8. As with Step 4, ask the group to share the factors that they identified most frequently. Record comments on a chalkboard or on chart paper.

9. Ask group members to reflect on the activity. Did they find it easier to fill in the at-risk stick figure or the resiliency one? How many found the at-risk part of the exercise easier to complete? How many found the resiliency part of the exercise easier to complete? Many will probably conclude that it was easier to identify deficits. If this is true for your group, ask members to discuss the implications.

10. Ask group members to talk about why it is so important to see their youngsters as possessing resiliency factors as well as risk factors. Could relationships with such youngsters be different if group members focused more on the strengths or resiliencies that they possess? Furthermore, would it make a difference in how these youngsters might see themselves? Could it increase the likelihood of their succeeding in school and in life?

SOURCE: This exercise was adapted from one N. Henderson originally developed.

The point of the exercise is clear: we relate to others based on how we perceive them. When relating with youngsters, we need to be particularly sensitive to this reality because they are still forming their self-images. As Shel Silverstein (1974) reminded us, we have a powerful ability to detract or build on children's potential for resiliency during their formative years:

Listen to the MUSTN'TS, child,

Listen to the DON'TS

Listen to the SHOULDN'TS

The IMPOSSIBLES, the WON'TS

Listen to the NEVER HAVES

Then listen close to me

Anything can happen, child,

ANYTHING can be (p. 27).

From which mind map do you operate? Is it "the impossibles" mind map or is it the "anything can be" mind map? What about your school's mind map and your community's mind map? These questions are important to think about because, in large part, what we see is what we get. Each of us has extraordinary strengths, capabilities, and potentials. We are not suggesting that problems are irrelevant. If they are real, they must be confronted, but we should not let them blind us to the potential for youngsters' growth and success.

As parents, educators, and community members, we are guides and role models for today's youth. What we say and do matters. We can add to their' difficulties, leaving them to cope on their own as best they can, or we can be positive forces in their lives, relating with them in ways that encourage wellness, confidence, and pride in positive achievements. Exercise 3.3 emphasizes the importance of how we respond to youngsters.

> If a child lives with approval, he learns to live with himself.
>
> —*Dorothy Law Nolte*

Exercise 3.3: A Judgment Test

1. This activity can be done individually, but it is best done with groups. Distribute copies of the case descriptions that follow (see Handout 4 in the Resource section).

Case A

A girl, age sixteen, was orphaned and willed to custody of her grandmother by her mother, who was separated from an alcoholic husband, now deceased. Her mother rejected the homely child, who had been proven to lie and steal sweets. She swallowed a penny to attract attention. Her father was fond of the child. The child lived in fantasy as the mistress of her father's household for years. The grandmother, who is widowed, cannot manage the girl's four young uncles and aunts in the household. The young uncle drinks and has left home without telling the grandmother his destination. The aunt, emotional over a love affair, locks herself in her room. The grandmother has resolved to be stricter with the granddaughter because she fears she has failed with her own children. She dresses the granddaughter oddly. She refuses to let her have playmates. She puts her in braces to keep her back straight. She was not sent to grade school. An aunt on the paternal side of the family is crippled, and an uncle is asthmatic.

Case B

A boy, who is a senior in high school, has obtained a certificate from a physician stating that a nervous breakdown makes it necessary for him to leave school for six months. The boy is not a good all-around student, he has no friends, teachers find him to be a problem, he developed speech late, he has poorly adjusted to school, and his father is ashamed of his son's lack of athletic ability. The boy has odd mannerisms, makes up his own religion, and chants hymns to himself—his parents regard him as "different."

Case C

A boy, age six, had a large head at birth. He was thought to have had brain fever (meningitis). His three siblings died before his birth. His mother does not agree with relatives and neighbors that the child is probably abnormal. The child is sent to school, and the teacher diagnoses him as mentally ill. The boy's mother is angry—she withdraws the child from school, saying she will teach him herself.

2. After reading the three cases, group members should discuss their predictions:
   - How will each of these young people function as they grow up?
   - Will they be gifted, average-normal, psychotic, neurotic, delinquent, or mentally deficient?
   - Will they excel or will they lead very difficult lives? Ask members why they have come to these conclusions.

3. Last, look at the additional information about these cases that Handout 5 in the Resource section provides and respond to the question posed there.

Adults' actions impact what happens to youngsters. What we say and do does matter. Youngsters can overcome obstacles. How they do so has been well documented. Emmy Werner and Ruth Smith's (1992) classic study of at-risk youth on the Hawaiian Island of Kauai is an extraordinary longitudinal study, spanning more than fifty years, that documents the human capacity to "overcome the odds." The following is a summary:

1. Their longitudinal study includes all of the survivors of the 837 individuals born on Kauai in 1955, from their prenatal period and, currently, into their fifties.

2. About two-thirds grew up with sufficient support to function as effective youngsters and as adults.

3. The other one-third was identified as "high risk" because they had multiple risk factors in their lives, including prenatal stress, chronic poverty, and family situations marked by parents with some mix of low education, alcoholism, and mental disturbance.

4. About one-third of these high-risk children seemed invulnerable to risk factors. They led healthy lives as adolescents and developed into normal young adults by the end of their teen years. Their human drive to survive and succeed apparently helped them overcome the adversities that high-risk individuals confront.

5. The rest of the high-risk children (about two-thirds) did develop problems by the age of ten (e.g., delinquency and mental health problems). However, the majority of the individuals in this group were doing well by the time they reached their thirties. *This is one of the most important findings of the study.* That is, although many of those who were identified as likely to exhibit high-risk behavior did indeed do so, *it was not a one-way street. Most found their way back by their early adult years.*

6. Only a small number of the original high-risk group (about one-sixth of them) continued to exhibit problems as adults.

What accounts for the fact that the majority of those who exhibited risk behaviors during their younger years turned out to be more resilient than anticipated? Werner and Smith (1992) drew a number of conclusions, the most important of which are these:

• Leaving their homes of origin gave many a new lease on life.
• Some joined the military and thrived within the required behavioral boundaries, gained new skills, were encouraged to achieve, and participated in experiences that were meaningful to them.
• Many married, became parents, and joined church groups.
• Someone along the way reached out with the message that "you matter" and "it doesn't matter what you have done in the past."
• They developed competencies that were valued by others.
• Sources of support were available to them—most often from neighbors, teachers, and youth leaders. Such support individuals or groups became, in effect, their extended families. The care and support provided are important elements that helped these high-risk participants make it through their hardest times.

> I have never taught an "at-risk" student in my life.
>
> —*Herbert Kohl*

The findings of Werner and Smith's (1992) ongoing Kauai study, and those of similar longitudinal studies (e.g., Anthony & Cohler, 1987; Benard, 2004; Elder, Liker, & Cross, 1984; Farrington, 1989; Higgins, 1985; Rutter, 1989) are important guides. What these studies tell us is what we should already know through our own life's experiences and through the lives of others that have come back from extremely deficit situations—*most people are amazingly resilient.*

The title of Werner and Smith's (1992) book, *Overcoming the Odds*, though not intended, implies that individuals who exhibit resiliency are on their own when trying to overcome negative environments. On the contrary, with positive support from the environment—schools, families, and communities—*we can change the odds.* We need to do this so that more youngsters avoid engaging in risky behaviors. For those who already exhibit risk behaviors, we need to help them work through their difficulties easier, faster, and with fewer negative repercussions, similar to the story of Chauncey Julius. He learned how to be resilient in his early years on the street, but it also took caring adults in his life as well as his determination to succeed to bounce back.

What happens when schools are unable or unwilling to help troubled youngsters? Some who drop out or are pushed out of school may find sufficient support in the alternative schools that have been developed. These alternative schools can be the kind of environments where such youngsters gain the balance they need to get back on track, succeed academically, and pursue meaningful and positive lives.

Others may find their way back from risk behavior by becoming involved in community-based organizations. McLaughlin, Irby, and Langman (1994) provided convincing evidence that "sanctuaries," varying from local storefront organizations to nationally known organizations such as the YMCA can encourage youngsters to become engaged in positive, proactive activities (e.g., theater or athletics). These organizations provide support, security, caring relationships, and opportunities for achievement. They do this without making judgments that can make the difference between a life fraught with problems and a life that is positive and productive.

> Likely as not, the child you can do the least with will do the most to make you proud.
>
> —*Mignon McLaughlin*

Many youngsters who attend alternative schools, participate in community-based organizations, or both, manage to do well and become more resilient. Why don't these same youngsters succeed in regular public schools? Many of them do much better in other settings, so it cannot just be the students' fault. We need to focus on the school environment. We need to change schools in ways that can help youngsters succeed as students and as people. What is called for is conscious efforts on the schools' part to develop youngsters' resiliency.

STUDENT RESILIENCY: THE COMMUNITY'S AND SCHOOL'S RESPONSIBILITIES

Promoting student resiliency is not just about doing something to make students feel good about themselves, although this is a worthwhile positive outcome. Beyond such feel good results, there is growing evidence that promoting resiliency for youngsters can also result in improved student retention, a more positive school climate, and improved academic outcomes.

Benard's (2004) review of research studies indicates that children with resilient attributes adapt better to challenging situations. They exhibit good planning and other problem-solving abilities and skills that help them avoid making poor choices. Many studies typify resilient youngsters as being flexible and resourceful, both of which are important attributes for coping with challenges and developing positive and meaningful lives. Such children are highly likely to have, as Benard noted, "a sense of purpose and a bright future" (p. 28).

But does this translate into academic success? Benard's (2004) review of Meier's (1995) and Mehan, Hubbard, and Villanueva's (1994) work seems to indicate so. Purposes and motivations challenge students to achieve. Research over the past two decades on successful schools and programs for youngsters in difficult situations has shown that high expectations, along with support, can decrease the number of school dropouts and increase the number of students who go on to college.

Waxman's (2004) review of recent studies (e.g., Alva, 1991; Gonzalez & Padilla, 1997; McClendon, Nettles, & Wigfield, 2000; Nettles, Mucherach, & Jones, 2000; Read, 1999; Reyes & Jason, 1993) also provides persuasive evidence of a direct and powerful relationship between academic achievement and the resiliency exhibited by students. As Waxman reported, a growing body of research points to the conclusion that students exhibiting academic success have family and peer support, have supportive teacher feedback, and are involved in school life. Conversely, students who exhibit low self-esteem have little parental support and involvement, are not engaged positively with their schools, are not usually motivated to succeed, and do not achieve good academic results.

Chapter 1 presented a list of internal and environmental protective factors (Table 1.1). The extent to which these factors exist in our lives directly affects our ability to exhibit resiliency, whether as children, adolescents, or adults. How can we help youngsters develop resiliency profiles that are replete with these factors? Changing the way we respond to students' resiliency needs begins with an honest assessment of how we interact with them now. Exercise 3.4 can provide an initial assessment of your school's current situation.

Exercise 3.4: Supporting Youngsters' Protective Factors

1. Distribute copies of Table 1.1 (Handout 2 in the Resource section). Ask group members to assess the extent to which "typical" youngsters in your school possess these internal and environmental protective factors. Which are most present? Which are least present?

2. How present are the internal protective factors among youngsters who seem to be at risk? How present are the environmental protective factors for the at-risk youngsters?

3. Are there differences between the extent to which (so-called) typical and at-risk youngsters possess protective factors? If so, discuss whether the school is doing anything that may be contributing to these differences.

4. Discuss what the school may need to do, or do more effectively, to help all youngsters acquire these resiliency factors.

Another way of finding out how many protective factors youngsters have in your school and community would be to assess their situation. Exercise 3.5 will provide more in-depth understanding of the protective factors they possess.

Exercise 3.5: What Do You Need?

The intention of this exercise is to have youngsters assess their own protective factors. The following directions are for the facilitator.

1. Distribute copies of Table 1.1 (Handout 2 in the Resource section) to each youngster in the group. Go over each item on the *Internal Protective Factors* list to ensure there is a clear understanding of the terms. Give examples when necessary.

2. Ask them to think about a time that was very stressful for them. It might be parents separating, a pet that died, or someone close who was in an accident. During that time what did they use to help get through it? Circle the ones on the internal protective factors list that helped get them through this tough time.

3. Ask them to take a few minutes and share with the person sitting next to them how these protective factors helped them.

4. Ask the group how many used at least one of the Protective Factors during a tough time. Ask them which one(s) and how it was helpful.

5. Ask them what they learned about themselves through the process. What relevance does it have for their lives?

6. Have them read the *Environmental Protective Factors* and be sure they are clear about them before continuing. Ask them to identify the ones that exist in their school.

7. Go through the list, one by one, and for each, ask if they think each factors is seen most of the time in their school. Proceed through all of them. Identify which ones were prevalent and identify those that do not appear to be prevalent.

8. Ask them what the school could do to change the environment to be healthier. Ask what they could do to make it healthier.

9. If there is more than one group, combine the results. Then meet with the staff to determine ways of enhancing the factors that support students' resiliency. Invite students to participate in the discussions.

10. Repeat steps 6–10, focusing on the community.

Another way of proceeding with this assessment is to use the approach developed by the Search Institute, a nonprofit organization based in Minneapolis, Minnesota. The Search Institute has surveyed parents and youngsters in communities across the country to identify what it calls *developmental assets*, which are similar in nature to the internal and environmental protective factors but are more specifically focused on the needs of young people (Scales, et al., 2006; Benson, 1997; Benson, Galbraith, & Espeland, 1995; Leffert, Benson, & Roehlkepartain, 1997; Roehlkepartain & Benson, 1996). The extent to which there is evidence of external assets (e.g., parent support, communication, involvement, positive school climate, and involvement in school extracurricular activities) and internal assets (e.g., achievement motivation, homework, helping others, assertiveness skills, and self-esteem) directly affects youngsters' levels of resiliency. The Search Institute has correlated such behavioral indicators as extent of alcohol use, early sexual experience, and school success with the number of assets that are present in the environment as well as within the individual. The more assets that are in existence, the less risk-related behavior will be evidenced and the more school success will be seen.

> This is our village
> These are our children
> Love them
> Teach them
> Guide them
>
> —*Anonymous, Battle Creek, Michigan billboard (2/15/98)*

Figure 3.1 Learning Barriers and Responses

Artist: Todd Tibbals, Los Ranchos, New Mexico

LEADERSHIP STRATEGIES THAT PROMOTE STUDENT RESILIENCY

In all likelihood, your school has probably already developed many responses to student resiliency needs. However, unless the approach is comprehensive and focuses on basic resiliency elements rather than on the symptoms that happen to be displayed, these efforts may lead to meager results. Figure 3.1 illustrates this clearly.

Our hope is that students will possess the positive characteristics noted in the upper left-hand corner of Figure 3.1. However, the sad reality is that many of them are burdened by the barriers to learning identified on the wall and the box of problems being dragged along.

With the best of intentions, we fund programs for certain classifications of students (e.g., at-risk and those needing compensatory education) and provide special programs (e.g., substance abuse and remedial reading) to try to meet their specific needs. What we need to do is take a holistic approach, placing things in a larger societal perspective, and recognizing that the specific manifestations we are observing are often symptoms of deeper problems. Students with low resiliency will always find creative ways of acting out, including exhibiting learning problems or other dysfunctional behaviors, such as low school attendance, bullying, substance abuse, teen pregnancies, gang activities, and violence. Certainly, we need to respond to these symptomatic realities but we also need to address the deeper problems that they represent. We need to get to the taproot, *the absence or paucity of elements that promote resiliency*, to reduce the potential of dysfunctional behaviors associated with low resiliency.

A number of suggestions follow for improving youngsters' resiliency at your school. We encourage you to engage educators and parents in discussions about these suggestions and how they can enhance the resiliency of youngsters in ways that are appropriate to your situation. We also encourage you and others to include additional suggestions that might be worth implementing.

Increase Positive Connections

> The key to effective prevention efforts is to reinforce within every arena, the natural social bonds between young and old, between siblings, between friends that give meaning to one's life and a . . . reason for commitment and caring.
>
> —*Emmy Werner*

If we do not provide opportunities for developing positive connections, youngsters will find other ways to satisfy their bonding needs. That is the way of human nature. Gangs exist because they fill a bonding void for many youngsters. Gang membership may be viewed as antisocial bonding, but it clearly fills the need to be connected. When many opportunities for positive connections that engage youngsters effectively are provided, gang membership becomes less desirable.

Leadership Strategies for Increasing Positive Connections

- Promote caring and consistent relationships with supportive adults as well as positive peer bonding opportunities within the school.
- Provide a variety of extracurricular activities before, during, and after school that appeal to different interests. The possibilities are rich and varied including athletics, theater and the arts, service clubs, and academic enrichment opportunities.
- Diversify teaching approaches by encompassing multiple intelligences to account for different ways of learning. Besides promoting academic success, diversification of teaching approaches can encourage students to become more involved with classroom and school dynamics.
- Encourage family involvement to promote a sense of shared purposes between parents, children, and the school. This is easier to accomplish at the elementary school level, but although more difficult, it is just as important to encourage parental involvement at the middle and high school levels. To do so, we need to identify relevant and real roles for parent involvement (e.g., as members of site-based management teams, teacher assistants, and mentors) and develop approaches that include them as part of their children's learning teams. We must reach out and contact parents much more regularly and more often. It is also helpful to emphasize sharing good news with them and place less emphasis on delivering bad news.
- Create smaller teacher-student groupings within schools to counteract the negative effects of large schools. Subunits such as "families" and "houses" can provide a sense of belonging as well as more opportunities for connecting.

Record other strategies to increase positive connections for students:

- _____
  _____
- _____
  _____
- _____
  _____

Set Clear, Consistent, and Appropriate Boundaries

Freedom, creativity, and growth are nurtured by setting realistic and appropriate boundaries that can give youngsters a sense of security and safety. Boundaries are especially important for troubled youth, who often view school as their only sanctuary from the chaos that otherwise dominates their lives. But a school can provide such a sanctuary only if attention is given to establishing boundaries that make it a safe and secure setting for students.

> Our aim is to discipline for activity, for work, for good; not for immobility, not for passivity, not for obedience.
>
> —*Maria Montessori*

Leadership Strategies for Promoting Clear, Consistent, and Appropriate Boundaries

- Develop boundary-related consequences that are clearly stated and appropriate.
- Involve students in the development of boundaries that are meaningful to them.
- Make caring and support the basis for the development of boundaries instead of viewing boundaries as discipline or punishment for misbehavior. This attitude is best reflected if boundary-related language is stated positively and focuses on positive academic and social behaviors. For example, "Students have the right to be drug free, to be respected, and to learn in conducive environmental conditions."
- Disseminate clear policies regarding boundaries to all involved—parents and educators as well as students—and actively seek their feedback and suggestions for improvements.

Record other strategies to promote clear, consistent, and appropriate boundaries for students:

- _____
  _____
- _____
  _____
- _____
  _____

Teach Life-Guiding Skills

Schools can be babysitting establishments that do little more than focus on containment; they can provide education for the basics—reading, writing, and math; or they can extend their efforts to include helping students develop life skills. Recently, there has been a growing recognition that youth are more likely to

> Too often, we give children answers to remember rather than problems to solve.
>
> —*Roger Lewin*

exhibit resiliency if they learn skills that equip them to cope effectively with the challenges of life. In fact, formal programs such as *Emotional Intelligence,* which focuses on helping students make their emotions work for them (Goleman, 1995), and *Character Counts,* which focuses on universal principles of ethics and character such as respect and responsibility (Lickona, 1991), have been developed to help guide schools in their efforts to bolster students' life skills. As we increase our consensus about what children need to learn and know beyond the academic basics so they can cope well as adults, we should see expanding efforts to provide opportunities for life skill development in schools.

Leadership Strategies for Fostering Life-Guiding Skills

- Emphasize cooperative learning approaches. Students can develop communications, conflict management, and assertiveness skills that will help them get along with others. They can also learn how to set meaningful goals and make better decisions through cooperative learning.
- Enrich the curriculum so that it focuses on life-guiding skills such as assertiveness, refusal skills, conflict resolution, decision making, problem solving, and stress management. This curriculum should be woven throughout the instructional program, but it can also be an integral part of specific courses such as civics or health.
- Integrate life skills into daily school activities—on the playground, in the lunchroom, and at extracurricular activities, as well as in the regular acadmic program.

Record other strategies that increase life-guiding skills for students:

- _____
  _____
- _____
  _____
- _____
  _____

Provide Nurture and Support

Nurture and support are key foundations of resiliency. If we are not cared for, we are likely to feel alone and alienated. Too many youngsters feel this way, especially those who are latchkey children or those who live in sterile or alienating homes and communities. Schools often add to their problems if they are excessively large or when high teacher-student ratios make it difficult to provide the focused attention that youngsters require. It is more difficult for educators to provide nurturance and support if they are responsible for larger numbers of students each day, particularly at the secondary level. However, even under these debilitating conditions, nurture and support can be provided.

> To have another individual express belief in you as a worthy human being in spite of your acne, awkwardness, and inexperience can be overwhelming.
>
> —James J. Fenwick

Leadership Strategies for Enhancing Nurturance and Support

- Know and call students by name.
- Identify and focus on individual students' needs and strengths.
- Be empathetic to students' school, home, and community situations.
- Encourage students to participate in learning situations.
- Provide opportunities for team or cooperative learning.

- Recognize and reward positive behaviors by, for example, showing appreciation for doing good class work.
- Encourage youngsters to share their concerns and provide positive feedback when they try to overcome them.
- Provide concentrated time blocks within the day and throughout the year for teachers and students to connect meaningfully.
- Schedule teacher assignments so they stay with their students, preferably for several years as students progress from grade to grade. At the elementary level, teachers may move with their students to the next grade level. At the middle and high school levels teachers may be in "families" or "houses" that promote students having teachers who know and care about them.

Record other strategies that enhance nurture and support for students:

- _____
  _____

- _____
  _____

- _____
  _____

Set and Communicate Purposes and Expectations

The message that needs to be sent is "You can do it, and I will support you in any way possible to help you do it!" It is too easy for schools to focus on control and orderliness and send the message, "Be quiet, behave well, do the minimum amount of academic work that is required, and you will get along and make it through school!" Many youngsters receive these same kinds of

> My idea of education is to unsettle the minds of the young and inflame their intellects.
> —*Robert Maynard Hutchins*

disincentive-oriented messages at home and in the community. The human spirit seeks opportunities for challenge, creativity, and growth. School should be a place where this spirit is encouraged, not dampened!

Leadership Strategies to Strengthen Purposes and Expectations

- Develop incentive programs that promote *every* student's potential to succeed. Create specific and realistic expectations for each student, and provide challenges that are both feasible and relevant. If students are allowed to participate in setting these expectations, they will be more motivated to accomplish them. The emphasis should be on competition with self rather than with others. This can be promoted by practicing and modeling cooperative learning principles and approaches.
- Make it clear that you believe your students can achieve and that you support them in their efforts to do so. A well-known example of this approach is Jaime Escalante's successful efforts to encourage his lower socioeconomic students to excel in math, particularly calculus, as described in the movie, *Stand and Deliver*. He believed that his students were capable of higher order thinking and he challenged them to do so. They responded and accomplished things well beyond what many believed they were capable of accomplishing.

- Encourage students to develop their interests and talents. Each of us has particular talents and skills that, if promoted, can build self-confidence as well as belief in our ability to achieve.
- Place responsibility for learning on students. Encourage them to set their own goals, search out appropriate learning content and activities, solve problems, and think critically so they can develop their own expectations for high achievement.
- Match teaching strategies with students' learning styles. For example, apply Gardner's (1983) schema of multiple intelligences, and vary instructional approaches to challenge students in ways that maximize their potentials to excel.
- Encourage students to support each other's successes in school and in life.

Record other strategies that strengthen purposes and expectations for students:

- _____

  _____

- _____

  _____

- _____

  _____

Provide Opportunities for Meaningful Participation

Students need to be viewed as participants in a learning community, not as the school's "customers." We get trapped in the student-as-customer mentality when we view educators as permanent residents and students as temporary participants.

> If [schools] are able to teach young people to have a critical mind and a socially oriented attitude, they will have done all that is necessary. Students will then become equipped with those qualities which are prerequisite for citizens living in a healthy democratic society.
>
> —*Albert Einstein*

Students play different roles than educators, but they have their own legitimate and important stakes in the life of the school beyond the classroom level. Thought of in this way, schools can be laboratories for social development. They are the places where students spend most of their waking hours for much of their young lives. They are the places where students, as well as educators, do their work. If we recognize this reality and see schools as laboratories for life skills development, we will seek ways of meaningfully engaging students.

Leadership Strategies for Improving Meaningful Participation

- Promote student participation in school governance. Examples of areas for meaningful student participation include discipline and extracurricular committees. Not so obvious examples include site-based management committees as well as curriculum committees. A review of policymaking needs and governance procedures and actions can likely lead to identification of numerous other possibilities.
- Develop service-learning initiatives, which have the added potential of enhancing partnerships between the school and the community.
- Provide opportunities to participate in communication initiatives such as school newspapers and school-based radio and television stations that students can organize and operate.

Record other strategies that improve meaningful participation of students:

- _____
  _____
- _____
  _____
- _____
  _____

BRINGING IT ALL TOGETHER AS AN OVERALL RESILIENCY-BUILDING APPROACH

In the real world, it is impossible to categorize these six resiliency elements tightly or to focus on them discretely. Rather, they cross over and affect each other directly and deeply. Ignoring any of them or placing too much emphasis on any single element can result in minimal positive impact. Resilient youngsters do not just happen—most need help in developing their resiliency. As your school initiates changes that are supportive of improving youngsters' resiliency levels in specific areas, give thought to how these changes relate to and are likely to affect other resiliency areas.

The resiliency contract that follows is an example of practicing what we have been encouraging in this chapter. Developing a contract between students, parents, and teachers can help promote a balanced, across-the-board approach to resiliency. It brings the three interested parties together to design an educational plan that fits each specific student's resiliency-building needs. Preferably, the contracting should be done at the outset of the school year and tailored to fit the student's priority resiliency needs. The process works as follows:

> The habits we form from childhood make no small difference, but rather they make all the difference.
>
> *—Aristotle*

- The teacher leads the student and parent(s)/guardian(s) through a brief discussion of the six resiliency elements.
- Together they assess the student's current situation regarding each of the resiliency elements, focusing on both strengths and areas to strengthen.
- They agree on goals and activities for each resiliency area that are relevant for the student to pursue.
- The teacher helps the student and parent(s)/guardian(s) understand the importance of all three contract signers' playing their appropriate roles in pursuing the goals and activities that will promote the student's resiliency, monitoring progress that is being made, making modifictions when appropriate, and celebrating successes as they occur.

Table 3.1 is a prototype of such a contract (see Handout 6 in the Resource section for a copy of the contract). Readers are encouraged to modify the categories in ways that may best meet their own particular needs. Taking the situation of each youngster into account and proceeding accordingly, we believe that even younger children have the ability to play a part in resiliency contract building.

This chapter has centered on the need to prioritize students' resiliency development needs and has provided strategies to help accomplish this important goal. There is growing evidence that schools can change and, in the process, positively support the resiliency of youngsters. For example, Henderson and Milstein (1996, 2003), provided examples of the process and impact of resiliency-building efforts in the Albuquerque Public Schools, and Krovetz (1999) documented resiliency strategies that have been applied in seven elementary and secondary schools in the area around San Jose, California.

However, this goal is not likely to be attained if we limit our efforts to student resiliency. Youth will not be encouraged to exhibit resiliency unless the adults in their lives act as positive resiliency role models. In Chapter 4, we turn our attention to the importance of promoting educator resiliency and explore ways to go about pursuing this important activity.

Table 3.1   Improving Student Resiliency: A Contract

Resiliency Element	Strengths	Areas to Strengthen
Positive Connections		
Clear, Consistent, and Appropriate Boundaries		
Life-Guiding Skills		
Nurture and Support		
Purposes and Expectations		
Meaningful Participation		

Signed by: _____ Student   Date:_____

_____ Parent

_____ Teacher

Meeting Dates: _____

_____

_____

_____

Exercise 3.6: Considerations for Leaders

Leaders who reflect on how they lead become stronger and more effective in moving others to take responsibility for their growth. Consider where you are in each of the following areas. Rate yourself from one (low) to five (high) in each of the areas. Remember to rate yourself where you are currently and not where you would like to be.

1. I see each student has having strengths and areas to improve.

2. My mind map is one of seeing potential instead of problems.

3. I can identify some of the students in my school and community who may fit on the "on any given day" list.

4. I help others at the school to support student resiliency daily.

5. I help others in the community to support student resiliency consistently.

6. I work with teachers to help them develop their ability to nurture student resiliency.

7. I believe that all youngsters can improve their resiliency.

What do your ratings tell you? What are your strengths? What are the areas you may need to develop further?

Chapter 4 focuses on educators' resilience. Resilient educators are better prepared to develop student resiliency.

Educator Resiliency

Nurturing the Nurturers

"A teacher affects eternity; no one can tell where his influence stops."

—Henry Adams

Fostering educator resiliency has to be a priority if we hope to have a positive impact on students and communities. Educators who are not resilient will be stressed, dissatisfied, frustrated, and poor role models for their students. In fact, they are likely to be roadblocks rather than pathways for the development of students' resiliency.

We need a healthy, self-confident, effective workforce if we expect educators to be willing and able to support the resiliency needs of students. More than two decades of continuous criticism and endless reform efforts have left the education workforce feeling embattled and under siege. Worst of all, many educators simply quit and seek alternative employment. For example, in California 22 percent of new teachers leave within the first four years of teaching. That adds up to eighteen thousand teachers quitting every year. When asked what caused them to leave, one out of three said that it was due mainly to lack of support from their schools. It is clearly important to focus on the resiliency of educators, both for their own well-being and for the well-being of students.

This chapter is devoted to helping educators develop and exhibit career resiliency so they can remain energized and motivated and can contribute positively to the goals of their schools. We begin by exploring three predominant *resiliency pathways that differentiate educators' effectiveness over the span of their careers.* Then we turn to the two variables that influence which pathway educators are likely to experience. The first has to do with *the ability of educators to perform well over time,* particularly regarding how well they respond to a widespread phenomenon, educator plateauing. The second has to do with *the impact of the school's environment on educators' resiliency*. Strategies will be suggested in the chapter that can be employed to make these environments more supportive of educator resiliency.

RESILIENCY PATHWAYS AND EDUCATORS' PERFORMANCE OVER THEIR CAREER SPAN

Educators' careers, like those of most any professional group, follow one of three paths. Some remain resilient throughout their careers; others begin their careers exhibiting resiliency, seem to lose it, but then manage to find ways to bounce back; and a third group seems to be unable to maintain enthusiasm or even function at minimally effective levels.

Educators in the first group always seem to exhibit resiliency. They remain enthusiastic about their professional activities year in and year out. They grow and adapt by employing a variety of strategies including modifying job content and how they deliver it, seeking professional development opportunities, taking on new challenges, and sometimes even new roles. A good example is those teachers who are senior in years of service but approach each new school year with an enthusiasm that is palpable. They encourage their students to excel and have an intuitive sense of the importance of continuing to grow professionally. They are usually highly regarded by their colleagues. They work at remaining resilient. They reflect on their professional and personal growth, and they seek ways to stay stimulated and engaged.

> Mere survival is an affliction. What is of interest is life, and the direction of that life.
>
> —*Guy Fregault*

The second group is composed of educators who initially exhibit resiliency, get off track, losing energy and enthusiasm, but somehow manage to find their way back to commitment, enthusiasm, and involvement. Sometimes such transformations come through purposeful decision making, as in the case of a highly senior teacher who served on seemingly endless school improvement committees early in her career, only to watch reform efforts come and go with little lasting impact. In time she began to feel frustrated and "burned out." However, after some time and reflection, she found an avenue back to her earlier resiliency: she decided that her students were too important to her and she could not abandon them. She refocused, made numerous home visits, and challenged them to succeed. Through these efforts, she once again became known as a caring educator and helped many youngsters who might otherwise have dropped out of school. She also took on the important role of positive critic and a sounding board for school improvement efforts, which tapped into her experience and ability.

> But if a man happens to find himself . . . he has a mansion which he can inhabit with dignity all the days of his life.
>
> —*James Michener*

Sometimes, finding the way back to resiliency may require a little help from others such as when the principal challenged a twenty-year veteran teacher who seemed to be going through the motions and coasting toward retirement to improve his classroom performance. The teacher confided that he had an idea for a curriculum unit that he had long wanted to develop but felt constrained to do so because it would require about $2,000 for materials and equipment. The principal thought this project might motivate him to do a better

> There are only two lasting bequests we can hope to give our children. One of these is roots; the other, wings.
>
> —*Hodding Carter*

job in the classroom and secured the necessary resources. After overcoming his initial disbelief that someone would actually listen to him and respond positively, the teacher became highly enthusiastic and proceeded to develop a good curriculum unit. In the process, he rekindled his excitement for teaching and spent the final five years before retiring supporting his students' growth and sharing his enthusiasm and expertise with other teachers. For a minimal financial investment of $2,000, this teacher was reenergized and the hundreds of students who passed through his classroom were affected positively rather than negatively. The school's expenditure of approximately $250,000 for the last five years of his teaching was used for good purposes. These are impressive results.

The third group is composed of educators who get stuck and remain that way, feeling miserable and doing a poor job in their assigned roles. It may sound like a line from a country western song, but we recently heard one downtrodden teacher comment about his work life in the following manner: "I mind my own business. Every day, I go from my truck to my classroom and back to my truck." We all know educators—administrators, teachers, and others—who seem to just plod between their car or truck and their classroom, taking care to avoid anything that some might view as a challenge or a risk. They also may not have supportive environments, which, in turn, continues to deplete their energies and resilience. They focus on counting the hours and minutes until the end of the day, the days until the end of the week, the weeks until vacation time, and the years until retirement.

> Things are not as bad as they seem. They are worse.
>
> —*Bill Press*

> And nothing to look backward to with pride, And nothing to look forward to with hope.
>
> —*Robert Frost*

Besides being unhappy individuals, they are poor role models who are hardly likely to promote resiliency among their students.

School leaders who provide varying kinds of support for staff members, depending on which of the three paths they are following can do a great deal to improve resiliency. Those who always seem to exhibit resiliency can often do even better if they are in supportive environments. Similarly, those who start with resiliency but who are detoured along the way can probably bounce back sooner if they are in supportive school environments. Those who do not exhibit resiliency require focused attention from school leaders or may even have to be counseled out of education (Henry & Milstein, 2004).

To promote a discussion about educator resiliency in your school, Exercise 4.1 encourages members of your group to reflect about past colleagues who typify these different resiliency patterns. Undoubtedly, educators who have spent some or all of their professional careers at your school fit into the preceding three career paths. Their stories can provide important lessons regarding what needs to be done by and for educators at your school today.

Exercise 4.1: Tell Your Stories

This exercise is most meaningful, both in richness of discussion and potential for change and improvement, if the school's staff as a group experiences it:

1. Think about educators who were on staff at your school at an earlier time. Some probably met challenges well and continued as effective educators. Some probably lost energy for the job or went into a slump but somehow regained enthusiasm and focus. Others may have felt defeated and unable or unwilling to regain their enthusiasm and focus. Can you identify particular educators who fit into each of these patterns?

2. Share stories about educators you are thinking about. How did they meet challenges? What are the differences regarding the responses of individuals from the three different career paths previously identified?

3. What can be learned from these stories? What impact did the stories have on you? What important lessons can you draw regarding educators in the school right now?

THE ABILITY OF EDUCATORS TO PERFORM WELL OVER TIME: COPING WITH PLATEAUING

Plateauing is what differentiates the three career paths previously discussed (Milstein & Bader, 1992). As such it is a phenomenon that can directly affect educator resiliency. To get a snapshot about your own plateauing situation, *we encourage you to respond to the questionnaire presented in Table 4.1 before you read what follows.* Respond as you believe things actually are and not as you might want them to be.

To obtain accurate results, be sure to follow the instructions closely as you complete the questionnaire and transfer your results to the scoring sheet (Tables 4.1 and 4.2 are also included as Handouts 7 and 8 in the Resource section for future use):

1. Be sure to put your responses in the correct spaces.

2. Reverse the scores for those items that are asterisked on the scoring form (i.e., a score of 1 becomes a 5, a 2 becomes a 4, a 3 remains a 3, a 4 becomes a 2, and a 5 becomes a 1).

3. After transferring all the scores, total up the three subscale scores and divide each of them by 10 to get your subscale mean scores for each.

4. Divide your total score by 30 for your overall mean score.

Before interpreting your scores, read the important background information that follows about plateauing. A good additional basic source is Bardwick's (1986) *The Plateauing Trap*.

1. Plateauing is a normal human experience. Throughout life, we vary between periods of high energy, change, and transformation and periods of calm, quiet, and reassessment, or plateauing. In the normal course of events, plateauing is that period when we reflect, recharge, and prepare for the next transformation or time of change.

2. Plateauing becomes problematic only when we feel stuck and have little hope of change or improvement (Milstein & Bader, 1992; Weiner, R. Remer, & P. Remer, 1992). When we find ourselves experiencing this kind of extended plateauing, we may feel dissatisfied and concerned about our situation, but

we rarely consciously or fully recognize what is happening as we slowly lose enthusiasm, feel less energized, and a sense of hopelessness sets in. Worst of all, because we are probably embarrassed about how we feel, we are unlikely to openly discuss our unease with others. In fact, we may believe that we are the only ones experiencing these feelings. It requires only a small jump in logic to conclude that there is probably something wrong with us.

3. As the survey scoring sheet indicates, there are three types of plateauing: content, structure, and life. Each is explained below.

Table 4.1   Educator Plateauing Survey

Select the response that best completes each item, using a scale from 1 to 5, with 1 indicating *strongly agree*, 2 indicating *agree*, 3 indicating *undecided*, 4 indicating *disagree*, and 5 indicating *strongly disagree*.

1. _____ The realities of my job come close to matching my initial expectations.
2. _____ I have high professional regard for those in leadership positions in my organization's structure.
3. _____ I feel trapped because I am unable to advance in my organization.
4. _____ My work is satisfying to me.
5. _____ I feel burdened with the many things I am responsible for in my life.
6. _____ I am bored in my current job.
7. _____ I usually start a new day with a sense of enthusiasm.
8. _____ To the extent that I am interested, I have opportunities to advance in my organization.
9. _____ Work is the most important thing in my life.
10. _____ My job is full of repetitive tasks.
11. _____ I feel like I have been passed over when advancement opportunities have occurred in my organization.
12. _____ I can usually find time to engage in leisure activities that I enjoy.
13. _____ I have little interest in advancing within my organization's structure.
14. _____ My life is too predictable.
15. _____ I participate in challenging and meaningful activities in my job.
16. _____ I believe I can achieve my career goals within my organization's structure.
17. _____ I have been in my job too long.
18. _____ I find myself being impatient too often with family and friends.
19. _____ I wish I had more opportunities to advance in my organization so I could do more meaningful work.
20. _____ I know my job too well.
21. _____ I rarely think of my life as boring.
22. _____ Although I would like to advance in my organization, given my abilities, my present position is the highest I can realistically attain.
23. _____ My job affords me little opportunity to learn new things.
24. _____ I am energized by the challenges and opportunities in my job.
25. _____ I consider myself a risk taker in my approach to life.
26. _____ Advancing further in my organization's structure would require that I give up many of the things I really like about my current position.
27. _____ I feel I perform successfully in my current job.
28. _____ My family and friends get irritated with me for being more involved with work than I am with other aspects of my life.
29. _____ My life is turning out as well as I hoped it would.
30. _____ I relate career success to promotion within my organization's structure.

Table 4.2 Educator Plateauing Survey Scoring Sheet

The numbers in categories A, B, and C correspond to the thirty statements in the Plateauing Survey. Transfer your responses to the blanks provided.

Note that those numbers followed by an asterisk (*) are reverse-scoring items. For these items, a score of one should be entered as five, two becomes four, three remains three, four becomes two, and five becomes one. Be sure to reverse these items as noted.

Category A	Category B	Category C
1. _____	2. _____	5.* _____
4. _____	3.* _____	7. _____
6.* _____	8. _____	9.* _____
10.* _____	11.* _____	12. _____
15. _____	13. _____	14.* _____
17.* _____	16. _____	18.* _____
20.* _____	19.* _____	21. _____
23.* _____	22.* _____	25. _____
24. _____	26. _____	28.* _____
27. _____	30.* _____	29. _____

Category Totals (add each column):   *Plateau Area:*

A = ___   Divide by 10 = _____   Content (work has become routine)

B = ___   Divide by 10 = _____   Structure (organization does not offer opportunity for growth or promotion)

C = ___   Divide by 10 = _____   Life (life is too predictable or not fulfilling)

Total = ___   Divide by 30 = _____   Overall plateauing

The higher the score is in each category and overall, the higher the level of plateauing is. This survey can be used to assess the need for resiliency building in any of the three plateauing categories or regarding overall plateauing.

Copyright © 1993 by Mike Milstein

Content

This type of plateauing has to do with your specific work role. After about three to five years in a job, most of us learn how to meet basic role expectations. That is, we become so-called experts. Being experts, we may be less likely to continue to learn, grow, and seek new challenges. If this happens, our jobs can start to feel routine and boring.

After enough time and experience, the learning curve inevitably goes down in any job. Unless we consciously and actively explore ways of responding to this reality, we can suffer negative consequences including loss of enthusiasm, reduced productivity, and less energy put into cooperative efforts and caring relationships.

Responses to this phenomenon vary from educator to educator. Those who are not aware of what is happening to them or who believe that there is no way out of the situation will feel frustrated and trapped in their roles and will slowly begin to disengage. Others who recognize that they are experiencing manifestations of plateauing and decide to do something about it will try to modify how they conduct their established roles so they can feel more motivated about their work. Some may even take on new roles, transfer to another school, change grade levels, or move into leadership positions, possibly even switching from teaching to administration. Change can break the routine and stimulate growth.

Structure

This type of plateauing has to do with the sense of not being rewarded appropriately for positive contributions, or not being able to grow or advance professionally in the organization. This perception can be minimized for teachers if opportunities are provided to take on new roles such as counselors, diagnosticians, or administrators. Some may seek recognition for their special abilities by becoming, for example, demonstration teachers or mentors for new teachers. Administrators at school sites can be offered the opportunity to take on leadership roles at another school or move into some other supervisory position. There is growing recognition of the importance of providing such opportunities. For example, in New Zealand, there is a movement to create new roles including advanced skills teachers, mentor teachers, and more leadership positions for teachers. Those seeking such positions are going to have to demonstrate that they have the skills, knowledge, and attributes to take on these roles and there will be additional compensation for those in these roles ("New Teacher Roles," 2007).

Opportunities can also be provided without having to change roles such as by promoting professional growth and recognition. Many teachers who have learned the basic requirements of their roles may remain enthused about them but also desire to expand their professional abilities through cutting-edge professional development opportunities.

Structural plateauing is experienced differently by different individuals, depending on personalities, perceptions, experiences, and interests. For example, teachers who are highly enthusiastic about teaching will probably have little interest in leaving the classroom for an administrative position but will likely have an interest in professional development opportunities that can be applied to their classroom activities. Others, especially those who have lost enthusiasm for teaching, may be attracted by opportunities to change job roles or by incentives to leave the profession and do something entirely different.

Life

This type of plateauing has to do with life outside the workplace, especially in reference to relationships with family, relatives, and friends. It also has to do with enthusiasm and motivation for avocations, service, and other normal aspects of life. It is about life's quality, not quantity, and about life's intensity and intrinsic worth, not material wealth.

> The ultimate value of life depends upon awareness and the power of contemplation rather than upon mere survival.
>
> —Aristotle

As might be expected, life plateauing affects educators differently, depending on their individual abilities and their work environments. Some of those who experience work-related plateauing may find that it can spill over and leave them with little enthusiasm or energy for high-quality nonwork lives. For such educators, all of life becomes a struggle. Others who plateau at work may focus on active engagement with life as an effective way of minimizing the most negative effects of the work situations. However, this does not mean that their professional engagement at work will improve.

Ironically, many of those who have found ways of avoiding plateauing at work may experience a significant cost in the form of life plateauing. Being highly engaged with work, they may have little energy left to put into nonwork situations. Spouses, children, and friends often adjust by keeping some distance, partly to honor these educators' desires to focus on work-related activities and partly out of self-defense, not wanting to place too much energy on relationships with others who may not respond in kind. Nobody wants to be put into a position where he or she is merely tolerated or ignored.

With this background information and with the plateauing instrument completed, you should now be able to assess your plateauing level. Exercise 4.2 can be done individually or by the group as a stimulus for support and as encouragement for change. (For future use, the instrument and score sheet are also provided as Handouts 7 and 8.)

Exercise 4.2: How Plateaued Are You?

The average score for educators who have taken the instrument is 2.6 (Milstein & Bader, 1992). This means that a score above 2.6 is higher than the average plateauing score and a score below 2.6 is lower than the average plateauing score. The further away your score is either above or below 2.6, the higher or lower your level of plateauing. An examination of your mean scores for each of the three subscales and for the overall questionnaire can provide a picture of your content, structure, and life plateauing, as well as your overall level of plateauing.

1. Check your overall score for a gross indicator of plateauing. Also check the three subscale scores. Which is highest? Which is lowest? Why do you think this is the case?

2. You may want to measure your scores against your own expectations for growth and development, as well as against the average results. In addition, whether your scores are lower or higher than the 2.6 indicator, there are probably some differences across the three scales, as well as for individual items within the scales, that you may want to think about.

3. Are there things about your scores that you feel good about? Are there things about your scores that you may want to consider changing?

Plateauing, as noted, is quite normal. We all experience it. For the main part, it can be a healthy time for reflection, and should not be viewed as a problem or an embarrassment. It, however, can become an issue if it leads to frustration and it feels insurmountable rather than as a place to pause and reflect before planning, making decisions, taking actions, and moving on.

> The important thing is not to stop questioning.
> —Albert Einstein

Finally, novice educators learn how to play their roles in a variety of ways, but one important way is through observing the attitudes and behaviors of senior colleagues. If these senior educators have plateaued, guess what newer teachers will learn? It is important to

> As I grow older, I pay less attention to what men say. I just watch what they do.
> —Andrew Carnegie

recognize this reality. Encouraging and supporting a resilient educational workforce means putting a good deal of effort into ensuring that senior educators remain resilient.

> Man is what he believes.
>
> —*Anton Chekhov*

THE IMPACT OF THE SCHOOL ENVIRONMENT ON EDUCATOR RESILIENCY

Chapter 1 included a summary of internal and environmental protective factors (Table 1.1). The more these factors exist as a part of our reality, the more we are likely to exhibit resilient behaviors. Internal factors that are individually developed and enhanced by our unique experiences, affect how we relate to others at work and in our personal lives. However, the ability to sustain our resiliency is also directly affected by the extent to which environmental protective factors exist in our lives.

Each of us develops and strengthens our internal protective factors in our own unique ways, but we do not do this in a vacuum: our environments affect the internal protective factors that support our resiliency. The reverse is also true: the extent to which we are able to display resilient behaviors can have negative or positive effects on our environments, one of the most important of which is our workplace, the place we spend the majority of our waking hours.

> The general tendency of things throughout the world is to render mediocrity the ascendant power among mankind.
>
> —*John Stuart Mill*

It is important to focus on the dynamic interplay that occurs between educators and their work environments if we expect to improve the resiliency-building capacity of these professionals. The challenge is to provide positive environments that promote each individual's internal protection capacities. This means creating and maintaining schools that promote professional growth, encouraging achievement, recognizing exceptional efforts, and focusing on optimism and hopefulness rather than on pessimism and helplessness. This requires risk taking and creativity as well as the will power to resist the criticism of naysayers.

It is helpful to ground the discussion in ways that can help you apply insights to your own reality. Exercise 4.3 encourages you to assess your own school's environment.

Exercise 4.3: Protective Factors and Educators at Your School

This exercise can be pursued by individuals, or preferably by groups if members are ready to explore educator resiliency at the school. Distribute Handout 2 (Table 1.1) to group members.

1. Approximately what percentage of the educators in your school exhibit healthy levels of the internal protective factors listed on Handout 2? How many of the factors do you exhibit? How do you think they (and you) have achieved this healthy level of internal protective factors?

2. Which of the internal protective factors are most evident among your school's staff members? Which ones are most evident for you? Why do you think these factors are most evident?

3. Are any factors in short supply and do they require growth and development on the part of the staff? How about for yourself?

4. Next review the list of environmental protective factors listed on Handout 2. Which of these factors do you think are most characteristic of your school environment? Why? Which are least characteristic of your school environment? Why?

5. Are there implications for needed changes at the school? Are there any changes you would like to make for yourself?

STRATEGIES TO OVERCOME SCHOOL-BASED BARRIERS TO EDUCATOR RESILIENCY

Many specific environmentally related barriers to educator resiliency are embedded in the ways we structure our schools. We created these situations and it is within our powers to modify them in ways that are more supportive of educator resiliency.

What are these barriers? What strategies can we use to reduce them? We have organized the discussion of barriers and strategies around the six elements on the Resiliency Wheel (Chapter 1, Figure 1.3) to encourage creative ways of thinking about improving educator resiliency. For each element, we summarize the most relevant barriers and offer strategies for improvement, as described in the following section. We encourage you and your colleagues to particularize and otherwise modify the suggested strategies to fit your own school's realities. We encourage you to add others that might be worth considering in your situation.

Positive Connections

Two barriers are frequently identified as inhibitors of positive connections among educators in schools. First, educators spend most of their workdays in isolation from other adults. Their time and efforts are devoted to working with youngsters, which leaves little room for adult-to-adult interactions. Furthermore, the time that does exist for connecting tends to be misused, leading to distancing rather than to closeness. Think about the informal interactions that take place in many teachers' lounges. Often they center on discussing students' shortcomings, complaining about working conditions, and gossiping. It is a place where teachers can let out frustrations in a relative safe place. Even when school staffs come together as formal groups, it is usually for meetings that are limited to brief periods of time and built around agendas (if indeed there are any) set by the principal. They tend to be one-way communication sessions, with little time devoted to collegial exploration, decision making, and feedback. Such meetings do little to promote togetherness. Given these barriers—work performance isolation, infrequent educator face-to-face interactions, and the misuses of even that minimal time—it is unrealistic to expect positive connections to occur naturally.

Second, role performance evaluations are almost totally based on individual efforts. It rarely includes evaluation of cooperative group or team efforts. What normally seems to matter regarding judgments about an educator's worth is how well specific professional roles are performed. As noted, these roles are typically conducted in isolation. A good example of this is the teacher evaluation process. Traditionally, they are focused on individually managed goals related to student achievement, safety, and security in the classroom. While cooperative efforts, such as involvement on site-based management teams are being introduced in some schools, they are not often given serious consideration in formal evaluation efforts. In other words, although working cooperatively promotes positive connections, there are few, if any, built-in organizational rewards for such activities. In fact, there are more likely to be disincentives because doing things cooperatively takes time away from individual role efforts, which is what counts most for evaluation purposes.

It is interesting to note that there are some beginning movements aimed at shifting the balance of evaluations and rewards of teachers away from a total focus on the individual to one that includes recognition and reward for efforts and outcomes of teams and the overall school staff. For example, Broward County Schools are adopting a merit program that is tied to teamwork and awarded equitably to all members of the team (Sampson, 2007).

Leadership Strategies for Increasing Positive Connections

The nature of the task of educating students places major constrictions on opportunities for positive connections, but there are ways for leaders to stimulate positive changes. Examples of ways to increase positive connections are the following:

- Promote team-teaching efforts and other teaming activities (e.g., curriculum development groups) to encourage positive connections. Adult teams also model and make cooperative learning more relevant for students. Reward team efforts by giving recognition to teams that work well together.
- Practice principles that emphasize the value of everyone's contributions and capabilities. This can be promoted through a variety of means including site-based management teams, study groups, instructional and curricular demonstrations and presentations, visitations to other schools, encouragement of teachers to participate in regional and national professional conferences and to share what they have learned with their colleagues.
- Bring the staff together to discuss, clarify, and update the school's vision, mission, and goals. This activity can promote a shared sense of purpose and a stronger sense of community.
- Experiment with opportunities for the staff to share ideas and lend support to each other. For example, senior teachers can be mentors for new teachers. This may be a new role for some staff members. It should be encouraged.
- Develop norms that promote cooperation and support. For example, collegial classroom coverage, peer feedback, and interpersonal support and recognition that support positive improvements in behaviors and relationships.

- Ensure that meetings are managed so they focus on meaningful issues and, when appropriate, provide opportunities for open discussion and consensus decision making.

Record other strategies that can increase positive connections for educators:

- _____
  _____

- _____
  _____

- _____
  _____

Set Clear, Consistent, and Appropriate Boundaries

Educators frequently live split lives when it comes to boundary setting. They have wide latitude to set boundaries within their specific roles, but they are not given much voice in decision making about the wider school outside of their classroom. Teachers establish many of the policies, rules, and expectations regarding behaviors for students in their classrooms. However, beyond the classroom, policies, rules, and expectations are usually set by the principal, other supervisors, or school boards. To one degree or another, the same high boundary-setting control within one's role and low boundary-setting control outside of one's role holds true for other educators, including diagnosticians, counselors, supervisors, and administrators.

> I am the decisive element in the classroom. . . .
> In all situations it is my response that decides whether a crisis will be escalated or de-escalated and a child humanized or dehumanized.
>
> —*Haim Ginott*

Policies, rules, and expectations can vary from minutely detailed to generalized and confusing, from consistently stated and enforced to arbitrary and contradictory, from logical to illogical, and from equitably applied to capricious and differentially applied. Often behavioral expectations are not even verbalized or put in writing, remaining as vaguely understood norms that emerge from the organizational culture and are only learned over time and through hard-earned experiences.

Leadership Strategies for Promoting Clear, Consistent, and Appropriate Boundaries

Growth, creativity, and achievement are important aspects of resiliency. For these things to occur one must first feel secure. This requires knowing the rules of the game, understanding their relevance, accepting them as appropriate, and believing that you can influence them. Strategies for creating healthy boundaries include the following:

> There is no conflict between liberty and safety. We will have both or neither.
>
> —*Ramsey Clark*

- Involve educators in establishing, interpreting, and implementing policies and rules. If they participate in these boundary-setting processes they will more likely understand, accept, and support them. For example, if there is need to review the criteria of the evaluation system that is used, include teacher input in the discussion and in decisions about any changes that are required and agreed upon.

- Communicate policies and rules clearly and frequently. This should be done in writing and checked to avoid misinterpretations.
- Make sure that norms are clarified, understood, and shared. Periodic clarification of norms by updating and discussing them can keep expectations clear. Most important, it can help newer staff members become acquainted with them without undue efforts.

Record other strategies that can promote clear, consistent, and appropriate boundaries for educators:

- _____
  _____
- _____
  _____

Life-Guiding Skills

Educators continuously need to hone their life-guiding skills. Even if their preservice education is adequate at the time, it soon becomes obsolete because of changing conditions and the increasingly complex tasks that educators are asked to perform. Coupled with this is the rate of growth that is marked by the explosion of technology, most of which impinge on what we do in schools and how we do it. Support for life-guiding skill development is a constant need, but the resources—money, expertise, and time—to provide such enrichment opportunities are often in short supply.

> Life is what happens to us while we are making other plans.
> —Thomas La Mance

> We are made to persist. That's how we find out who we are.
> —Tobias Wolff

Leadership Strategies for Fostering Life Skills

We need to provide opportunities for educators at all career stages—novices, mid-career, and those with long-term service records—to upgrade their present skills and learn new skills if we expect them to function effectively and promote life-guiding skills for their students. Strategies to consider include the following:

- Broaden the definition and scope of professional development. Professional development offerings are often narrowly designed around role-related content and skills. However, life-guiding skills that are important for educators to learn transcend role requirements if they are going to be able to carry out their responsibilities and enhance their students' life-guiding skills. Goal setting, problem solving, conflict management, and communications are life-guiding skills that need to be learned, updated, and practiced by educators. In fact, if we view educators as whole persons with potential for growth and development rather than just as role holders and support this potential as fully as possible, professional development will be defined more broadly. Broadening the definition and scope would include such things as learning about avocational interests and effective strategies for health enhancement.

> Show me a thoroughly satisfied man— and I will show you a failure.
> —Thomas Alva Edison

- Survey your school's educational workforce about what they think they need in the way of professional development initiatives and activities. This may require a major shift in thinking—away from distant policy centers to site based and individual educator involvement in decision making about relevant professional development activities.

- Practice adult learning principles. Educators need to be engaged in the development of life-guiding skills in ways that are consistent with what we know about adult learning. This includes positive focus on improvement, alternative learning opportunities based on individually defined needs, active engagement in problem solving, trust, relevancy, respect, collaboration, interaction, continuity, integration, and follow-up.

> The art of teaching is the art of assisting discovery.
> —Mark Van Doren

- Provide needed resources and create more on-the-job time for professional development opportunities. The school sector lags far behind the business sector in money and time reserved for professional development. School leaders need to search for means to provide these necessary resources from within their local budgets as well as from regional and nationally funded programs and private philanthropic sources. Prioritization of time for professional development can send a powerful and positive message to educators.

- Encourage exceptional educators who have demonstrated their capability to apply important life-guiding skills effectively to share them with other educators. For example, they can team with faculty members from the local university to enrich preservice teacher preparation programs. At least two important benefits can be achieved through such an arrangement. First, novice teachers who are prepared by exceptional educators at the outset of their careers will be more likely to form good life-guiding skills and habits and practice them successfully. Second, positive recognition and meaningful rewards can be gained by exceptional educators who participate in these activities.

Record other strategies that can foster life-guiding skills for educators:

- _____

  _____

- _____

  _____

- _____

  _____

Nurture and Support

Nurturing youngsters is a demanding task. It requires an enormous amount of energy and a seemingly endless supply of care and support. Most educators are nurturers by nature, but they cannot continue to give over the years without having their own nurturing and support needs met. Like our car batteries, educators need regular recharging if they are going to have the energy to support students' needs.

However, there are barriers that stand in the way of educators receiving sufficient nurturing and support. First, as noted, there is not much time available for adult-to-adult interactions. Second, even the little time available is often squandered on negative criticism of students, teachers, and administrators rather than on positive and supportive feedback about efforts and achievements. Third, teacher evaluations are usually limited to the minimal number of visits from the

> We must have . . . a place where children can have a whole group of adults they can trust.
> —Margaret Mead

supervisor required by the contract and focused on improvements that are needed much more than on supportive feedback that celebrates positive efforts and achievements. Furthermore, administrators usually conduct these evaluations with little, if any, collegial teacher-to-teacher input. In short, many schools' working conditions do little to support the development of care and support among educators on many levels.

Leadership Strategies for Enhancing Nurturance and Support

Demonstrations of nurturing and support are critical cornerstones for self-worth, connectedness, and belonging. This is true for educators at all career levels, from novices to those who have served a long time and have, too often, received little positive response, extrinsically or intrinsically, for their efforts. Some strategies that can change the situation include the following:

> Kind words can be short and easy to speak, but their echoes are truly endless.
>
> —*Mother Teresa*

- Provide purposeful and regular feedback that sends messages of support. This behavior, if practiced regularly and sincerely by leaders as well as among colleagues, can improve self-perceptions and promote the belief that one's role is important and, if performed well, is helpful and appreciated by other adults in the school.

> The race advances only by the extra achievements of the individual. You are the individual.
>
> —*Charles Towne*

- Create and support special events that recognize and celebrate educators' efforts. These symbolic events let educators know that what they do is important and appreciated. This is especially true when colleagues recognize each other's challenges and are supportive of each other's efforts and achievements. A powerful way to start the school year is to celebrate accomplishments of the staff over the summer or from last year.

- Establish processes to ensure members' life events, such as birthdays, marriages, illnesses, and family activities, are recognized. Schools that have done this regularly have found it to be an effective way of demonstrating nurturance and support.

> Faults are thick where love is thin.
>
> —*James Howell*

- Encourage positive regard and support between educators and the community and discourage negative criticism. Provide information to the local newspaper about the good things that are happening at the school and who the individuals are who are responsible for doing them. Another idea is to establish a community-school appreciation day that brings the broader community into the school for activities that focus on positive support and shared feedback.

Record other strategies that can enhance nurturance and support for educators:

- _____
  _____

- _____
  _____

- _____
  _____

Purposes and Expectations

The dominant message in many schools is "don't rock the boat." It should be "go for it!" "Don't rock the boat" is what administrators tell teachers when they prioritize maintaining order over taking risks and challenging students to grow and achieve. It is also what teachers hear from their unions and associations when these organizations emphasize the need for unity and for behaving within agreed-upon boundaries (i.e., "don't be a rate buster") rather than emphasizing the need for individual members to take initiatives and do all they can to achieve meaningful goals. The impact of such messages is compounded by the less than motivating reality of the matrix-based salary compensation formula that is prevalent. Under this system, salaries are formulated on the basis of number of years of service and academic hours and degrees obtained, not the quality of role performance. Teachers need to be encouraged to take risks and be provided with a supportive safety net for them to achieve.

> You cannot teach and empower children to be successful if you do not hold yourself to be so. Everything you are and all that you believe is transmitted to your students at some level
>
> —*Michel de Montaigne*

Leadership Strategies to Strengthen Purposes and Expectations

The extrinsic reward system in education does little to recognize or support individual efforts. Minimal expectations also significantly deter motivation to achieve. Here are some strategies that can counteract these barriers:

> I know well what I am fleeing from but not what I am in search of.
>
> —*Michel de Montaigne*

- Encourage regular feedback from colleagues and formal leaders that show appreciation for efforts and recognition of achievements. Set up a system where teachers gain the skills to give useful feedback and the time to provide it to their colleagues.
- Involve educators in the development and clarification of the school's vision, mission, and goals to promote a shared sense of purpose and expectations for achievement. If educators participate in defining these expectations, they are more likely to be enthused about them and to understand how they can contribute to their achievement. Given the isolating nature of most educators' work roles, it is important to bring them together regularly to set goals and the development of motivation to achieve them.
- Promote cooperation and expectations for excellence by reducing the isolation associated with educator role performance. Encouraging regular professional interactions can be quite helpful in this regard. Team teaching and other cooperative efforts can stimulate accomplishment of special projects. Similarly, job sharing and job expansion can be challenging to individual educators, support cooperative efforts, and promote school-wide achievement.

> Is not life a hundred times too short for us to bore ourselves?
>
> —*Friedrich Nietzsche*

- Maximize on-task time by reducing the extent of low priority maintenance activities such as filling out extensive records and forms. This communicates that the organization's leaders will do what they can to help educators focus their time on helping students achieve positive educational outcomes.
- Change extrinsic reward systems in ways that emphasize achievement and recognition of individual efforts. Given the deeply embedded reality of the matrix system and of union protection of members, it is not likely that this constraint on high expectations will ever be fully removed. However, there are ways of modifying the problem. For example, grants can be awarded to teachers to develop innovative teaching units; extra pay can be awarded to teachers who are able and willing to help

students in need of support outside of regular school hours; and funds can be reserved for professional development opportunities, including tuition for courses at local universities or travel money to attend local, regional, and national educational conferences for those educators who are identified by their peers as making important contributions to the school.

Record other strategies that can strengthen purposes and expectations for educators:

- _____
  _____

- _____
  _____

- _____
  _____

Provide Opportunities for Meaningful Participation

Once they achieve basic role competence, many educators seek new challenges. They recognize that opportunities for growth and development are vital to their well-being. One way for them to grow is to participate more broadly in organizational life in ways that transcend the limited requirements of their assigned roles. Many seek these experiences because they want to be part of something bigger and give back to the organizations they serve. It also is stimulated by the adult learner's need to grow and take on new challenges.

> A life spent in making mistakes is not only more honorable but more useful than a life spent in doing nothing.
>
> —*George Bernard Shaw*

It is difficult to find sufficient opportunities to participate meaningfully in broad-scale activities if educators' roles are defined narrowly, that is, teachers teach, counselors counsel, and administrators administer. In addition, few career development opportunities are made available, so it is difficult for educators to change roles and explore alternative ways of participating. There are few promotion possibilities, for example, as demonstration teachers or staff developers, within the teaching role. The possibility of changing roles by becoming a diagnostician, counselor, or administrator is limited by the flat hierarchy and the attendant low supervisor-supervisee ratios that typify how schools are organized. Furthermore, given resource constraints for professional development, especially in knowledge and skill areas beyond one's direct role, there are not enough opportunities to learn skills necessary for meaningful participation. For example, to participate effectively on site-based management teams, educators need to acquire basic team management skills. Even with skill development and the best of intentions, there is scant time available during the workday to contribute beyond daily role expectations.

> There is no meaning to life except the meaning man gives his life by unfolding of his powers.
>
> —*Erich Fromm*

Leadership Strategies for Improving Meaningful Participation

Educators need adult learning opportunities and school leaders need all the help they can get to accomplish purposes. Therefore, it is important to focus on developing ways to participate meaningfully. Strategies for doing this include the following:

- Practice site-based management approaches that promote participation by educators (as well as by community members and students). To promote educator participation, organization-wide responsibilities need to be built in as part of members' role expectations, for example, by participating on curricular and extracurricular committees and other school-wide responsibility areas. But it is important that the focus be on things that are meaningful to participants. Discussing educational goals and curriculum development is more relevant to teachers than discussing the lunch menu and grounds maintenance. Motivation to participate in school-based decision making depends on whether there is a sense of value and ownership for the content of the discussion. There should also be comparable rewards for participating. Released time is one way to reward it. Recognition in the evaluation process for participating in school-wide activities is another way.

- Promote team planning and team teaching. One example is to provide time prior to each term to focus on team planning activities. Such cooperative efforts and role sharing can encourage the development of creative ideas and provide motivation to become more involved in meaningful activities.

- Promote participation by changing the way meetings are managed. Agendas that are given to staff members prior to the meeting can encourage thinking about issues ahead of time. At the meeting limit the number of items on the agenda so there is more time for discussion; avoid using valuable meeting time to share information that can be disseminated by other means; emphasize consensus decision making; encourage volunteerism for task accomplishment; and most important, ensure that decisions lead to actions so members recognize that participating in meetings is relevant. Agendas that are organized to be more strategic engage everyone.

Record other strategies that can improve meaningful participation among educators:

- _____

  _____

- _____

  _____

- _____

  _____

Over time, you and others on your school's staff have probably given thought to many of the resiliency barriers discussed in this chapter. Exercise 4.4 can be used as a means of encouraging the staff to share these thoughts and develop suggestions to overcome educator resiliency barriers.

Exercise 4.4: Responding to Educator Resiliency Barriers

1. Distribute the Barriers to Educator Resiliency sheet (Handout 9 in the Resource section) and lead a discussion about the barriers. Do members understand them? Do these barriers seem to be relevant at your school?

2. Divide the staff into six subgroups. Assign each group to a separate workstation. Put a piece of chart paper at each work station, with a different resiliency element at the top of each sheet (i.e., positive connections at the first station, boundaries at the second, life-guiding skills at the third, nurture and support at the fourth, purposes and expectations at the fifth, and meaningful participation at the sixth).

3. Give each group about five minutes to review the handout about barriers related to the resiliency elements on their sheet of paper and briefly brainstorm ways of improving the situation at your school. A recorder should be assigned and asked to write the group's ideas on the chart paper.

4. Ask each group to pass its chart papers on to the next group, in a clockwise manner, so that there will be a new resiliency element to explore at each workstation. Ask the groups to take about five minutes, first to read the ideas that the previous group suggested and then to add their own ideas.

5. Continue the process by asking the groups to continue the brainstorming exercise and to pass their chart papers clockwise to the next group until all groups have responded to the six elements on the chart papers. Pass them on one more time so that the groups have the chart paper with the resiliency element they worked on initially. The task is for each group to review all the ideas suggested regarding improving their particular element. After the review, group members should discuss and agree on the overall ideas suggested and list them at the bottom of the paper.

6. Recorders from each group should take turns sharing the basic strategies that were identified. With further discussion and agreement by the large group, these strategies can become the basis for school-wide action planning. Is there is interest in implementing any or all of them? Ask for thoughts about next steps.

Just as students need resiliency to develop and thrive at school and in life, educators need resiliency to develop and thrive as professionals and as people. Career resiliency characteristics include "teamwork, effective communication, adaptability to change, positive and flexible attitudes, continuous learning, self-confidence, willingness to take risks, and a commitment to personal excellence." (Brown, 1996, p. 1)

Exercise 4.5: Considerations for Leaders

Leaders can make a big difference in the resiliency of educators. The more they purposefully support the well-being and growth of their colleagues the greater the likelihood is that they will be resilient and provide positive role models for students. What rating, on a scale of one (low) to five (high) would you give to the knowledge and capabilities of your school's leaders to develop and maintain schools that promote resiliency?

1. Support the resiliency development of other educators over the span of their careers.

2. Differentiate support strategies depending upon whether educators are
   A. resilient throughout the span of their careers.
   B. exhibit resiliency, seem to lose it, but then regain it.
   C. not resilient.

3. Help educators deal effectively with the negative manifestations of plateauing. They differentiate strategies for educators who are
   A. content plateaued.
   B. structurally plateaued.
   C. life plateaued.

4. Promote positive environmental conditions in the school so that educators experience opportunities to become evermore resilient, regarding
   A. positive connections.
   B. clear, consistent, and appropriate boundaries.
   C. life-guiding skills.
   D. nurture and support.
   E. purposes and expectations.
   F. meaningful participation.

School faculties can be motivated to institutionalize behaviors and beliefs that enhance resiliency for them as well as for their students. But they cannot do it alone. They need to work in schools that are organized in ways that promote student and faculty resiliency. In the next chapter, we will focus on schools and explore ways that leaders can organize and manage them in ways that are more supportive of resiliency building for students, faculty, and community.

5

School Resiliency

Creating Supportive Environments for Students, Educators, and Communities

"At a gut level all of us know that much more goes into the process of keeping a large organization vital and responsive than the policy statements, new strategies, plans, budgets, and organization charts can possibly depict. But all too often we behave as though we don't know it. If we want change, we fiddle with the strategy. Or we change the structure. Perhaps the time has come to change our ways."

—Peters & Waterman, 1982, p. 3

Most schools do things right but that is not the same as doing the right things (Bennis, 1989; Sergiovanni, 1990). Schools, like most organizations, have deeply embedded and strongly held belief systems about what should be done and about how it should be done. When communities were sedentary and expectations were clear and predictable, it may have been sufficient to take a "business as usual" stance about purposes and about how they should be pursued in our schools. But this stance will not suffice now or for the foreseeable future because challenge and change are the dominant reality.

Schools need to be sensitive to community expectations and responsive to community demands. This is difficult enough to do when demands are clear and there is widespread agreement about what schools are supposed to do, but it becomes increasingly challenging when demands are unclear, intense, broad in scope, and

> An old error is always more popular than a new truth.
>
> —German proverb

often contradictory. In fact, in most communities, there is no longer a clear agreement about the role of schools. Given this lack of clarity, school districts need to *be proactive. That is, they must continuously upgrade themselves to meet changing realities.*

This chapter focuses on schools as organizations that, if they make the choice and commitment, can promote the resiliency of students and educators and become more accessible to and supportive of their surrounding communities. The chapter explores why changing the way a school functions is often quite difficult, suggests ways that leaders can plan for change, and provides strategies that they can use to improve the potential to promote resiliency for students, educators, and communi-

> There is nothing permanent except change.
>
> —Heraclitus

ties. The chapter also provides exercises that encourage readers to examine the status quo regarding their school's ability to support resiliency development.

DOES YOUR SCHOOL SUPPORT RESILIENCY?

Resilient schools encourage exceptional performance expectations and produce extraordinary outcomes. Does your school do these things? A good place to begin is with an assessment of your school's current situation. Exercises 5.1, 5.2, and 5.3 are intended to help guide your group through this assessment. They relate and build on each other. If time permits, ask the group to proceed through them in the order in which they are presented. This will help move the group toward shared understandings and agreements. Exercise 5.1 should help clarify your school's impact on student, educator, and community resiliency.

Exercise 5.1: Your School's Resiliency

In what ways does the school *promote* resiliency among students, educators, and community members? In what ways does the school *deter* resiliency among students, educators, and community members?

1. Ask members to complete the survey presented in Table 5.1 (Handout 10 in the Resource section).

2. Develop a composite score sheet for the group by making an enlarged copy of Table 5.1 on a chalkboard or on chart paper and filling in members' scores. Compute the group's mean scores and put them in the "overall" column.

3. Discuss the implications of the mean scores. What is the overall sense of the group regarding whether the school supports or deters resiliency? How far apart are the highs from the lows?

4. Are there distinctive differences regarding the school's support of resiliency for students, educators, and community members? If there are, ask group members to discuss why they think these differences exist.

5. Last, ask group members to share the comments they wrote about the six resiliency elements. Check for the extent to which they agree about these comments.

Table 5.1   My School: Does It Deter or Support Resiliency Development?

1. The six resiliency elements are listed in the following table. If definitions are needed, refer to Chapter 1.
2. To what extent does your school deter or support the development of the six resiliency elements among students, educators, and community members? Use the following five-point scale to record your judgment in each of the columns:

Supports Resiliency   5   4   3   2   1   Deters Resiliency

3. Think about how the school does overall and record your judgment in the "Overall" column.
4. Add any comments you may want that support your judgments.

Resiliency Elements	Students	Educators	Community	Overall	Comments
Positive Connections					
Clear, Consistent, and Appropriate Boundaries					
Life-Guiding Skills					
Nurture and Support					
Purposes and Expectations					
Meaningful Participation					

In all likelihood, the exercise and discussion will result in perceptions that the school is doing better regarding some resiliency elements than it is regarding others and, perhaps, with some more than with others. It may be viewed that the school is doing a good job of supporting everyone's resiliency, or it may be viewed that it is doing a poor job of promoting everyone's resiliency. Just as likely, the group may conclude that the school varies in its impact with students, educators, and community members. Every school situation is different. The important thing is to check for agreements about yours.

Exercise 5.2: Beliefs About Schools and Resiliency

1. The following statements should be posted on a chalkboard, on a flip chart page, or from an LCD projector:

   There is widespread belief that the school's role should be limited to teaching the basics and keeping youngsters academically engaged during their formative years.

   Or

   There is widespread understanding of the important role the school plays in developing youngsters' capacities to cope with life's challenges.

2. Ask the group to discuss which belief is most characteristic of your school. What are the implications for the school's ability to enhance student resiliency? What, if any, changes in beliefs need to be encouraged?

3. Next, post the following statements about the school and educator resiliency:

   Educators are viewed as professionals who are responsible for their own growth and development. They take care of themselves.

   Or

   There is recognition that educators need to be provided with regular growth opportunities so they can help their students be more resilient. The school plays an important role in educators' professional development.

4. Ask the group to discuss which belief is most characteristic of your school, the implications of this belief, and whether any changes in beliefs need to be encouraged.

5. Post the following statements about school and community member resiliency:

   The school views educating youngsters as its specific responsibility. This is best accomplished with minimal involvement by members of the community.

   Or

   There is a clear understanding that the larger community has an impact on the school's effectiveness, and the school promotes community members' involvement in school life.

6. As in Step 4, ask the group to discuss which belief is most characteristic of the school, the implications of this belief, and whether any changes need to be encouraged.

7. Ask the group to synthesize the discussion. If your school members selected the second statements, then you have a healthy outlook of your school. If there is a mixture of responses, then clarification and unity are needed to improve the balance. Does the school support student, educator, and community resiliency? Are any actions called for?

Does the group believe that your school needs to promote resiliency more purposefully? Beliefs also crystallize perceptions of who is involved, who takes responsibility, and who is committed to a healthier place and need to be clarified and agreed on if necessary changes are to be pursued. Exercise 5.2 can help group members promote reflection, clarify beliefs, and encourage them to become more sensitive about the importance of the role of the school in supporting the resiliency of everyone involved.

All schools are candidates for change in ways that can improve their capacities to promote resiliency. What matters most is to recognize this potential and take meaningful actions to help the school fulfill it. With perceptions and beliefs clarified, as suggested in Exercises 5.1 and 5.2, Exercise 5.3 can help the group clarify the school's current state of readiness to support members' resiliency.

Exercise 5.3: What Do We Do Well? What Do We Do Okay? What Do We Need to Start Doing?

How does the school promote resiliency? In what ways does it fall short? What else may need to be done to improve its resiliency-building capacity?

1. Ask group members to identify *what the school is presently doing well* to promote resiliency among students, educators, and community members. Encourage them to think broadly. For example, resiliency can be promoted through governance structures, policies and procedures, communications, instructional approaches, curriculum, and outreach efforts. Ask members to record their agreements on chart paper or on a chalkboard.

2. Next, ask group members to identify *what the school is doing "okay" but could do better to promote resiliency*. Again, encourage them to think broadly. List things they agree about on a chalkboard or chart paper. Ask the group to identify what needs to be changed to promote student, educator, and community resiliency.

3. Last, ask group members to identify *things they know about (or may have read about) that can promote resiliency but are not presently the way things are being done in the school.* After a list is generated, ask group members to prioritize suggestions. Which would be most likely to promote resiliency if they were to be introduced at the school?

(We encourage you to keep the three lists for later reference as the group moves ahead with resiliency improvement efforts.)

IMPROVING SCHOOL RESILIENCY MEANS CHANGING SCHOOLS

Once the group completes Exercises 5.1, 5.2, and 5.3, the picture should be clearer regarding beliefs about the school's current situation and changes that may be necessary. However, beliefs alone will not lead to a better tomorrow, even if there is agreement about the need for change, a sense of what needs to be done, and a plan to bring about agreed-upon changes. Goodwill and readiness are important starting points, but as anyone who has been involved in educational reform efforts knows, they probably are not sufficient. Barriers to change need to be confronted and overcome. Three barriers in particular are likely to be encountered:

1. *Change means loss and destabilization.* Whether related to current beliefs and ideologies or practices and behaviors, change requires letting go of something. Change dissolves meaning as new purposes and processes are explored and put in place. It also represents uncertainty and the likelihood of some discomfort. Change requires risk taking as participants gain new knowledge and learn new roles and skills, all of which require efforts as well as trust to follow unknown paths.

   > Man has a biological capacity for change. When this capacity is overwhelmed, the capacity is in future shock.
   >
   > —*Alvin Toffler*

   Individuals who have a difficult time with the destabilization that accompanies change are often labeled *resistant*, an oversimplified label that may be wrong and certainly can be dysfunctional.

   > Traditionalists are pessimists about the future and optimists about the past.
   >
   > —*Lewis Mumford*

2. *Change is confusing.* Enthusiasm dissipates quickly without clear purposes and strong support during the implementation process and confusion can take its

place. When leaders try something new they need to define and clearly communicate what they are doing. Further, it is one thing to declare a new direction, but quite another to make it happen, particularly without evidence of support in such forms as resources and public support by key players.

3. *Change upsets power relationships.* Organizations are political systems. They are engaged with the acquisition and distribution of scarce resources, including funds, space, and time. As such, shifts in the balance of power are likely to occur, which can stimulate resistance that has nothing to do with the content of the change itself. Leaders need to understand and manage power or else the power concerns that people have can negatively affect the outcomes of the change efforts. Those who have status, central roles, or control of resources may fear that they will lose their power advantage if change comes about. Similarly, those who do not have power may view the destabilization that accompanies change as an opportunity to gain it (Milstein, 1993).

Loss, destabilization, confusion, and power relationship games are likely to be experienced in most any significant school change effort. They can be viewed negatively as insurmountable barriers or simply as normal realities of any organizational change. With a bit of creativity, they can even be viewed positively as the stuff from which school resiliency can be built. After all, resiliency is all about being able to bounce back from stressful and adverse situations. Exercise 5.4 should help members of your school community develop a greater understanding and sensitivity about the dynamics of organizational change. It should also help them prepare for and be more realistic about planning to enhance the resiliency-building potential of the school.

Exercise 5.4: How Does Your School Cope With Organizational Change?

1. Ask group members to think about past change efforts at the school. The focus of these efforts might have been on governance, structure, instructional approaches, curriculum content, or any other school-related areas. Post situations that members identify on a chalkboard or on chart paper.

2. Ask the group to review the situations and pick one to explore that many of them have participated in or with which they are at least familiar.

3. Post the three change barriers identified earlier—loss and destabilization, confusion, and power relationships—on a chalkboard or on chart paper. Provide a description for each.

4. Ask group members to share stories about the situations they selected. How did they experience these barriers?

5. If time permits, do the same activity for another change situation the group has identified.

6. Guided by the following questions, ask the group to draw conclusions from the discussion:
   a. Given the three barriers to change and their occurrence in past situations, are they likely to occur if efforts to enhance the resiliency-building capacity of the school are initiated?
   b. If so, what might be done to respond to them effectively?

7. Ask the group to synthesize and record their agreements so they can be referred to during future change initiatives.

There are things that we need to consider about organizational change generally and about changing schools specifically. Understanding the dynamics of organizational change can help us respond effectively to barriers that are likely to be encountered as school resiliency-building initiatives are initiated:

Focus on leadership. Successful change requires committed and effective leadership to shape and communicate values, visions, and expectations. Those who lead such efforts need to model expected behaviors, to support and reward those who participate, and to keep the focus on purposes. The emphasis should be on the *function of leadership*, not on *leaders* per se, to encourage shared responsibility and initiative taking and to promote members' resiliency as they assume responsibilities and engage in the change effort.

> Leadership is *action*, not position.
> —*Donald H. McGannon*

Change perspectives by changing the culture of the school. The culture of the organization, is defined as "the norms that inform people about what is acceptable and what is not, the dominant *values* that the organization cherishes above others [and] the *basic assumptions and beliefs* that are shared by members" (Owens, 1991, p. 28). Many schools have cultures that are characterized by a focus on conformity, rules, discipline, and regularity. In such schools motivation for growth and risk taking are likely to be in short supply. Schools with such cultures are marked by high absenteeism, low participation in school-wide activities, minimal parent involvement, negative comments in educators' lounges, teachers leaving immediately at the end of the school day, and poor building maintenance.

> The perpetual obstacle to human advancement is custom.
> —*John Stuart Mill*

Changing such maintenance-oriented cultures requires shifting perspectives. This means changing the culture:

- from doing things right to doing the right things;
- from isolation and individualism to cooperation, teamwork, and relationships;
- from behaving reactively to behaving proactively;
- from catching members doing something wrong to catching members doing something right;
- from quick-fix solutions to broad-based, long-term responses to complex problems; and
- from viewing innovative efforts that fall short as "failures" to viewing them as learning opportunities that come with most any significant change efforts.

Build capabilities and confidence by providing opportunities to learn required skills. Skill development is important for any successful change, not just the promotion of resiliency. A good beginning place might be to provide opportunities to obtain relevant information about strategies that promote resiliency. Building on this knowledge base, opportunities can be provided to learn and practice facilitation skills that are needed to implement resiliency-promoting behaviors (e.g., goal setting, conflict management, communications, and decision making).

We use the term *skill development* rather than *professional development* because we believe that this activity should be made available to all participants, not just educators. If students, educators, and community members are to participate effectively as partners, status differentials must be minimized and skill development must be provided. Leadership activities that facilitate and support participants' skill development are described in Chapter 7.

Emphasize the way things will stay the same as well as the way things will change. Continuity is a necessary foundation for security. This is particularly true when we are asked to make significant changes. Individuals will more likely have the confidence to take necessary risks if they believe that there will be sufficient continuity and that known points of reference will be maintained regularly and meaningfully. In other words, they will feel more secure if a balance between security and risk taking is promoted.

Resiliency development is a change that is particularly well suited to promoting continuity because *it is more about changing our approach to our work than it is about changing the work itself*. That is, resiliency is an attitude, a state of mind, about how to behave in learning communities. With this understanding in place, attitudinal changes that may be required for the school to become more supportive of resiliency are not likely to be perceived as so disorienting to group members.

> The art of progress is to preserve order amid change and to preserve change amid order.
>
> —*Alfred North Whitehead*

Monitor progress. Even the best laid plans can go astray. Keeping on course toward agreed-upon goals requires regular and meaningful assessments of progress (see Chapter 7). Strategic adjustments that may be needed can only be made if clear, agreed-upon goals are developed and good assessment measures are put in place to monitor the extent to which the goals are being achieved. Assessment efforts can also help to maintain commitment and motivation. If participants see evidence of positive movement and results, they are more likely to have a sense of achievement and to continue their involvement.

BACKWARDS PLANNING

It is one thing to believe that a school should be reconfigured in ways that promote resiliency for all members, but it is quite another to move the organization in ways that make this a reality. To support this goal, we suggest backwards planning as an approach that can help you and others at the school become clearer about what needs to be changed and how to go about changing it.

What should your resilient school of tomorrow look like? Backwards planning emphasizes the importance of agreeing about and clarifying the vision of the future you hope to create before making decisions and taking actions. Exercise 5.5 (expanded from Henderson & Milstein, 1996) can help the group clarify school goals that can lead to increased support for the resiliency of its members. With end goals in mind, plans can be developed to bring them about.

> ### Exercise 5.5: A Backwards Planning Activity: Take the Roof Off the School
>
> Ask group members to respond to the following statement: *It is now five years into the future, five years since efforts were started to improve the resiliency-building capacity of your school. There have been struggles with implementation, but most everyone believes that the effort has been highly successful. What does "success" look like?*
>
> 1. Ask group members to imagine they are hovering over the school. Ask them to imagine that they are able to take the roof off of the school and peer down to see what is going on in it. What do they believe they will see five years from now in their more resilient school? For example, what kinds of interactions will be going on? What will classrooms and other areas of the school look like? What will be displayed on the walls? Ask group members to share their images. As they do, post them on a chalkboard or on chart paper.
>
> 2. Ask the group to review the posted images. Encourage them to clarify and modify the images and add any others that might be useful.
>
> 3. Share the six resiliency elements (see Figure 1.3) with the group. Ask members to check their list of images against the six elements. Are all of the resiliency elements adequately addressed by their list? If not, ask members to think of things they want to add to their lists, especially for those elements that may be absent or underrepresented.
>
> 4. Last, ask the group to identify the major characteristics that define the school as it becomes more supportive of resiliency. Review the agreements, and ask the group to translate them into goal statements that reflect what they want to achieve. Post the agreements and the goals. Save them for future reference.

Backwards planning is an approach that starts with agreements about preferred futures. Knowing what you want the school to become and agreeing on a vision of what it will look like is a positive and powerful starting place for getting there. With this vision in mind, it is easier to set goals and identify strategies that can support their achievement.

SCHOOL RESILIENCY-BUILDING STRATEGIES

Although each school is unique, there are common organizationally based dynamics that cut across school levels and geographic locations. School leaders need to understand the dynamics of modifying attitudes, structures, and behaviors and respond to them effectively. If they do, they can make a positive difference for students, educators, and the community. If they do not, they can inhibit growth and development.

> So much of what we call management consists of making it difficult for people to work.
>
> —Peter Drucker

To help leaders with these tasks, organizationally based dynamics that need to be considered when promoting each of the six resiliency elements are discussed. Strategies for responding to them in ways that can improve the situation are also offered. We encourage you and your group to modify and add to these suggestions to meet the particular needs of your school's situation.

Positive Connections

Supportive school climates and cultures promote positive connections. Organizational climate is like the weather. It can be a major challenge to basic survival if it is cold and unsettled. It can also be a major strategy for community building and bonding if it is warm and sunny. A school's culture is less observable, but it can have an even greater impact on resiliency building. Some organizations have cultures that promote status differences and foster the kinds of behaviors that lead to distrust, inhibit connectedness and teaming, and promote fear and reprisals. Other organizations have cultures that promote empowerment and equality, encourage learning and growth, and recognize individual and group accomplishments.

> A school can create a "coherent" environment, a climate, more potent than any single influence—teachers, class, family, neighborhood—so potent that for at least six hours a day it can override almost everything else in the lives of children.
>
> —*Ron Edwards*

Cultures change slowly because they are so deeply embedded over long periods of time, but with focused attention and patience, they can be positively affected.

Leadership Strategies for Increasing Positive Connections

Efforts to modify and strengthen the school's climate and culture can positively affect members' connections. Useful strategies include the following:

- Model and encourage respect, cooperation, support, and trust. These behaviors promote positive relationships and send a powerful message: people are important and their well-being is an organizational priority.
- Encourage members to discuss and craft vision and mission statements or to review and modify them as needed if they already exist. This exercise can stimulate the process of organizational change and promote resiliency by emphasizing and clarifying shared values, shifting resource allocation priorities, and institutionalizing important governance, structural, and educational modifications. It also can promote a shared sense of purpose.
- Emphasize cooperation, teaming, and support whenever possible. Many ways to do these things have already been suggested in the book.

Record other strategies that can increase positive connections at your school and in your community:

- _____
  _____
- _____
  _____
- _____
  _____

Set Clear, Consistent, and Appropriate Boundaries

School boundaries are set in two ways: policies and rules that are formalized and norms that shape behavioral expectations informally. Both are necessary. They inform students, educators, staff, and community members about how they should interact with each other to accomplish given ends. There is no problem with boundaries if they are reasonable, understood, and supported, but if they are capricious, inconsistent, unclear, or arbitrarily developed by a few rule makers for many others, they can be serious impediments to members' resiliency. For example, *students* can easily become alienated from the school if the rules are perceived to be unreasonable or unfair. In fact, if this happens, they may turn to peer-developed norms, which are likely to promote behaviors that directly challenge those fostered by school policies and rules. *Educators and staff* are usually granted wide latitude for rules that affect their own roles, but they usually do not have much control over behavioral expectations outside of their role domains. This control dichotomy can lead to confusion and frustra-tion. *Community members* are typically confronted by formal and informal rule structures at the school that are not of their own making and that often send a clear and negative message: "Stay out unless we ask you to come in!"

> Integrity has no need of rules.
> —Albert Camus

Leadership Strategies for Promoting Clear, Consistent, and Appropriate Boundaries

If boundaries are clear and school members own them, everyone knows how they should behave and can concentrate on teaching, learning, relating, and cooperating. If they feel safe and secure, they can take the risks required to grow and develop. Feeling safe and secure can be promoted by the following:

> The fact, in short, is that *freedom* to be meaningful in an organized society must consist of an amalgam of hierarchy of freedoms *and* restraints.
> —Samuel Hendel

- Clarify the school's vision, mission, and goals so that everyone understands purposes and priorities.
- Share behavioral expectations with staff, students, families, and others from the community, and encourage positive behaviors that, over time, can be embedded intrinsically.
- Clarify role expectations and the ways they interrelate and provide opportunities for questions and concerns to be raised.
- Base rules and policies on research, information gathering, and best practices.
- Provide regular opportunities for members to review, modify, and otherwise update policies and rules that affect them.
- Follow through to ensure that equitable implementation of agreed-upon boundaries occurs.

Record other strategies that can promote clear, consistent, and appropriate boundary setting for your school:

- _____
  _____
- _____
  _____
- _____
  _____

Life-Guiding Skills

Schools that narrowly focus on academic basics and are preoccupied with maintenance tasks such as budgets and books, miss the opportunity to support the development of student, educator, staff, and community members' life-guiding skills. School leaders need to take a comprehensive perspective about their role in life-guiding skill development, a perspective that views all participants as members of learning communities. Learning communities are concerned with the growth needs of all, not just some, of the members.

Leadership Strategies for Fostering Life-Guiding Skills

Strategies that can promote members' life-guiding skills include these:

- Model expectations for life-guiding skill development. Send consistent messages that change and renewal are necessary for all members of the learning community, and for the well-being of the school itself. Leaders model these expectations when they practice and promote involvement in problem finding, diagnosis, decision making, problem solving, conflict management, intervention, and change practices and when they make efforts to monitor and evaluate outcomes. Involving students, faculty, and community members in these activities can provide unique opportunities for participation, learning, and growth.
- Respond to challenges from students, staff, parents, and other community members proactively, creatively, and openly rather than reactively, defensively, and guardedly and seek feedback rather than cutoff inputs.
- Provide opportunities for all members' life-guiding skill development in areas such as critical thinking, effective problem solving, and conflict management so they can participate in school-wide improvement efforts effectively and with confidence.
- Encourage cooperative efforts such as consensus decision making, goal setting, and teaming for organizational improvement. Learning these life-guiding skills as a learning community promotes commitment and motivation to practice them as a group. As an added bonus, once learned, these life-guiding skills will likely become part of the ongoing repertoire of those who participate.

Record other strategies that can foster life-guiding skills at your school:

- _____
  _____
- _____
  _____
- _____
  _____

Nurture and Support

Schools vary along a continuum from places that emphasize control and where members feel isolated and alienated to places that emphasize inclusion and where members feel connected, cared for, and sup-

> Once we believe in ourselves, we can risk curiosity, wonder, spontaneous delight, or any experience that reveals the human spirit.
>
> *E. E. Cummings*

ported. School leaders who emphasize control believe that regimented daily routines, compliance, and micromanagement of resources are required because students, educators, and community members will not otherwise cooperate or participate positively. Good school leaders focus less on compliance and control and more on members' care and support.

Leadership Strategies that Promote Nurturance and Support

To promote nurturance and support, it is important to institutionalize strategies such as the following:

- Develop a school climate that emphasizes positive feedback, cooperation, and caring.
- Spend most of the school day out in the school promoting care and support rather than in the office. Leaders who are engaged within the school will roam the building, talk regularly and by name with students and staff, welcome community members, respond to members' concerns, reach out to students' families, and send powerful messages that nurturance and support are highly valued in the school.

> Kindness in words creates confidence. Kindness in thinking creates profoundness. Kindness in giving creates love.
>
> —*Lao-Tsu*

- Avoid favoritism and distribute resources equitably to demonstrate that there is concern for the well-being and growth of all members. Creative ways to engage all aspects of the school are needed to ensure that resources are known and distributed equitably.
- Shift the emphasis from external locus of control of members' behaviors to an emphasis on shared values, norms, and expectations. In the process, a community of learners that encompasses all members will be promoted. Through frank and open exchanges, members can come to understand each other better, empathize with each other's needs and hopes, and view each other as respected partners rather than distrusted competitors.
- Celebrate members' rites of passages, including student progress and achievements, staff members' professional accomplishments and career development initiatives, and community members' support and contributions to the school. At one school, a teacher who was close to retirement finished her master's degree. At the awards celebration at the end of the year, the teacher was presented to the school in her cap and gown. The teacher who continued to grow was recognized for her work. The students were given a positive image of this teacher.
- Publicize members' efforts to reach out and help, for instance, by serving on school-wide committees and recognizing others who make similar contributions to the school. Recognizing these outreach activities sends messages that they are highly valued.

Record other strategies that can enhance nurture and support in your school:

- _____
  _____
- _____
  _____
- _____
  _____

Purposes and Expectations

Schools function like the worst stereotypes of organizational bureaucracies when they focus on meeting minimal performance expectations and producing minimally acceptable outcomes. Such schools are places noted for competing forces that require bargaining and trade-offs rather than places noted for supportive and symbiotic forces that build on each other in ways that promote win-win opportunities and high achievement. Worst of all, the focus is on defending and preserving rather than on taking risks and creating.

> A subject for a great poet would be God's boredom after the seventh day of Creation.
>
> —*Friedrich Nietzsche*

This mentality can lead to school dynamics that depress the basic human desire for challenge and growth. Such schools are places where

- students get messages that they need only meet minimal standards to pass on to the next grade;
- educators receive little positive feedback, their extrinsic rewards are limited to lockstep salary schedules, and they are often required to participate in professional development activities that do not take their own perceived needs for growth into consideration; and
- community members are given the message that they should not "interfere" in school matters.

The potential for mediocre performance, as well as a lack of self-confidence, is great in such schools.

Leadership Strategies for Strengthening Purposes and Expectations

The following leadership strategies can foster positive and challenging purposes and expectations:

> I believe that anyone can conquer fear by doing the things he fears to do, provided he keeps doing them until he gets a record of successful experiences behind him.
>
> —*Eleanor Roosevelt*

- Permeate the school with "can do" messages. Norms need to change from acceptance of nonengagement, minimal effort, and low expectations to norms of support for achievement. "You can do it, and I will support your efforts to do it!" is a message that may be stimulated initially by the school's leaders, but ultimately needs to be believed and practiced by everyone—students, educators, staff, and community members. It is a simple and potent message.

- Encourage goal setting and achievement for everyone. This can be pursued in many ways. School leaders can set the tone by making sure that the school's vision, mission, and goals are translated into meaingful operational plans with clearly established responsibilities and time lines. Teachers can prepare annual professional development plans and share them with their colleagues and administrators. Parents and students, as noted in Chapter 3, can contract with teachers to establish and accomplish learning expectations. Parents and other community members can be asked to participate in site-based governance activities and to volunteer their time and talents for school and classroom improvement efforts. Given appropriate challenges and sufficient support, risk taking, and experimentation, everyone can experience meaningful achievements.

> The mind, once expanded to
> The dimensions of larger ideas,
> Never returns to its
> Original size
> —Oliver Wendell Holmes

> If at first you don't succeed, you're running about average.
> —M. H. Alderson

- Monitor progress and achievements regularly. Conducted properly, monitoring can send clear messages that everyone's success matters. Supportive feedback for efforts that are made and suggestions for improvement can help promote success.

> Treat people as if they were what they ought to be and you help them to become what they are capable of being.
> —Johann W. von Goethe

- Encourage learning opportunities that legitimize giving and receiving help. With such encouragement and some practice, fear and distrust will begin to subside and, as members cooperate and support each other, they will become more involved and more encouraging of everyone's success.

> We are told that talent creates its own opportunities. But it sometimes seems that intense desire creates not only its own opportunities, but its own talents.
> —Eric Hoffer

- Celebrate achievements and tell stories about "heroes"—students, edu-cators, staff, and community members—who, with support, focus, and motivation, have overcome the odds to succeed in school and in life.

Record other strategies that can strengthen purposes and expectations for your school:

- _____
- _____
- _____

Provide Opportunities for Meaningful Participation

There is continuous recognition that widespread involvement in site-based decision making is important. Students, educators, and community members have concerns, ideas, and energies that are relevant and can contribute to the school's success. As they participate in school-wide agendas, they also enhance their own resiliency. However, they will be

> A school should not be a preparation for life. A school should be life.
> —Elbert Hubbard

motivated to contribute to school improvement efforts only if their participation in discussions and in decision making is perceived as valued.

Widespread participation can strengthen the relationships and foster a foundation of mutual support for the school and community but only if four aspects are changed from barriers to assets. First, site-based activities need to be understood if people are going to become involved. This requires leaders who have the skill to facilitate open and clear communications, relevant goal setting, purposeful conflict management, and positive team development. A good way to squash site-based activities are to have them perceived to be pro forma and micromanaged by leaders rather than relevant and open equitably to all participants. Such leaders limit participation because they are uncomfortable about sharing authority, particularly if they are going to be held responsible for outcomes they do not control.

Second, participation is encouraged because all are viewed as legitimate partici-pants in the process and relevant to the decisions made. Educators discourage involvement when they think of students, parents, and other community members as clients or customers to be served rather than as important partners and partici-pants in the process.

Third, teacher involvement in school-wide problem solving and decision making is important. In fact, there is evidence that in schools where the staff works together cohesively, student achievement is positively affected (Wheelan & Kesselring, 2005). An example of this is the recognition given in the San Diego Union-Tribune ("Teacher collaboration," 2007) to nine San Diego County, California schools that have been identified as the state's "best of the best." These schools all emphasize teacher collaboration. But such collaboration is not likely to be fostered if these activ-ities are viewed as the prerogative and responsibility of administrators. Teachers' preparation and experience, which is mainly limited to classroom-level curriculum and instruction, also constrains it. These activities are usually performed individu-ally and in isolation from others, which does not foster group skills or encourage cooperative efforts.

Fourth, recognition and rewards for students, teachers, parents, and other com-munity members cannot be overrated. Most people help because of intrinsic rewards they gain from the experience. Such contributions require time and effort that is sim-ply added to everything else that must be done. Celebration of what people have given and done fortifies the link between the individual and the school. Unfortunately, celebrations are usually rare or sporadic rather than seen as a part of the school fabric. Leaders need to plan for it.

Leadership Strategies to Improve Meaningful Participation

Meaningful participation can promote learning communities in which all mem-bers' inputs are sought and valued, engagement becomes the norm, and successful change is more likely to occur. Leaders can foster meaningful participation in a num-ber of ways:

- View students, parents, and other community members as legitimate and important participants rather than as clients. *Students* learn best when their participation in school affairs is actively solicited because they have legiti-mate and relevant roles to play. The school should be a living laboratory in which students practice life-guiding skills such as communication, goal set-ting, and decision making. *Parents* and other *community members* are more likely to participate when they are viewed as partners with legitimate concerns and important contributions to make to the school's educational processes. This does not deny the fact that educators play a centrally important role in the maintenance and development of schools, but schools *belong to the community and are established to serve community-identified needs. They do not belong solely to educators.*

- Promote the attitude that participation is important to the school. Everyone has information, suggestions, energy, and skills that can contribute to more effective educational outcomes at the school. In like manner, members need to believe that they are engaged in activities that matter to them. That is, they will feel ownership for what is going on if they value the goals being pursued and they see the potential of positive results, both for themselves and for the community.
- Establish healthy norms for conflict management. Conflicts about ideas are legitimate, but personality attacks are not!
- Offer skill development that prepares members to participate effectively. This includes information gathering and dissemination as well as skills focusing on goal setting, teaming, communications, meeting management, consensus decision making, and conflict management.
- Provide sufficient time for participation and be creative about find-ing meeting times that are responsive to members' time constraints. The time constraints of all members, not just of educators, need to be taken into consideration.

Record other strategies that can improve meaningful participation in your school:

- _____
  _____
- _____
  _____
  _____
- _____
  _____
  _____

Exercise 5.6: Putting the School Roof Back On and Getting Started

1. In the "Take the Roof Off the School" exercise presented earlier in the chapter (Exercise 5.5), group members were asked to review the six resiliency elements and apply them to the vision of their resilient school of the future. Ask the group to take a few minutes to review the results of that exercise.

2. Next, ask the group to review the strategies suggested for each of the resiliency elements in this section of the chapter. Are some of these strategies worth considering for improving their school's resiliency-building capacity? Are there others they may want to add? If so, record them.

Exercise 5.6 provides an opportunity for the group to think about strategies that can enhance the school's resiliency-building capacity.

Schools can change in ways that promote resiliency. We created them and we have the capacity to recreate them to meet changing needs. In fact, we have the obligation to do so if our assessment indicates that students, educators, and community members are not being well served in ways that promote their long-term resiliency. This chapter has provided a variety of responses to the significant barriers that stand in the way of school resiliency building. We encourage readers to look closely at their own schools, draw relevant conclusions, make plans, and take actions that can improve the resiliency-building capacity of these settings.

> Civilization is a race between education and catastrophe.
>
> —H. G. Wells

Exercise 5.7: Considerations for Leaders

Leaders play a central role in the ability of schools to promote resiliency for students, educators, parents, and other community members. They set a tone that either supports this goal or becomes a barrier to its realization. What rating, on a scale of one (low) to five (high) would you give to the knowledge and capabilities of your school's leaders to develop and maintain schools that promote resiliency?

1. Facilitate change-related activities
   A. shaping values and expectations
   B. improving the culture of the school
   C. emphasizing continuity as well as change
   D. monitoring progress

2. Facilitate backwards planning activities

3. Facilitate positive connections strategies

4. Facilitate clear, consistent, and appropriate boundary development strategies

5. Facilitate life-guiding skills

6. Facilitate nurturance and support

7. Facilitate purposes and expectations development

8. Facilitate meaningful participation

The environments we live in significantly affect our resiliency. In Chapter 6, we turn our attention to the environment that surrounds our schools—the communities in which we live and work. Ultimately, the community is the locus in which the long-term ability of our schools to promote student and educator resiliency is determined. If active partnerships of schools and communities are forged, resiliency can be promoted for everyone.

6

Community Resiliency

Developing Partnerships

"Never doubt that small groups of thoughtful, committed citizens can change the world. Indeed, it's the only thing that ever has."

—Margaret Mead

There are many ways in which individual citizens can help make the community more resilient, but this is rarely the message citizens hear when they try to make a positive difference in their neighborhoods.

It may seem insurmountable for many to make a positive difference, but together we can indeed do so. A community service announcement on television captured the point. It began with the silhouette of a person talking about how sure he was that he *could not make a difference* because he *was just one person*. Another silhouette appeared repeating the same phrase. Within thirty seconds, the television screen was filled with silhouettes lamenting the "fact" that they *could not* make a difference because of being just one person. The message was clear: yes, each of us is just one person, but *together* we *can* make a difference.

> Even weak men when united are powerful.
>
> —*Friedrich Schiller*

There are many examples of courageous people who have accomplished extraordinary things. The civil rights movement of the 1960s could never have become a reality without people like Martin Luther King, Jr., Bobby Kennedy, and Rosa Parks, who each in his or her own way spoke out about the need for fair treatment and human dignity for everyone. Mahatma Ghandi became the leader of his country because he acted on his beliefs.

> I like the dreams of the future better than the history of the past.
>
> —*Thomas Jefferson*

The citizens of Afghanistan, the Czech Republic, Hungary, and Poland rose up to confront the Soviet Union's occupation of their countries and the control of their lives. There are countless examples of how citizens have united for a cause with the result of positive influence for the greater good.

Similarly, schools and communities are composed of individuals who may be ordinary people, but together they can do remarkable things. For a community to be healthy and resilient, it takes collaboration. Unfortunately, many schools and communities do not partner in productive ways. In fact, they may even view each other as adversaries. Educators and communities can choose to recognize their common destinies and create partnerships for mutual benefit, or they can choose to struggle along in isolation from each other.

> It really takes a community to raise children, no matter how much money one has. Nobody can do it well alone. And it's the bedrock security of community that we and our children need.
>
> —*Marian Wright-Edelman*

Resilient schools and communities work together as partners. They work at understanding each other, finding common ground, building a shared commitment, and fostering the skills needed to make the partnership effective. The focus of this chapter is on building this kind of relationship between schools and their communities. The chapter explores ways to increase awareness of the need for partnerships between schools and communities as well as strategies to make this happen. First, we differentiate between a community that exhibits high levels of resiliency and a community that exhibits low levels of resiliency. Second, we explore the importance of the community and school supporting each other in their success and well-being. Next, using the six resiliency elements, we present strategies for expanding school-community partnerships and making your school and community more resilient. Last, we give strategies for leaders to promote partnerships between schools and communities.

BUILDING RELATIONSHIPS BETWEEN SCHOOLS AND THEIR COMMUNITIES

Leaders who work at meeting the needs of students recognize the importance of building positive relationships with the community. They understand the value of supportive connections and invest time and effort in forging them.

Why aren't there more of these partnerships formed and continued in productive ways? Several factors contribute to the problem. In large measure, this is an outcome of the constant drumbeat of negativity that has come out of policymaking centers over the past several decades. A plethora of reports have declared that schools and, by inference, our communities are at risk and that they are making little positive progress. In the United States, the *National Commission on Excellence in Education Report* (1983) and, more recently, the No Child Left Behind Act or Public Law 107-110 (U.S. Department of Education, 2001) spotlighted schools that were identified as not meeting standards. The NCLB's yearly report concludes that the number of schools that do not meet standards is increasing at an alarming rate.

Many of our schools and communities are in trouble, in part at least because of the negative tone of these efforts and the deficit thinking they represent. Goleman (1995) captured the dilemma well:

"Over the last decade or so "wars" have been declared, in turn, on teen pregnancy, dropping out, drugs, and most recently, violence. The trouble with such campaigns, though, is that they come too late, after the targeted problem has reached epidemic proportions and taken firm root in the lives of the young. They are crisis interventions, the equivalent of solving a problem by sending an ambulance to the rescue rather than giving an inoculation that would ward off the disease in the first place." (p. 256)

This is an important time because of the shift in the public's thinking about schools and because of the resources allocated or not allocated based on these perceptions. For the most part, the reports and subsequent contributions to the debate have led many of us to believe that we need to "fix" individuals and schools that exhibit at-risk behaviors. The good news is that many schools and communities are not in need of being fixed.

COMMUNITIES WITH CHARACTERISTICS OF RESILIENCY

How many communities can you name that are resilient? More than likely, you know of communities that are close by that confront issues and continue to grow. How many are recognized in the media for the work they are doing and the positive results they are achieving? If we look to our media, the numbers are limited, but if we talk with people who are engaged in their communities, we find many that have had difficulties, learned from them, and become stronger and healthier.

We are quite good at identifying what does not work, but how much do we know about what does work? What are the characteristics of a community that exhibits extensive resiliency? In contrast to nonresilient communities, resilient communities tend to exhibit the characteristics listed in Table 6.1. Resilient communities are not free of problems, but they are more likely to confront problems effectively.

> Do what you can with what you have, where you are.
>
> —*Theodore Roosevelt*

COMMUNITIES THAT NEED RESILIENCY IMPROVEMENT

With all of our efforts to improve the health and well-being of young people and our communities, we still have a long way to go. It is not difficult to find examples of communities that need resiliency improvement. Stories appear daily in newspapers, on TV, and on the Internet, reminding us of the lack of community resiliency. For example, we regularly hear about communities in which young people do not practice protective sex because, given the profusion of crime and violence that exist in their neighborhoods they believe that they will not live long enough for what they do to matter (McLaughlin, Irby, & Langman, 1994). Similarly, we hear about teenagers who find life so negative that they are committing suicide.

> The game of life is not so much in holding a good hand as playing a poor hand well.
>
> —*H. T. Leslie*

Table 6.1 Examples of a Community With Characteristics of Resiliency

Increase Positive Connections	Set Clear, Consistent, and Appropriate Boundaries	Teach Life-Guiding Skills	Provide Nurture and Support	Set and Communicate Purposes and Expectations	Provide Meaningful Opportunities to Participate
Citizens engage in meaningful discourse	Norms for participation and decision making are established	Human services collaborations exist	Widespread collaboration on community projects exist	Community supports positive vision for the future	Many civic clubs exist with broad membership
An infrastructure exists that promotes cooperative efforts	Proactivity and acceptance are practiced	Lifelong learning opportunities are available	Respect for law and order is widespread	Quality of life is a high priority	Volunteerism is encouraged
Celebrations and rituals exist	Participatory governance exists	Intergenerational programs are operating	Intergenerational connections are made	High standards of acceptable behavior are set	Community vision is shared and pursued
Interorganizational activities are common	Emphasis is on community	Preventive programs that are proactive are widespread	Services to others is encouraged	Family and community spirit is prevalent	Leadership training is available and effective
Community symbols are evident	Regular and clear communications exist	Support groups are established		Recognition for efforts and achievements are common	
Meaningful partnerships are nurtured					
Past and current cultures are celebrated					

A community in need of resiliency can do irreparable damage to the hopes and dreams of those who live in it. Table 6.2 depicts some of the characteristics that typify these communities.

The negative examples illustrated in Table 6.2 are typical of communities that need to grow and become stronger. Do any of these examples represent your community? Are there others you think should be added to Table 6.2 as related to your community?

We each have our own perceptions about the resiliency of the communities in which we live and work. Exercise 6.1, which follows, can be used in a variety of ways: as a community survey, a large group activity, a small group activity, or as an individual assessment for each of the stakeholders.

Table 6.2 Examples of a Community Needing Resiliency Improvement

Increase Positive Connections	Set Clear, Consistent, and Appropriate Boundaries	Teach Life-Guiding Skills	Provide Nurture and Support	Set and Communicate Purposes and Expectations	Provide Meaningful Opportunities to Participate
People are isolated	Laws, policies, and rules are applied inconsistently	There is denial of problems	Few community services are available	Status quo orientation is maintained	Apathy is evident
Streets are unsafe	Few opportunities for community input	Poor problem-identifying and problem-solving skills are apparent	There is need for much greater resources than are made available	A sense of hopelessness prevails	The focus is on differences
A culture of fear and discrimination exists	Tension exists among ethnic, racial, and other groups	There is little evidence of cooperation	Absence of partnerships is the rule	Widespread poor self-esteem/self-concept	Minimal infrastructure for citizen input
There is a lack of effective programs	Favoritism is the norm	Ineffective conflict management is common	Individuals feel anonymous	There is little evidence of mutual trust	There is little or no celebration of successes
Little effort to communicate is made	A sense of community is not shared	Teenage pregnancy and other risky behaviors are prevalent	There is an absence of community celebrations	There are few cooperative or cohesive efforts	Few if any community improvement initiatives are undertaken
Lack of trust is common		Bullying exists	Leadership is not visible	There is an absence of community vision	
Factions thrive within community			Leadership lacks vision		

Exercise 6.1: Do You Know How Resilient Your Community Is?

1. Duplicate and distribute Tables 6.1 and 6.2 and answer sheet (Handouts 11, 12, and 13 in the Resource section).

2. Ask each person to rate the community's resiliency for each of the six elements. Use the following scale:

Low Resilience   5   4   3   2   1   High Resilience

3. Develop a group score and identify elements that are low and high in resiliency.

4. List the characteristics that people saw as making the community more resilient.

5. List the characteristics that people saw as making the community less resilient.

6. Agree on priorities that the group may want to discuss further.

Resilient communities not only believe that difficulties can be met but that they can grow stronger if they address them. They are aware of the interdependencies that exist between individuals, families, schools, voluntary organizations, and government agencies. Resilient communities know what their problems are, strive for continuous improvement, and nurture their assets. Genuine participation is invited and listened to seriously. Broad-based support is developed and maintained so that coalitions can be formed, problems can be addressed, and assets can be strengthened.

> The world has narrowed into a neighborhood before it has broadened into a brotherhood.
>
> —Lyndon B. Johnson

COMMUNITY ASSESTS

We know that the community in which a school operates can make a significant difference in its effectiveness (Carter, 2007). Over the past decade, the impact a community can have on its schools and the youth who attend them has been well documented. One of the leaders in this effort is Peter Benson, president of the Search Institute in Minneapolis, who believes that providing the young with strong foundations during the first two decades of their lives is an important community responsibility (Benson, 1997; Benson, Galbraith, & Espeland, 1995; Scales et al., 2006). Based on the data the Search Institute has collected across the country, Benson and colleagues (1995) identified internal and external assets from birth to adulthood. Their conclusion is that support, boundaries, expectations, empowerment, constructive use of time, educational commitment, positive values, social competencies, and positive identity are eight essential categories to healthy youth development. In 2006, they solidified their research into five core areas, which they described as the five promises: caring adults, safe places and constructive uses of time, a healthy start and healthy development, effective education for marketable skills for life long education, and opportunities to make a difference through helping others (Scales, Benson, Bartig, Streit, Moore, Lippman, et al., 2006). These five promises provide a solid foundation for communities to foster their youth and apply their resources effectively.

COMMUNITY SUPPORT IS NEEDED FOR SCHOOL RESILIENCY

Partnerships work best when those involved believe they serve their interests. In the past, the roles of the school and community were clear and distinctly different. Communities were responsible for providing students, a plot of land, a building for a school, and funds to pay for operational costs while educators were responsible for molding the young into contributing community members.

However, these roles have become blurred and relationships have changed from ones noted by trust to ones noted by skepticism. This has become more pervasive as modern societies moved from agrarian small towns to large urbanized communities coupled with more funds generated from state and national governmental levels, which also created more external controls on schools. The growing size of communities and the dynamics of outside control have made school and community partnerships more tenuous. Many parents and community members perceive that they no longer have a say in their schools. A current example is the strain NCLB has placed on schools and communities to perform at expected standards without accompanying resources to help educators improve education for all students. Over time, many schools and communities have increasingly moved apart from each other. In some instances, they have even become adversarial in their relations.

Schools that place a priority on improving partnerships with their communities can create more positive relationships. The need to do so is extremely pressing, not only because of the importance of partnering effectively but also because schools are being pressed to do more with fewer resources. When normal sources of support are limited or inadequate, educators have to seek more resources from their communities. This need is driving even more schools to tap community resources and to work more collaboratively with them. In almost all communities, there are extraordinary resource people who are ready and able to provide voluntary services. For example,

- many senior citizens have the time and interest to work with young people;
- young retirees, in particular, often want to contribute their energies and talents and give something back their community;
- accomplished individuals may want to "give back" by mentoring others; and
- skilled professionals may want to share their interests with students.

Reform and restructuring efforts have required educators to rethink the ways they operate and see the necessity to partner with their communities. In particular, site-based management and shared decision making are formats that encourage school leaders to collaborate with the community.

Schools that open their doors to community participation for site-based management activities have experienced positive results. Slowly but surely, attitudes begin to change. Schools that have taken this route have discovered that they can do a better job of preparing students when they recognize and act on the need to use all available resources—from the community as well as from within the school.

SCHOOL SUPPORT IS NEEDED FOR COMMUNITY RESILIENCY

Schools have the potential to provide extensive support for the development and maintenance of resilient communities. Fulfilling this potential is quite a formidable task, particularly because many schools and communities tend to apply quick fixes for complex problems. For instance, "just say no to drugs" may send a clear message, but it does not build the life skills that are necessary to support the intent. Words need to be accompanied with deeds or little will happen. Undeterred drug abuse, crime, and other antisocial behaviors that contribute to the schools' problems require community-wide responses.

The school can play a pivotal role in changing the course of events and enhancing the potential for community resiliency. The following are some ways:

- Prepare the community's youth, through academic and vocational development, to play positive roles as adults. They can do so by developing mentoring programs, providing opportunities to shadow a career person for a day, and promoting apprenticeships for different professions that students want to explore.

> Why should society feel responsible only for the education of children, and not for the education of all adults of every age?
> —*Erich Fromm*

- Encourage students and staff to engage in service activities that directly support community development such as high schools students who tutor primary age students.

> The man who has ceased to learn ought not to be allowed to wander around loose in these dangerous days.
>
> —M. M. Coady

- Be a community focal point by promoting pride and a sense of connectivity through its academic and extracurricular accomplishments.
- Be a center for learning for *all* community members by developing a learning community whose members inform and learn from each other.
- Develop life skills and leadership skills for parents and other community members.

FROM REACTIVE TO PROACTIVE COMMUNITY RELATIONSHIPS

Schools that have reached out to their communities recognize the importance and value of doing so. This may call for changes in how we do business and additional resources reserved for the effort but, with determination and commitment, it can happen. In fact, Chapter 8 provides information about many communities around the country where it is happening.

> That which seems the height of absurdity in one generation often becomes the height of wisdom in another.
>
> —Adlai Stevenson

What do mutually beneficial partnerships between schools and their communities look like? To visualize such partnerships, we summarize how schools have limited their involvement with communities in the past and identify the trends that are currently evolving toward more positive and effective partnerships.

Table 6.3 graphically displays a reactive-to-proactive scale of school and community relationships. It illustrates five types of relationships, varying from those that typified school-community interactions of the past, *reactive* or *with tolerance*, to those that are becoming more common now, *involvement*, to those we believe will emerge in more school-community interactions: *connectivity* and *outreach*.

Reactive ◊ Tolerance ◊ Involvement ◊ Connectivity ◊ Outreach

Reactive Systems

Schools on the closed end of the continuum are *reactive*. They minimize contacts with community members, viewing them as bothersome and intrusive. Parents and other community members are seen as adversaries rather than partners and critics rather than supporters and as incapable of making meaningful inputs rather than being relevant and equal voices at the table. They believe that the important task of educating youngsters should be left to those qualified to do this—educators. In short, parents and community members should assist schools but only when they are asked to do so. The message communicated to the community is to stay out. Community members may continue to push for engagement with educators, but when parents and others ask for information and when they want to partner with schools, they are often shut out (Mathews, 2007).

Table 6.3   School and Community: From Reactive to Proactive Relations

	Reactive	Tolerance	Involvement	Connectivity	Outreach
Beliefs	• Locked down mentality	• Grudging acceptance of legitimate, but limited, role of parents in school	• Community support for school sought and encouraged	• Active networking to develop community-wide, comprehensive, integrated programs	• Mutual support and partnerships
Expectations	• Minimal involvement of parents (controlled by school staff) • Limited time set aside for engagement	• Limited and formalized engagement in school affairs for parents and possibly others in community	• Parents and others actively involved • Social agencies encouraged to collaborate on youth-related activities	• Extensive open, flexible, and ongoing relationship between community and school	• All community elements represented • Equal access for initiation, involvement, and decision making
Governance structures	• Explicit and detailed policies or rules for parent involvement set by the school	• Advice sought from select group of parents (PTA or PTO) • PTAs or PTOs dominated by educators • School-dominated governance and decision making	• School sets parameters but seeks active involvement with parents and community	• Schools and other agencies focused on youth meet together regularly to set priorities and monitor activities	• Interagency councils • Nonbureaucratic and fluid structures that promote mutual influence
Communications	• Highly limited and one way, from school to parents	• Primarily one way, from school to parents and community	• School-initiated feedback encouraged from parents and community • Invitational and regular to parents and community	• Two way and formalized with youth-related agencies and other organizations	• Multichanneled • Two way • Frequent
Resources	• Minimal resources set aside for relationship purposes • Parents or community resources not pursued	• PTA/PTO fund raising for school priorities • Room Mothers or Fathers with limited roles • Focus limited to students and classroom needs	• Resources for the school identified and solicited	• School facilities made available for community use • Community facilities made available for school use	• School personnel and students engaged as community volunteers
Activities	• School calls on parents when student-related problems arise • Formal and limited parent committees	• Structured and limited parent committees • Principal apprises parents and others of school activities	• Students mentored by community members • Volunteers sought for school programs • Social service agencies function in the school	• Shared use of facilities (e.g., meeting rooms, libraries, and computers) • Summer programs developed cooperatively to meet community needs	• Agreed-upon joint initiatives that focus on community improvement • Service learning

Tolerance

To the extent that these schools find themselves pressed to interact, they relate with *tolerance*. They posture about involvement but keep tight control on the process. For example, many school Parent Teacher Associations (PTAs) or Parent Teacher Organizations (PTOs) send signals that only a select group of parents are valued and that even with this limited group, educators will provide the leadership and be the dominant force. Schools operating from the tolerance approach may request parental involvement but typically only when academic or disciplinary problems regarding their children arise. Educators who function this way provide only the information they want community members to have and do so in ways that limit feedback and discussion. Newsletters are sent only to parents and without an invitation to present or discuss ideas. When parents and caregivers do participate, they are usually not recognized or rewarded for their input.

> When an individual is kept in a situation of inferiority, the fact is that he does become inferior.
>
> —*Simone de Beauvior*

In the past, most community members may have been willing to accept this situation, but not many do today. When there is apathy or adversarial relations between the school and the community, the cost is tremendous: community support is diminished and defensive, and isolated schools proliferate, detracting from support for the welfare of the larger community.

> In the end, education must be education toward the ability to decide.
>
> —*Victor Frankl*

As tasks associated with schooling become more complex and more controversial, parents and other community members are less willing to acquiesce to educators. Instead, they are demanding a more direct role for themselves in the process.

Involvement

Many schools are putting energy into the development of mutually beneficial relations with their communities. They believe that reactive systems are outdated, as is the expectation that meaningful education can occur without engaging the energies and participation of community members.

These schools understand the important role of the family and the community in raising and educating children. This is particularly true today because families and communities are more mobile and more geographically extended, communities are larger, and community boundaries are becoming blurred. In addition, traditional institutions such as the church and the home seem to be less able or willing to play their parts in keeping the community together.

This reality has led to experimentation with different configurations in which there is purposeful nurturing of community involvement on the part of schools. The number of efforts that encourage communities to bring their resources to bear on improved services for children are increasing. In fact, schools are becoming one-stop shopping centers for parents seeking child-related services. Some schools invite welfare and mental health agencies, budget advice services, and health clinics to set up shop. The intent is that working cooperatively in a single setting these agencies, in partnership with schools, can better coordinate services to meet the needs of children and support for parents and caregivers.

There are also increasing efforts to enlist community resource people. These resource people can be senior citizens and young retirees who have the time and interest to work with children, mentors who provide positive role modeling by spending quality time with one or two children, tutors who work with children on a one-to-one basis, and individuals who share special talents and life experiences with young people.

Further efforts that emphasize schools are here to serve communities are becoming more prevalent. For instance, community-wide celebration days, open houses, coffee hours for realtors, bicycle roundups, and celebration of education and community are just a few of the ways this effort to serve is being expressed.

Connectivity

As community involvement proves to be effective and expands, a new level of proactive relations between schools and communities, *connectivity*, is spreading. Connective relations are those in which schools and other youth-related agencies cooperate and coordinate to develop comprehensive community-wide programs for youth and adults. Connectivity means opening schools for mutually beneficial program endeavors. These include summer programs for youth and other community members, adult learner initiatives, and making school facilities available for community uses and community facilities available for school uses. The influence of the community on the school and the school on the community expands through connectivity.

Outreach

Moving to the cutting edge of the continuum, *outreach* efforts that can have a direct and positive impact on the community are being initiated by some schools. These schools promote service learning, encourage staff and students to participate in community improvement efforts, and take initiatives to bring diverse agencies and volunteer organizations together for mutual understanding, problem solving, and comprehensive improvement efforts. Such schools recognize that both they and their communities have much to gain by helping and working together. Joint interest is evident, efforts are cooperative, and successes are mutually celebrated.

> People should think things out fresh and not just accept conventional terms and the conventional way of doing things.
>
> —Buckminster Fuller

Outreach is still an illusive goal for many schools. We are most likely to do those things for which we will be rewarded. Schools do not frequently reward educators for reaching out to the community. As important, community leaders do not often see the relevance of working with educational leaders for mutual assistance. These dynamics can change, but it will take individuals and groups who have the courage to think and act differently and who are willing to develop cooperative plans and strategies to improve everyone's resiliency.

It is a long journey to move from a reactive school to an outreach school. It means changing behaviors as well as beliefs. The journey will have to be taken one step at a time. It will require considerable time and effort to make the shift from one end of the continuum to the other. But it is a worthwhile goal if we expect to meet the challenges faced by schools and communities. The purpose of Exercise 6.2 is to help your group assess where your school and community currently are on the reactive-outreach scale and identify what may be needed to move your school and community closer to the proactive end of the scale.

> You have not done enough, you have never done enough, so long as it is still possible that you have something to contribute.
>
> —Dag Hammarskjöld

Exercise 6.2: Making Proactivity a Part of Your Day

This exercise is intended to help participants be clearer about the ways the school and community related in the past, how they related now, and how they would prefer them to relate in the future.

1. Distribute copies of Table 6.3: School and Community: From Reactive to Proactive Relations (Handout 14 in the Resource section). Ask members to review it and determine which column most closely represents the current situation. Ask the group to come to a consensus about the closest fit for your school and community.

2. Ask the group to explore why the current situation exists. What has the school done that has led to it? What has the community done that has led to it? Ask someone to write agreements on chart paper or on a chalkboard.

3. Where the group views relationships between the school and the community as being reactive, what changes may be needed to move away from this direction? What resources will be needed? List changes and resources needed on chart paper or the chalkboard.

4. Where the group categorizes school and community relationship as being on the proactive side of the scale, what do you think it will take to remain at this level or, better yet, become even more proactive? List strategies and resources.

STRATEGIES FOR IMPROVING COMMUNITY RESILIENCY

Planning, timing, and readiness are important considerations when initiating community resiliency efforts. For example, if a critical mass of supporters is not in place, progress will probably be slower. We know that the fewer the number of people that are committed to positive change, the more the likelihood that negative dynamics such as low academic achievement, gangs, drugs, and violence will be widespread. Without sufficient support, efforts that are pursued are likely to be isolated rather than comprehensive, with little likelihood of positive networking and connectivity across the larger community. Similarly, without sufficient coordination, when schools receive funds for cross-agency projects, there is still no guarantee that they will proceed systematically or that they will involve representatives from the community. When one school we worked with listed all the agencies working with a particular family, they identified twenty-six, each doing its own thing without reference to the efforts of the others. Once the school figured this out, they promoted collaboration and sharing of resources.

If there is commitment to building resiliency for schools and their communities, there are ways to do so. The road may have more bumps along the way for some communities than for others, but they all have the potential to be more resilient. For starters, assessing current capabilities can help prepare community members to proceed with improvement efforts.

To help readers who are ready to implement resiliency-building strategies in their communities, we return to the elements on the Resiliency Wheel (see Figure 1.3). The discussion of the barriers and strategies for each of the six elements is intended to stimulate thinking about the situation in your community and how best to improve it. Readers are encouraged to modify suggested strategies and add others that might be helpful in making their communities more resilient.

Positive Connections

Connections become meaningful when people get to know each other. People are motivated to work together when they have positive relationships. The challenge is to foster positive connections where few seem to exist due to things like large populations and geographic dispersal, cultural differences, and the daily exodus to work from bedroom communities to urban centers. However, many school and community leaders have discovered creative ways of responding to such realities and, as a result, have found ways to unite people behind improvement efforts.

Leadership Strategies for Increasing Positive Connections

Caring adults exist in every community. The key is to find ways to expand the core group of highly active adults engaging others who have not yet become involved. Communities that can tap into these latent resources are more likely to become healthier and stronger.

Positive things can happen when people connect with each other. Connectivity can result in unleashing untapped resources for community improvement efforts. Here are some leadership strategies to consider:

- Connect young people with individuals in the community who are positive role models. They can be found in organizations such as Big Sisters, Big Brothers, PTOs, and PTAs. Or they may just be individuals in the community who are able and willing to be mentors. Thinking of such connections as expanding the circle of friends may help stimulate similar connectivity initiatives.

> The family you come from isn't as important as the family you're going to have.
>
> —*Ring Lardner*

- Identify groups of people who can be called on to help. For example, retired persons are excellent resources. They can be invited to help in the school, work in the library, be mentors for students, give demonstrations regarding subjects they are knowledgeable about, and they often have more time to take leadership roles in change efforts.
- Create opportunities for communities and schools to connect positively by outreach activities such as extending community access to school facilities and putting on school-community fairs.
- Promote multiage and intergenerational connectivity through rewarding activities. For example, continuing education opportunities can bring people from across the community to learn together. Similarly, basketball courts in urban centers that are available for extended hours can bring people of all ages together to meet and talk while shooting hoops.
- Bring community members together in settings that promote positive discussion about important issues and initiatives. Town-hall-type meetings can involve leaders from the local government, schools, higher education institutions, businesses, voluntary organizations, as well as other interested citizens.
- Provide a directory of organizations that support the community's mission and goals. This low-cost activity can identify resources that are available in the community and let people know how to access them.

Record other strategies that can increase positive connections for your community:

- _____

_____

- _____
  _____
  _____
- _____
  _____

Clear, Consistent, and Appropriate Boundaries

The larger the community, the more likely it is to exhibit diversities of cultures, values, and traditions. These differences can be a rich resource but only if they are brought together effectively. The more diverse the community, the more boundaries are needed to clarify behavioral expectations. Many communities either do not have adequate boundary-related structures in place to address community issues or else they are not used effectively. Often expectations for behaviors may be unwritten, unclear, or even contradictory.

Leadership Strategies for Promoting Clear, Consistent, and Appropriate Boundaries

Communities can define boundaries that help citizens interact safely and effectively with each other. For this to happen, all voices need to be represented when laws, policies, rules, norms, and other expectations are discussed and agreed on because involvement creates ownership and understanding. Strategies to promote effective and agreed-upon boundaries include the following:

- Promote rules that emphasize taking care of each other and that promote opportunities for growth and development, not rules that focus on disciplining people. Families need to set rules and consequences to promote positive relationships; neighbors need to take responsibility for monitoring youth behaviors; schools need to establish clear rules and consequences, positive and negative, for students and the adults who work with them; and communities need to set rules that promote acceptable behaviors for such things as people congregating together and for people driving a vehicle.
- Encourage community involvement in clarifying and resolving school-based issues. For example, one school in a high crime area had a persistent problem with teachers' cars being broken into or stolen. When the school enlisted the help of neighborhood families whose homes bordered the school, the thefts stopped. Neighbors called the police when they saw anything going on and got the word out in the community for it to stop. In a very short time, it did.
- Conduct town hall meetings that can be used to set norms and expectations for the community. Be sure to identify best times for the majority of the community to meet. Do not assume that an evening meeting time is best for everyone.

Record other strategies that can promote clear, consistent, and appropriate boundaries for all members of your community:

- _____
  _____
- _____
  _____

Life-Guiding Skills

Navigating life in our complex society can be treacherous without the ability to communicate, make decisions, and manage conflict effectively. These skills, along with having a sense of purpose, are particularly needed in large and diverse communities. It is not realistic to expect effective participation if community members do not possess necessary skills. It is also problematic when some members such as government and school leaders have them but others do not. Such disparities in skill levels often lead to conflict and distrust.

Leadership Strategies for Fostering Life-Guiding Skills

The well-being of a community is highly dependent on the ability of its members to interact with each other effectively, particularly in efforts to improve the community's resiliency-building capacity. In turn, the ability to interact effectively is based on skill development for all participants. Strategies to bring this about include the following:

- Train community leaders, both youth and adults, in key skill areas. For example, Leadership Academies for youth are available in many areas. These academies give the support and guidance for youth to be positive role models for their peers. Similarly, the National PTA offers a comprehensive program for parents who want to learn to be better leaders. Such programs are most helpful if they are based on a "training of trainers" model, wherein participants learn skills and then help others learn them.
- Identify resource people within the community who have skills and experiences that can be of help to others. For example, community volunteers can help youngsters develop life skills through career day programs. Community organizations can encourage interested members to lend their skills to help others in the community. Cross-organizational planning and coordination of needed services can enhance efficiency and effectiveness. Most important, equitable access to services should be promoted so that those who need them the most receive them.
- Teach assessment techniques so the community can identify both strengths and areas of improvement needed in life-skill areas and can make good decisions about the use of its resources.
- Develop communication skills that keep the dialogue going, particularly when risks are taken that may lead to conflicts that need to be managed.
- Provide life-skill learning opportunities through continuing education classes.

Record other strategies that can foster life-guiding skills for all community members:

- _____
- _____
- _____

Nurture and Support

Communities that provide nurture and support for everyone—young people, the elderly, and those in between—develop strong connections that can help individuals, families, schools, and neighborhoods through hard times. When nurture and support are practiced in the home, the neighborhood, the school, and the community, people feel that they matter, less isolated and less fearful of each other.

Leadership Strategies for Enhancing Nurture and Support

Leaders who want to get people involved in resiliency initiatives need to promote a sense of belonging. Learning to care about others is what makes the difference in building connectivity and community. This is true whether referring to students and staff in schools or adults and children in families, neighborhoods, and communities.

Some strategies to promote nurture and support include the following:

- Identify caring members in the community who can be on call to provide support for others, whether they are youngsters or adults, who may need help. This group can be expanded over time as others come forward and make the commitment to volunteer.
- Place high value on caring. This can be promoted formally through the use of such things as billboards, radio, and television announcements or informally by good role modeling of leaders.
- Provide recognition for positive behaviors. Catching people doing things right ought to be the bias, rather than catching them doing things wrong. For example, efforts of students and community members who take care of themselves and take the time to care for others can be publicized and celebrated.
- Work with the media to get stories that demonstrate caring and support out to the public. For this to happen, relationships with the media must be nurtured and developed over time, not just when a favorable story needs to be broadcast: invite the media to cover important school and community stories, respond quickly when they call for information, and be empathetic to their constraints. They have deadlines that you can help them meet.

Record other strategies that can enhance nurture and support for community members:

- _____
  _____
- _____
  _____
- _____
  _____

Purposes and Expectations

The words we use and the attitudes we have can make a huge difference in the results we get. Saying "we can" and "we will" instead of "we can't" and "we won't" or saying "when we . . ." instead of "if we . . ." creates hope and motivation instead of fatalism and minimal efforts. Putting the emphasis on "we" rather than "you" sends a powerful message.

The language that is communicated has an extraordinary impact. Some schools and communities tend to use positive, encompassing, and inviting language, while others tend to use negative and divisive language.

> Nothing splendid has ever been achieved except by those who dared believe that something inside them was superior to circumstances.
> —Bruce Barton

Regardless of sociodemographics or other unique factors, people need to believe in themselves, be supported by others, and join together to form viable communities. Reaching out to build belief in capabilities within and across neighborhoods sets a tone for growth and development of communities. Schools and neighborhoods need to reach out and see each other for mutual supports rather than conclude that they have to cope with issues on their own.

Leadership Strategies for Strengthening Purposes and Expectations

Changing attitudes is the starting place. Before action takes place people need to share the belief that the community can become what they want it to be. Improvement needs to be viewed as a necessity, not an option. Most of all, creating high expectations for a community means promoting

> Improvement is a necessity, not an option.
> —Bill Blokker

dialogue. Community members cannot remain silent or accept the ways things are and still expect great things to happen. Changing the "can'ts" to "cans," the "wants" to "wills," and the "ifs" to "whens" requires the following kinds of strategies:

- Promote service. Youth, adults, and senior citizens can all give in ways that improve the community. Students can engage in service learning and adults can be encouraged to volunteer their time, skills, and talents. Service-oriented communities are those in which all age groups help others achieve in meaningful ways.

- Create rituals and celebrations that honor efforts and achievements of individuals, groups, schools, voluntary organizations, neighborhoods, and the local government. Community celebrations are important. They send the message that there is pride in members' achievements. It also reminds members about what they hold in common and that the community's resiliency vision is being pursued.

- Work with the media to publicize progress and positive outcomes by individuals, groups, neighborhoods, schools, and the entire community. There are few things more exciting than witnessing the transformation of a community. Making it happen is a major task, of course, but telling the story is also vital. Sharing positive results builds ownership and increases participation. Besides, it reflects the resiliency message, turning the focus from finding the negative to finding the positive. This culture-modifying activity is a difficult task, but it can happen if everyone involved focuses on getting the message across and supports each other's efforts.

- Changing communities means moving into unknown territory and taking risks. Therefore, it is necessary to develop and promote projects that are meaningful and challenge community members. Aiming for short-term results as well as long-term outcomes is important as these provide convincing evidence that things are moving forward.

- Encourage everyone—adults as well as the young—to try their best and to succeed. All of us—educators, parents, and community members—can become more resilient if we participate, gain confidence, and commit to supporting efforts. "You can do it and I'm going to help you in any way I can" is a powerful resiliency-building message.
- Clearly identify 3 reasons that your community needs to work together. Slogans, mottos, visuals, and other devices should be developed to keep the purposes of resiliency initiatives in front of everyone.

Record other strategies that can strengthen purposes and expectations for community members:

- _____
  _____
- _____
  _____
- _____
  _____

Provide Opportunities for Meaningful Participation

Community problem solving, decision making, and goal setting are most effective when all facets of the community are represented, not just formal leaders or those connected to them in some influential way. When core issues are addressed, decisions should be made after engaging a wide representation of the community. Too often showcase meetings are held and we are left with the feeling that our time is being wasted. If our experiences are positive, we are more likely to participate and may even make the commitment to take on leadership roles. If our experiences are negative we are likely to withdraw. We may even become opponents of the initiatives that are being taken.

Two essential elements are necessary to promote meaningful community participation: *quality time to engage in the conversation* and *trust between members*. Educators often become so focused on content delivery and engagement in school improvement efforts that they do not give sufficient time to the need to stay connected with the community. If staying connected is not valued and practiced the activity becomes mere ritual.

It is also important to remember that many community members work and do not have the opportunity to meet with educators during the daytime when schools are in session. This is a bigger problem today than ever before, in part because of increasing numbers of households with single working parents and in part because even where there are two parents, in many instances both are likely to be working and unavailable during the day to meet with educators.

Time for dialogue is a precious resource for meaningful participation. If communities have set sufficient, appropriate times to meet and they are clear about purposes, then meetings can be productive.

Leadership Strategies for Improving Meaningful Participation

Reaching out to involve community members can seem like an overwhelming task because there are so many people to engage and so many voices to be heard. However, the payoff of working together can make a notable difference. Some useful strategies include the following:

> We are not going to be able to operate our spaceship earth successfully nor for much longer unless we see it as a whole spaceship and our fate as common. It has to be everybody or nobody.
>
> —*Buckminster Fuller*

- Hold a series of town-hall-type meetings, bringing representatives of all segments of the community together to create a vision, priorities, goals, and expectations for positive contributions by community members. The process is just as important as the product; it promotes networking and support. Summarize and disseminate the results to spread the word. This can make the mean-ing more tangible and provide the basis for further discussions and planning for ongoing improvement.

- Invite the media's involvement. The media can get the message out to people and provide a forum for the exchange of views. Community members can also write editorials. But for all of this to happen, the media needs to become an active partner.

- Develop responses to people's difficulties about becoming involved. For example, people with children who would like to participate can be provided with child care not only to increase their involvement but also to model a service-learning community approach. Community members who do not have access to transportation can be brought into the dialogue through carpooling arrangements. Simply holding meetings at alternative times and at more convenient locations can also make a big difference for busy citizens.

- Develop ways of connecting that emphasize the personal touch. Some ways to connect are to include different community voices and perspectives during planning, to be knowledgeable about cultural differences, and to honor them by providing translators when some community members are non-English speakers. Learn basic greetings in the other languages. Tap into local organizations that have experiences with diversity to provide needed assistance. In addition, tapping in to technological tools such as Web sites and instant text messaging can expand the potential for information and dialogue to be shared by those who are not able to participate face-to-face.

> The good neighbor looks beyond the external accidents and discerns those inner qualities that make all men human, and, therefore, brothers.
>
> —*Martin Luther King, Jr.*

- Move beyond conversation to make plans and take specific actions. Community members are more likely to continue to participate if they believe there will be positive actions that will follow. Attending to the priorities that are set so that outcomes are generated is just as important as getting the process started. For example, if a weekly coffee klatch is instituted to talk about community issues and a list of ideas is generated, it is important to share progress reports at future gatherings. Reports that include descriptions of plans and activities that have been initiated can fuel momentum and build interest and enthusiasm.

- Develop a common language system that defines terms related to healthy, resilient communities. Shared meaning is a critical foundation. We need to understand each other before we can come together to support shared purposes. This can be promoted by creating teams of school and community-based volunteers to carry the message to the rest of the community. In fact, such a team approach models the process for building community resiliency while it provides opportunities for people to become conversant with the basic elements of resilient communities.

Record other suggestions to improve opportunities for meaningful participation:

- _____
  _____

- _____
  _____

- _____
  _____

Community resiliency building requires broad-based commitment and support. This is more likely to happen when successes are celebrated, strengths are noted, and shortcomings are dealt with. Getting started means making a realistic appraisal of where things are currently.

> Nothing in life is to be feared. It is only to be understood.
> —Marie Curie

Exercise 6.3 focuses on the priorities needed to increase your community's resiliency. It can move participants a step closer to agreement about resiliency-building strategies to apply in the community.

Exercise 6.3: Moving a Step Closer to a Resilient Community

It will be helpful if a cross section of community members is involved in the exercise. Groups of six to eight people work best. Ensure that everyone has a copy of Table 6.4, which is a form that can be used to promote the discussion (Handout 15 in the Resource section).

1. Ask group members to identify resiliency-building activities that are presently going on in the community. Have them list things they agree about in the "Now" row of their copy of the handout.

2. What are the community's greatest strengths? How did these things evolve? Does the discussion provide any insights for future resiliency-building initiatives?

3. Review the strategies presented in the chapter. Are any of these relevant for your community? Ask members to write things they agree about pursuing in the "Tomorrow" row.

4. Ask the group to review and prioritize the strategies on which it would like to focus your community's energies and resources. How can these priorities be put in place?

5. What priorities will the group take on to move resiliency into the forefront? Who will take the lead in making it happen?

Table 6.4 Building Resiliency in Our Community: Now and Tomorrow

	Increase Positive Connections	Set Clear, Consistent, and Appropriate Boundaries	Teach Life-Guiding Skills	Provide Nurture and Support	Set and Communicate Purposes and Expectations	Provide Meaningful Opportunities to Participate
Community as it currently exists						
Community of the future						

If community members work together to become stronger, healthier, and more resilient their voices can be like chimes in the wind, blending together to make a beautiful melody.

Strategies to promote community participation in resiliency initiatives require leadership and oversight. Leadership is needed for diverse groups to work together and to ensure that something positive will result from the effort. Exercise 6.4 provides considerations that leaders might use to increase the level of success with their efforts.

Exercise 6.4: Considerations for Leaders

Think about how well you believe you do as a leader in the areas listed below. Rate your efforts from one (low) to five (high) in each area. How would parents, staff, and other community members rate the school and community in the following areas?

1. How strong are the links between the community and the school?

2. How strong is the infrastructure to support dialogue, risk taking, and places to meet and work as a unit?

3. What are your resources and how do you find them?

4. What is the attitude, real or perceived, toward being proactive? What contribution and support does the school have in developing and maintaining the proactivity? What part does the community have?

5. What are you doing that works well and that you want to keep? What needs to be refreshed?

Chapter 6 built on the foundations created in previous chapters to suggest ways of harmonizing the voices of students, educators, and other members of the community. Chapter 7 focuses on facilitation of the effort and assessment of progress, two processes that are necessary if this is going to happen. Facilitation brings people together to work on improving school and community resiliency while assessment clarifies the current status and potential for community resiliency building, monitors activities, and establishes results.

PART III

Making It Happen for Schools and Communities

7

Leading Resiliency Development Initiatives

Strategies for Managing and Assessing Change

"Even if you're on the right track, you'll get run over if you just sit there."

—Will Rogers

BRINGING IT ALL TOGETHER AND LEADING RESILIENCY DEVELOPMENT INITIATIVES

Part I focused on the concepts of resiliency and community. Part II delved into specific challenges and strategies related to building resiliency for students, educators, organizations, and communities. In both parts, exercises were suggested to help readers gain a clearer understanding of how schools and communities grow healthier. The next step is to bring it all together for the benefit and well-being of students, staff, parents, and community members. To help leaders who are ready to facilitate this challenge, Chapter 7 concentrates on two vitally important tasks: implementing resiliency-building strategies and monitoring and evaluating the effectiveness of the change effort. Five important areas are highlighted: (a) stages of change, (b) group development, (c) leadership needs, (d) facilitation skills, and (e) assessment and evaluation of progress. Strategies are suggested to help leaders improve the chances of successful implementation of resiliency initiatives.

Leadership should not be narrowly defined as being the role and responsibility of the principal. The principal should certainly play a central part in school improvement effort, but for effective change to be introduced, accepted, and institutionalized, leadership must also come from teachers, students, parents, and other community members. The broader the base of leadership is, the more likely the probability of effective change and improvement.

Think about leadership as a function, not a person. It is about performing tasks that achieve desired ends. These tasks can be accomplished best when those who are most motivated and capable perform them. Broadening the base of leadership expands ownership for outcomes and models the intent, which is to encourage resilient behaviors on the part of everyone. Identifying and recruiting individuals who are willing to provide the time and energy to take on leadership roles is an important first step, but it is also necessary to provide them with the conceptual tools and facilitation skills they require to lead resiliency development efforts.

THE FOUR STAGES OF CHANGE

> Trust yourself in the deep, uncharted waters. When there is a storm it is safer in the open sea. If you stay too near the dock you will get beaten to death.
>
> —Sam Keen

Understanding the stages of change is critical to efforts that build resilient communities. It is easy to get stuck if people who are leading the efforts do not recognize and proceed with courage through the four stages of change: initiation, implementation, institutionalization, and refocusing (Fullan, 1985, 1991, 1993; Hord, Rutherford, Huling-Austin, & Hall, 1987; Houston, Blankstein, & Cole, 2007; Reiss, 2007; Senge et al., 2000).

Initiation

The *initiation* stage focuses on personal concerns and building readiness to become engaged in the change effort. Increasing awareness, providing information, making resources available, demonstrating relevance, developing motivation and agreeing on next steps are key considerations at this stage. People need to know why it is important to build resiliency and how it will affect them. At this stage, many of their questions will center on costs and benefits.

At the outset only a small group of people may be ready to move forward. These early joiners see the importance of positive change and are willing to put energy into accomplishing it. Most significant change efforts begin with the active participation of a small but critical mass of people who get things started and tip the scales toward positive change.

> A man convinced against his will is not convinced.
>
> —Laurence J. Peter

Others may need to be encouraged to join the effort, or at least not actively block it. Leaders need to build ownership and trust with as many students, teachers, support personnel, parents, and other community members as they can if change efforts are to get off the ground and be institutionalized. Information needs to be provided, multiple times and multiple ways, using different media formats, to address personal concerns. Miles's (1987) review of major research studies found "that a combination of strong advocacy, need, active initiation, and a clear model for proceeding characterized . . . successful startups" (p. 62).

Strategies to Consider During the Initiation Stage

- Check for signs of readiness. What do people know? What is the level of understanding? Most important, are there more supporters than there are detractors?
- Develop a critical mass of people who are supportive and willing to take active roles in implementing resiliency initiatives. This can be facilitated by meeting with key people in the school and the community; conducting town-hall-type meetings for the purposes of helping people learn about resiliency and the positive impact it can have on the community; and initiating planning activities. Be sure to include representatives from different segments of the community in these deliberations. It will be important to have representation from as many facets of the community as possible.
- Recruit people who, in turn, can bring others onboard.
- Build in early successes. Early successes promote participation.
- Provide information to key stakeholders. The message cannot go out too many times for it to be heard.
- Help participants understand that implementing positive change is likely to be a long-term process.

Implementation

Implementation, the next stage of change, "consists of the process of putting into practice an idea, program, or set of activities and structures new to the people attempting or expected to change" (Fullan, 1991, p. 65).

During this stage, leaders need to get people to focus on getting tasks completed. Implementing a resiliency effort will be a new experience for most people. False starts, mistakes, and confusion are likely to occur. Intensity will probably be heightened and conflicts will likely arise, as will impatience about the time it takes to make and implement plans. Some members may become uncomfortable because of these uncertainties. It may feel like building a rocket while it is in flight. This uneasiness must be effectively managed. Leaders need to help group members understand the process of change and the dynamics that can occur so they can cope with them effectively.

> Change means movement, movement means friction, friction means heat, and heat means controversy. The only place where there is no friction is in outer space or a seminar on political action.
>
> —*Saul Alinsky*

Strategies for Leaders to Consider During the Implementation Stage

- Help participants understand that "mistakes" are an important part of the learning process, rather than "failures."
- Focus on visioning questions that help build understanding and perspective. For example, stimulate discussion about what will be different if the school and community become more resilient?
- Identify key players in the change process (e.g., from the school, local government, higher education institutions, voluntary organizations, and informal community members) and connect them with each other so they work cooperatively rather than in isolation.

- "Early rewards and some tangible success are critical incentives during implementation" (Fullan, 1991, p. 69). Reinforcement of new behaviors is a powerful force, so it is important to identify and celebrate early successes and provide positive feedback to encourage continued involvement in the effort.

Institutionalization

The start-up and implementation of plans to build a more resilient school and community can be energizing and exciting, but it is only the beginning. The next

> I was taught that the way of progress is neither swift nor easy.
>
> —*Marie Curie*

stage is *institutionalization*, which focuses on moving initiatives from innovations to being embedded within the school and community structures. This is an important and difficult stage and few initiatives survive to become part of the school and community fabric. Many initiatives falter and are discontinued at this stage. Therefore, leaders need to put continued focus and time on guiding initiatives through the institutionalization process.

Strategies for Leaders to Consider During the Institutionalization Phase

- Foster collaboration so that resiliency becomes central to members' daily lives. Supporting and connecting people who are ready to collaborate sustains and expands the level of engagement.
- Secure resources. For example, secure funding as feasible in the annual budget; write grant requests; and promote corporate and community sponsorship. Although resources are needed at all stages of change, they are particularly important to secure during institutionalization. This is when things are regularized and that requires ongoing support.
- Keep interest high so the energy and initiatives do not falter. This requires involving stakeholders from the community through such devices as celebrations, assessments, evaluations, and fundraising.
- Build and share resiliency institutionalization plans, structures, budgets, policies, and procedures that promote continuation of the resiliency initiatives.
- Help people see the links between continuing resiliency-building efforts and community improvements.

Refocusing

Refocusing, the fourth stage, emphasizes two areas: making necessary process improvements and sharing the good feelings that come with positive outcomes. Like the old saying, "The storm comes before the rainbow appears." By this stage, the

> Start with what they know. Build with what they have.
>
> —*Lao Tsu*

community will have weathered many storms and have grown through challenges and opportunities. People will have grappled with the meaning of change and they will have learned new skills. It is now time to reflect on the journey, focus on steps needed to improve performance, and celebrate outcomes.

In the initiation stage, the journey began because enough people believed that the community could be healthier and stronger. Now, at the refocusing stage, newly learned behaviors need to be reinforced to sustain and spread these beliefs. A foundation for ownership needs to be fostered by including different stakeholders, providing relevant information, and encouraging ever-broader participation of community members.

Refocusing is about confirming outcomes and considering ways of improving on them. At this stage of change, people should have a sense of pride, feel good about what they are doing, and be ready to focus on refining processes and outcomes and, if appropriate, developing further resiliency initiatives.

A few cautions are in order. First, change is not a linear process. More than likely, some late comers will just be at the initiation stage or the implementation stage while others are at the refocusing stage. Care should be given to plan for participation by people who enter the process at different times. Second, significant systemic change does not occur rapidly. Members need to understand that many goals will not be realized during the first months or even the first year. In reality, it may take three to five years or more for the overall resiliency process to become institutionalized. Third, many initial assumptions may not hold true.

Leadership Strategies to Consider During the Refocusing Stage:

- Although a plan is needed to make change happen, the process will turn out to be somewhat different from how it was planned.
- There will be disagreements and conflict.
- People will change their positions and beliefs, sometimes in ways that are not predictable.
- Despite great efforts, not everyone will be able or willing to accept the changes.
- There will be multiple reasons why change may not be embraced, including lack of understanding, resources, time, and skills.

GROUP DEVELOPMENT

Understanding the stages of change is critical to efforts to build resilient communities but it is also important to be aware that groups that must work together effectively conduct community resiliency development. Groups that work cooperatively for common causes are relatively unique. They need to be nurtured, supported, and learn relationship skills or they will be in constant turmoil.

> Few, if any, forces in human affairs are as powerful as a shared vision.
> —Peter Senge

It is great fun to be a part of an energetic and productive group. If people within a group have similar values and beliefs and have compatible work ethics and skills, the group will probably function at a productive level. If they do not, it can result in chaos and jeopardize resiliency initiatives.

Groups develop by predictable stages. Whereas the stages of change focus on the overall plan, group development is about building capacity through relationships. According to Tuckman (1965), there are five phases of group growth: *forming, storming, norming, performing,* and *disbanding.* Positive group development requires careful facilitation and leadership during each of these phases.

The first phase, *forming,* is when people get to know each other as they join together to achieve common purposes. At this phase, they have not yet become a team. They are not focused on tasks. They wait and watch until they develop an understanding of what is expected and what their roles will be. Leadership challenges have to do with encouraging involvement and cohesion.

The second phase, *storming*, is characterized by conflict—vying for power, leadership rights and behaviors, and control issues within the group—as members begin to address hard issues. If members learn conflict management skills, this phase may be easier to process. But if leaders try to control conflicts, the group will not have the chance to develop and sort out their issues.

> Working with people is difficult, but not impossible.
>
> —*Peter Drucker*

The third phase, *norming*, focuses on establishing norms, procedures, and policies. Group members are motivated to explore roles and learn how to work through conflicts. Structures are established so that people can work together without constant storming. Acceptable norms of behavior are agreed on, including establishing expectations for how meetings will be conducted—starting on time, preparing and being ready to participate effectively, and following established procedures. A group identity is formed as expectations for group behavior and sanctions for group members who fail to meet these expectations are developed.

The fourth phase, *performing*, emerges as conflicts are resolved and structures are established. At this stage, group members are able to work together well—everyone is actively involved, accomplishing tasks and objectives and supporting norms and structures. At this stage, the group should be focused on performance and outcomes.

Many groups never reach the performing phase. In fact, some never get past the forming phase. Groups may require outside assistance to help them work through issues and move on to the next phase of development, and groups may need to develop group skills before members can work together effectively. Furthermore, as new members join the group, time needs to be allotted to help them move through the four phases. Effective groups take time to help new members through the phases. It is better to make this a regular up front activity than have to deal with it later if problems arise.

Last, groups that are formed around special purposes need to *disband* when tasks are completed. Members need to be released so that they can focus on other ongoing activities and emerging tasks. Human resources are at a premium, especially for voluntary initiatives such as community resiliency building. As initial resiliency priorities are institutionalized, it may be time to move on to other priorities. This will probably require the redeployment of group members.

Groups can become productive, grow, develop interdependence, and collaborate effectively. But it takes time to create such groups. In this regard, it might be useful for group members to reflect on the well-worn but still relevant story, *The Sense of a Goose* (Handout 16 in the Resource section). When working with groups, we have to help each other make the journey by sharing leadership, being empathetic when others have problems, and supporting each other through the process.

LEADERSHIP NEEDS

Leadership, especially within voluntary, self-managed teams, is extremely important. Leadership is needed to ensure that members share authority and responsibility and that work is coordinated. Self-managed teams need leadership to establish "clearly defined objectives, appropriate task design, appropriate size and membership, substantial authority and discretion, an adequate information system, appropriate recognition and rewards, strong support, adequate interpersonal skills, and appropriate socialization of

> Like effective parents, lovers, teachers, and therapists, good leaders make people helpful.
>
> —*Warren Bennis*

members" (Yukl, 1998, p. 363). In addition, diversity must be appreciated and nurtured by group leaders.

Leadership can have a major effect on building resiliency. How leadership evolves and functions will play a significant role in who participates, how effectively they participate, how teams are managed, how people are motivated, and whether they will be empowered during the process. Here are some key leadership functions that need to be considered.

Key stakeholders, including those who are critical of the effort, should be recruited and involved. Selecting only people who will be supportive or at least will not be resistors can create a false sense of effectiveness. Just as we need challenges to become more resilient, so do we need people to push our thinking to implement solid, well thought-out plans and actions. Knowing who the critics are and why they can be expected to resist is as important as knowing who the supporters of the change are. No one person or elite group of people can create a vision and plan for diverse communities. All key stakeholders need to be involved.

People will be motivated to participate if goals and activities are relevant to them. The leader has to communicate a vision that is clear and meaningful, that is, resiliency building is needed not just for some but for everyone. Creating a sense of urgency about the need for change promotes the development of a learning community that can support and nurture the process and the outcomes. In short, it is necessary to "build a broad coalition to support the change" (Yukl, 1998, p. 449).

> The salvation of mankind lies only in making everything the concern for all.
> —Alexander I. Solzhenitsyn

"People learn new patterns of behavior primarily through their interactions with others, not through front-end training designs" (Fullan, 1993, p. 68). This means that ongoing involvement, positive relationships, and continuing skill development need to be fostered.

People must be prepared for the realities of change. They must know that change is like a roller coaster ride; there will be highs, lows, progress, and setbacks. It is important for leaders to help people understand the process by letting them know about the problems that are likely to crop up. This can ease the trauma of change.

> Change without stability is chaos and stability without change is death.
> —Alfred North Whitehead

The stress of change can be managed better when group development is encouraged.

Change must be supported continuously through all stages. Support is motivating, especially during difficult times.

Keep everyone informed. This leadership task may be difficult when community building involves large numbers of people, but it is imperative.

Treat surprises, shortcomings, and mistakes as opportunities to learn instead of as "failures" and disasters. This will make it more acceptable for group members to take risks and grow.

Empower group members by giving them authority and responsibility to make decisions. The old saying, "If you want it done right, do it yourself," represents an attitude that disempowers people. Empowerment in building resilient communities models preferred states and helps people move toward shared values and purposes.

> Three-fourths of the miseries and misunderstandings in the world will disappear if we step into the shoes of our adversaries and understand their standpoint.
> —Gandhi

Leaders must support their words with appropriate actions. People believe in leaders who do what they say they will do.

Many leaders hesitate to share authority and control, particularly if they doubt that others share their values and goals. This may be understandable, but it gets in the way of reciprocal influence and empowerment, which are critical elements in resiliency building. Facilitation skills are essential when developing shared values and goals.

Stronger communities are developed through opportunities for leadership development around meaningful goals and action plans. People must know that their leaders value their participation and care about, support, and trust them. In other words, leaders need to facilitate inclusion.

FACILITATION SKILLS

Leaders need to model and practice good facilitation skills if they expect other participants to do the same. The intention of this section is to summarize key facilitation areas that can enable or inhibit community resiliency-development efforts.

Volumes have been written about facilitation skills (e.g., Harshman & Phillips, 1996; Houston et al., 2007; D. W. Johnson & F. P. Johnson, 1991; Napier & Gershenfeld, 1993; Schmuck & Runkel, 1994; Senge et al., 2000). The following discussion is by no means comprehensive. Rather, it is intended only to suggest ways of avoiding many of the problems that might otherwise arise during resiliency development efforts by focusing on helping leaders facilitate the process. Facilitation skills that we believe are particularly important regarding resiliency initiatives are vision building and goal setting, communication, problem solving, decision making, managing meetings, and conflict management.

Vision Building and Goal Setting

Vision building about what a resilient community will look like clarifies beliefs and how these beliefs can be turned into a better future for the community. Building a vision should not be done by a select few or developed by formal leaders. Understanding and ownership requires widespread dialogue about beliefs before vision statements are agreed upon and put in writing. It takes time, reflection, and involvement to formulate a clear and agreed-upon vision. Fullan (1993) reminded us, "[U]nder conditions of dynamic complexity one needs a good deal of reflective experience before one can form a plausible vision. Vision emerges from, more than it precedes, action" (p. 28). Given adequate time for this activity, vision building for a resilient community can be a powerful and driving force.

An effective way to begin might be to have participants share their views about the community and their concerns and hopes for the future. This exploration can reveal how participants feel about the community and their vision of what it can become. With each participant's personal vision shared, preferences can be established because personal visions are reflections of valued beliefs.

As important, similarities of beliefs can be clarified through such discussions and, to the extent that they are similar, shared visions can emerge from such interactions between members of the community. Senge (1990) described shared visions as being vital for development of learning communities. Vision statements focus energy for learning. "Generative learning occurs only when people are striving to accomplish something that matters deeply to them. In fact the whole idea of generative learning—will seem abstract and meaningless *until* people become excited about some vision they truly want to accomplish" (p. 206). The emphasis is on *shared* visions: "People with a strong sense of personal direction can join together to create a powerful synergy toward what I/we truly want" (p. 211).

The process is as important as the product when it comes to understanding beliefs and building ownership of a vision. Forming, shaping, and reshaping a vision can build ownership, but the community must experience the process of creating a vision before this can happen. While different paths for arriving at goals and action plans can be taken during the process, the sequence usually includes sharing belief statements, developing a vision statement and a mission statement, and creating goals that the group agrees on. Each step of the process continuously narrows the focus and more clearly defines the direction in which the community wants to go.

> Creating a vision forces us to take a stand for a preferred future.
>
> —*P. Block*

A mission statement, which has to do with intent or purposes, is based on the vision. When decisions are made about use of resources and energies, they should support the mission statement. Goals are derived from vision and mission statements and provide more specific directions for action. Keep them focused and limited. Generally, four to six goals may be all that are manageable. Including key stakeholders is necessary throughout the process. Most important, people who are expected to operationalize goals should be included in their development.

Leadership Strategies to Promote Vision Building and Goal Settings

- Involve community representatives. Building a shared vision is not a top-down activity.
- Listen to views of others and be prepared to modify and adapt vision as needed.
- Recognize that there may be different points of view between participants as a vision statement is being developed. Embrace and incorporate the diversity of views and develop ways to channel these tensions so they strengthen the vision.

Communication

"Inquiring minds want to know" is a message that needs to be heeded, particularly when it comes to initiating something as different and important as building community resiliency. Inadequate information sharing or waiting too long to share information are pitfalls to be avoided, especially given the complexity of getting relevant information into the hands of participants in most communities. Messages that are clearly articulated, involve key stakeholders, build understanding, and develop ownership require effective communication practices. However, more often than not, communications are handled in expedient and efficient ways but not necessarily effective ones. Focusing on efficiency in communication often leads to information giving rather than active listening and sharing.

Covey (1989) identified communication as one of seven effective habits. The essence of this particular habit is to seek to understand and to be understood. This requires effective practice of good communication skills. For example, paraphrasing is important to ensure understanding, descriptions of behaviors help pinpoint what is being observed, and sharing feelings helps members understand how others perceive things and what motivates them (Schmuck & Runkel, 1994).

Leaders need to communicate clearly, regularly, and frequently because information can easily be misinterpreted, especially when people are likely to be going through the stages of change at different times and at different paces. This takes constant focus to be effective, but it can make all the difference in identifying and overcoming problems and improving the quality of relationships within the community.

> Seek not to understand that you may believe, but believe that you may understand.
>
> —*Saint Augustine*

There are three forms of formal communication: *one-way, one-way with feedback,* and *two-way* (Schmuck & Runkel, 1994). When they are used appropriately and effectively, communication can be strengthened. *One-way communication* (e.g., newsletters, newspapers, memos, and TV and radio notices) can be an efficient way of disseminating information that does not require feedback. This form of communication is useful when information is routine and content is understood and agreed on. In such situations, using valuable resources, people, and time to conduct a dialogue is not required to keep everyone informed. However, one-way communication is inappropriate when information is about nonroutine matters that require discussion, clarification, and buy-in.

One-way communication with feedback (e.g., surveys, tear-off sheets, and encouragement of paraphrasing to promote understanding) is best used when there is widespread agreement about purposes and actions, but it is important to ensure that members understand what needs to be done and how it is to be done. It is inappropriate to use one-way communication with feedback when modification and improvement of plans require open discussion or, on the other hand, when information is clear and agreed on, and it is not necessary to get feedback.

Two-way communication (e.g., open dialogue at town meetings, explorations at planning sessions, shared vision building, and discussion about appropriate policies) is an effective way of communicating, but it is costly in terms of the skill and time that is required. This form of communication promotes fluidity between participants when information is being shared. In fact, it may be difficult to tell who is sending and who is receiving information because these roles flow back and forth among participants. Two-way communication is most useful when dealing with new initiatives, policy development, and commitment building because the personal contact involved promotes understanding and ownership. It is inappropriate to use two-way communication for routine information dissemination, because it is time consuming and not necessary. Two-way communications require time and skills. Therefore, this method should be used sparingly.

Leadership Strategies that Enhance Effective Communication

- Use the form of communication that appropriately matches the intended results. Both effectiveness and efficiency should be considered when choosing the communication form to use.
- Assess the ratio of use of one-way, one-way with feedback, and two-way communication. Generally, the majority of communication should be one-way or one-way with feedback. Two-way com-munications should be used least frequently and reserved for important issues that require agreement and clarification.
- Deliver consistent messages to avoid confusion. Also realize that some members will need to hear a message two or three times before they process it.

Problem Solving

Problem solving is a central process in community resiliency building. If done well it can bring information together about the status quo and generate proposals for improvement. Problems can be seen as obstacles or as opportunities to learn and grow, depending on how we respond to them. They need to be treated as a natural part of the change landscape.

If problems are dealt with superficially, then people fight for turf, appearance becomes more important than substance, disagreements will not be explored effectively, blame will probably be laid on those who disagree, and there will likely be resistance to revealing underlying differences (Senge, 1990). Unwillingness to deal with problems reduces chances for improvement. Change is rarely smooth, proceeding as anticipated without a hitch. Communities that are serious about becoming healthier need to confront problems and deal with them effectively.

Leadership Strategies for Effective Problem Solving

- Resist the tendency to delay resolving problems in hopes of attain-ing full information. Getting all the information that is desired for problem solving is not likely to occur.
- View problem solving as an ongoing and continuous process because change is dynamic and targets shift.
- Establish structures and procedures that encourage periodic checks to determine how problem solving is proceeding.
- See problems as opportunities and act accordingly. Remember that "life doesn't follow straight-line logic; it conforms to a kind of curved logic that changes the nature of things. . . . Problems then, are not just hassles to be dealt with and set aside. Lurking inside each problem is . . . a vehicle for personal growth. This entails the need for a shift; we need to value the process of finding the solution—juggling the inconsistencies that meaningful solutions entail" (Pascale, 1990, p. 263).

Decision Making

Making decisions is about making choices. The issue for community resiliency building is when to use which decision-making processes. There are three basic decision-making process options: decisions made by individual persons or small groups,

> Long-range planning does not deal with future decisions, but with the future of present decisions.
>
> —Peter Drucker

decisions made by groups through majority vote, and group decisions made through consensus. Each form is useful, depending on what is appropriate at the time.

An individual person or small group decision is efficient and can be appropriate if it is necessary to respond to an emergency situation, when the decision is to be based on previous group agreements, or if it is focused on a routine matter. It is inappropriate when decisions are policy related and will have a lasting impact on how the school and community organize and operate or when involvement and ownership are important.

Group decision making by majority rule may be appropriate if efficiency is of the utmost importance, there is limited time, the group is cohesive, or everyone does not have to participate in implementing the decision. However, if the group is divided and agreement is important, majority rule can lead to polarization.

Group consensus decision making takes time and requires good communications and conflict-management skills, so it needs to be used sparingly. It should be used when full deliberation is important, as is often the case regarding the development of new policies and goals procedures. It is best used when everyone is willing to support the decision even if they do not fully agree with it. On the contrary, it is inappropriate to practice group consensus decision making when the matter is routine or mandated or when expertise and skill in decision making is what is most needed.

Tannenbaum and Schmidt (1958) identified six decision-making levels from high leader control to high group control of the process; which is most appropriate is dependent on how routine the decision is, the time available for consultation, and the preferences of leaders and group members:

- Telling: the leader makes the decision.
- Selling: the leader makes the decision and tries to persuade others to agree with it.
- Testing: the leader presents a proposed decision for group input before making the final decision.
- Consulting: the leader asks for input before making decisions and shares the rationale for using or not using the input.
- Joining: the leader is an equal member in the group that makes the decisions.
- Abdicating: the group makes the decision either because the leader delegates it or by default.

The telling and selling end of the continuum is both efficient and appropriate to employ when decisions are about routine and agreed-upon matters. However, when important, controversial, or newly suggested ideas are on the table and group commitment and motivation are important, the consulting, joining and abdicating end of the continuum is a more appropriate decision-making approach to use. For this reason, group involvement in decision making is recommended for community resiliency-building initiatives. But for this to work well, information must be shared openly and members need to develop skills required to make decisions as a group.

Leadership Strategies for Promoting Effective Decision Making

> The hole and the patch should be commensurate.
>
> —*Thomas Jefferson*

- Provide decision-making skill development for group members.
- Encourage group input and participation in decisions.
- Develop an understanding with the group about which decision-making format—individual or small group, majority vote, or consensus decision making—is appropriate for which purposes.

Meetings

We have all suffered through frustrating and ineffectual meetings. However, if conducted well, meetings can be an important means of developing and sharing values and purposes, informing members, building relationships, solving problems, making decisions, and taking actions. The productivity of meetings depends on a number of factors including clarity of purpose, size of group, time constraints, compatibility of members, status differences, physical location, and facilitation skills of leaders. The frequency of meetings and the time of day they are held also affect meeting effectiveness.

Schmuck and Runkel (1994) identified four features of effective meetings that leaders need to facilitate.

Focus on both tasks (content) and maintenance (group development). Creating a balance between task accomplishment and group maintenance promotes effective meetings. People need to believe that they are valued, that they will be able to interact positively and effectively (interpersonal maintenance) at meetings, and that agreed-upon tasks will be accomplished. Meeting management structures that provide for both maintenance and task accomplishment are necessary. Members can easily derail meetings through confusion or by various forms of misbehavior if group maintenance is not prioritized. Similarly, to function effectively as a group, members need tasks to be clarified and agreed upon and leaders need to encourage follow-through so that decisions can result in meaningful actions.

Group-orientated agendas. People who have personal agendas, which are often hidden and are not addressed, will likely exhibit unproductive behaviors such as blocking, fighting, sandbagging, and withdrawing. To promote a group orientation, time must be given to resolve issues that have created disturbances to the group's work so that energy can be focused on goal achievement.

Shared leadership. Shared leadership distributes meeting functions so more members get to participate and challenges are shared. Leadership can be shared regarding planning and other preparation activities, building agendas based on goals, coordinating tasks, keeping records, promoting positive interpersonal dynamics, providing feedback, evaluating the effectiveness of meetings, and planning follow-up activities. In short, shared leadership can result in greater participation and group ownership of goals and activities.

> No one is useless in this world who lightens the burdens of another.
> —*Charles Dickens*

Follow-through. Follow-through is necessary after meetings are finished. Follow-through includes getting meeting minutes processed and distributed, getting tasks moving and completed, and preparing for future meetings. Fast and consistent follow-through builds confidence among group members as well as trust with the leadership.

Some Leadership Strategies to Make Meetings More Effective

- Honor those who come on time by starting on time.
- Set a time frame for conducting business items and keep to it.
- Distribute agendas in advance so that people can come to meetings prepared.
- Arrange the room to match the purposes of the meeting. An informational meeting can be set up theatre style, with presenters using visuals to explain key points. If interaction is important, the room and seats should be set up so that face-to-face discussions can take place (e.g., in a circle, a rectangle, or small groups around tables).
- Finish at the agreed-upon stopping time. Time is precious for everyone.
- Focus more on strategic agenda items instead of operational items. When the majority of the meeting focuses on operational items, little movement forward is made.

Conflict Management

Conflicts are inevitable when introducing significant changes like resiliency initiatives. Moreover, the good news is that they often provide the impetus for growth and breakthroughs. Conflicts can range from misunderstandings or disagreements over important issues to emotionally charged struggles over limited resources.

Most people are not accustomed to open confrontation of conflicts, especially given

> It is one of the beautiful compensations of life that no man can sincerely try to help another without helping himself.
>
> —*Ralph Waldo Emerson*

the diversity that exists in most communities. However, conflicts that are brought into the open and dealt with effectively can result in improved performance of group members. For this to happen, trust and constructive openness needs to be promoted. Confronting conflicts in such a manner requires leadership with good facilitation skills.

Different types of conflict require different responses. There are alternative ways of categorizing conflicts. Schmuck and Runkel (1994) identified three types of conflicts. *Factual conflicts* occur when there is disagreement over facts or there is unequal distribution of information about them. Some facts can be determined easily such as the number of buildings that exist on campus, but some are more difficult to discern such as opinions held about the health of the community. *Strategy conflicts* occur when there is disagreement over the best methods to use to accomplish a goal. *Value conflicts* can be quite intense because they occur when there is disagreement about beliefs and values.

Carney (1979) proposed four types of conflict and effective strategies for dealing with them. These conflicts and his proposed solutions are illustrated in Table 7.1. What is important is to diagnose the kind of conflict that is occurring and develop responses that fit the situation.

Table 7.1   Conflicts: Sources and Responses

Sources of Conflict	Solutions
• Meaning of words: Language may not be understood or may hold different meaning for different individuals.	• Clear up meaning: Make sure everyone understands the terms that are used.
• Evidence: People may have different information, or some members may have access to more information.	• Get the same information to everyone: Provide it in understandable terms.
• Reasoning processes: People may reason differently, based on their own unique experiences, thought patterns, etc.	• Check reasoning: Have members share their reasoning with each other.
• Values: People may hold deeply felt and different values.	• Agree to disagree: If it is okay that all do not agree, recognizing differences can promote care and respect. If disagreement is not possible, it may be necessary to separate those involved.

SOURCE: Adapted from G. Carney (personal communication, May 1979)

Some Leadership Strategies for Managing Conflict

- Collect data about conflicts from a variety of sources and use different methods, including questionnaires, interviews, and observations.
- Devise procedures and rules for resolving conflicts that group members agree on *before* conflicts arise.
- Clarify issues and confront them until they are resolved. This may intensify them temporarily but covering up conflicts usually only makes them worse.
- Recognize that change can bring out the worst in people (e.g., greed, power needs, autocratic styles of leadership, exclusionary behaviors, and heightened fears of the unknown).
- Conduct periodic reviews to keep the process in balance.
- Look below the surface for the potential of hidden conflicts.
- Consider whether the tension that is created by the conflict enhances productivity or inhibits it and respond accordingly.
- Determine whether the conflict interferes with the group's goals. If it does not, confrontation may be unnecessary or can perhaps be delayed.
- Determine if those involved in the conflict really need to work together. If not, separating them may be sufficient.
- Create structural responses—reorganizing, modifying, or shifting roles; increasing resources; and changing schedules.

ASSESSMENT, MONITORING, AND EVALUATION

> There is something I don't know
> that I am supposed to know.
> I don't know what it is I don't know,
> and yet am supposed to know.
> And I feel I look stupid
> if I seem both not to know it
> and not know *what* it is I don't know.
> Therefore, I pretend I know it.
> This is nerve-wracking since I don't
> know what I must pretend to know.
> Therefore, I pretend I know everything.
>
> —R. D. Laing

Assessment, monitoring, and evaluation are activities that can help keep resiliency initiatives on track. They can also identify and determine successes and failures of efforts to improve school and community resiliency. Unfortunately, these activities are often developed post facto instead of as an ongoing process to establish how well resources are being invested.

Clarity is needed about the purpose of information gathering. Is it for accountability? Does it determine program worth? Is it knowledge building and sharing? Is it capacity building? Or is it for other reasons? The purposes of assessment, monitoring, and evaluation should be to strengthen the process of resiliency building by providing information that can

> Research is to see what everybody else has seen, and to think what nobody else has thought.
>
> —Albert Szent-Gyorgyl

guide the community toward greater health. Knowing what is and what is not working well is important for such growth. However, many people—including leaders—fear that such scrutiny will bring attention to inadequacies. If this fear is not responded to effectively, initiatives may wander off target and self-serving judgments can take the place of meaningful feedback about the status quo, progress, and outcomes of them.

The remainder of the chapter focuses on assessment, monitoring, and evaluation, including practical methods of making these methods work in diverse situations. We discuss efficient and effective ways for leaders to collect, analyze, and report findings for review and decision making in the policy arena.

Meaningful assessment and monitoring (formative information gathering) and evaluations (summative information gathering) require clearly defined purposes and time lines, as well as the skillful use of appropriate information gathering methods. Assessment, monitoring, and evaluation are how we can know that resiliency-building plans are actually followed and supported.

Assessment

Assessment is about clarifying and agreeing on starting points: For instance, is the community ready to launch a resiliency-building effort? What are the most critical needs? What are some good vantage points from which to start the effort?

It is also helpful to keep outcomes in mind so information that is gathered can be assessed against intent. Clarifying where you want to go and what the community might look like in the future can be facilitated by using the "Roof" exercises (5.5 and 5.6) introduced in Chapter 5.

There are different ways to assess the initial situation. Selecting tools that are flexible and that can improve the possibilities of identifying problems and meaningful goals requires effort and skill. The important point is that *there is no one right way*. In fact, several complementary methods may be the best approach. A few examples of information-gathering tools and ways of using them follow. For the most part, these tools can be used during all three information-gathering phases—assessment, monitoring, and evaluation.

Assess the Current State of Community Resiliency

This should be done early. See exercises introduced earlier in the book for straightforward ways of doing these assessments (Exercises 1.1, 1.2, 2.1, 3.1, 6.1, 6.2, and 6.3). Conducting these exercises in heterogeneous groups can promote widespread involvement of diverse community groups, clarify resiliency concepts and processes, promote ownership and trust, and build the intensity and motivation needed to launch resiliency-building efforts.

Conduct Interviews

This is another method for assessing the current state of the community. Probing questions can be asked of individuals to get at in-depth information. People should be encouraged to express their ideas and perceptions if they are going to believe that their opinions matter. It takes time and money to conduct interviews, but the payoff can make the effort worthwhile.

Conduct Focus Groups

A group-based interviewing technique such as focus groups (Krueger, 1994) can clarify community stakeholders' perceptions. A trained outside facilitator can conduct these interviews or an internal committee can be formed and trained to do so. A set of questions can be developed to guide focus group interviews that are about six to eight people in size. Diverse representative groups can be interviewed, probing questions can be asked, layers can be peeled back , and group dynamics can be observed .

Conduct Surveys

A survey that addresses the six resiliency elements can be an efficient way of establishing a general sense of community attitudes about issues. After surveys are designed, completed, and returned and results are collated, outcomes can be disseminated to the community. Many people can participate, and important issues can be identified through surveys. Of course, care must be taken about survey item construction and sampling needs to be representative and of a sufficient size so results will be accurate and meaningful.

Make Observations

Observations of meetings and other interactions that relate to the effort can provide reflective feedback on the process. Group dynamics can be observed and analyzed, and suggestions for changes and improvements can be developed.

Analyze Documents

Analysis of documents can establish what is known and how it is perceived. Useful documents to collect and analyze include school and community demographic summaries and analyses, government agency and voluntary organization publications, as well as clippings from the local newspaper.

Involvement of community members is essential to the information-gathering process to get different perspectives and judgments, as well as to build participation and ownership. Another outgrowth of involving community stakeholders might be the promotion of more closely shared perceptions.

Monitoring

The purpose of monitoring is to identify whether there is a need to make incremental adjustments so that plans and actions do not go awry. If major adjustments are required, it is better to learn about them early rather than discovering them later through trial and error.

Monitoring is an ongoing process of determining the extent to which goals are being implemented. It is a formative activity, a systematic examination of the process that ensures results are not left to chance. Monitoring generates understanding, identifies strategies for improvement, and encourages continued growth.

People want to know where they are going and whether they are actually proceeding along the desired way. If they have a sense of movement, they will be more willing to continue to participate. Therefore, once plans have been set into motion, a system for monitoring

> If you don't know where you are going, you will probably end up somewhere else.
> —Laurence J. Peter

progress is critical to success. Achieving a balance between too little and too much monitoring is essential. Monitoring for resiliency development is similar to monitoring factors for the growth of a tree: checking the soil for nutritional value—acidity, alkaline balance, or dampness—too much or too little water, the right amount of sunlight, and the availability of wind to strengthen the tree. But pulling the tree out of the ground to check for growth would be detrimental, in much the same way that stopping resiliency-building efforts to check for progress would be detrimental.

Benchmarking has become a popular method for monitoring the progress of activities and the level of implementation of initiatives. Benchmarks, or preferred states, are predetermined prior to implementation and are based on the best practices that have been established. For present purposes, this means identifying best practices from community resiliency development efforts that are viewed to be successful (see Chapter 8 for a sample of such efforts).

Some Leadership Strategies for Monitoring the Progress of Resiliency Efforts:

- Establish periodic checkup points to understand and assess the process.
- Build opportunities into improvement plans for regularized problem identification.
- Procure a trained external evaluator, who can give formative feedback about the process, probably once or twice a year.
- Identify potential obstacles and, as they arise, develop alternative plans.

Evaluation

The purpose of evaluation is to determine the extent to which goals have been accomplished and whether outcomes are worth the efforts that have been made. This should give policymakers the kind of information they need about initiatives to make good resource allocation decisions. Evaluation is summative in nature, focusing on long-term outcomes.

Selection of appropriate methods to evaluate resiliency initiatives is critical in determining strengths and areas of growth that are required. Data can be collected in a variety of ways (see methods listed under the Assessment section), depending on the purpose and goals of the evaluation.

Some Leadership Strategies for Evaluating Resiliency Efforts:

- Define criteria for evaluation before beginning change initiatives.
- Recognize that goals and plans for evaluation should be reviewed, developed, and communicated early rather than waiting until the end of the effort to think about evaluation.
- Understand the political forces that may impinge on the evaluation process.
- Secure the services of a knowledgeable external evaluator who can advise the school and community about the best way to proceed and conduct evaluation activities as appropriate.
- Conduct evaluations at the end of each phase of the initiative to serve as a basis for continued improvement and any changes that may be required.

Assessment, monitoring, and evaluation are important activities if we hope to know what is happening and what has been accomplished. Identifying challenges and successes motivates continuing participation by community members. Besides testing progress and documenting outcomes, assessment, monitoring, and evaluation can build understanding, trust, and ownership in the resiliency-building process. These are a necessity if communities are going to be able to move toward increased resiliency. The results of assessment, monitoring, and evaluation can strengthen plans for growth and resiliency.

> Society is always taken by surprise at any new example of common sense.
> —*Ralph Waldo Emerson*

Exercise 7.1: Considerations for Leaders

In order to realize the goals of resiliency-building initiatives leaders need to understand change, guide group development, and facilitate the process effectively. What rating, on a scale of one (low) to five (high) would you give to the knowledge and capabilities of current leaders to do these things in your community?

1. Understanding the following four stages of change:
   A. initiation
   B. implementation
   C. institutionalization
   D. refocusing

2. Guiding the stages of group development:
   A. forming
   B. storming
   C. norming
   D. performing
   E. disbanding

3. Facilitation activities
   A. vision building and goal setting
   B. communications
   C. problem solving
   D. decision making
   E. effective meetings
   F. conflict management
   G. assessment, monitoring and evaluation

Chapter 8, which follows, provides examples of rural, small town, suburban, and urban communities that have taken the initiative to build resiliency among their members. These communities are taking risks, developing different ways of relating, and achieving results that can be meaningful to other communities that are initiating similar activities. Additional information about other resilient community initiatives, along with helpful resources for managing the process, are also presented.

8

School and Community Resiliency Initiatives

"We don't accomplish anything in this world alone . . . and whatever happens is the result of the whole tapestry of one's life and all the weavings of individual threads from one to another that creates something."

—Former Justice Sandra Day O'Connor, first woman on the U.S. Supreme Court

In this final chapter, we turn our attention to a sampling of schools and communities that have made the commitment to become healthier places to live and work. Many "real life" examples of communities are consciously improving resiliency for their members, adults, and youth. These initiatives can serve as a catalyst for your own community's thinking and planning. The intent of the chapter is to help communities that are ready to take action by showing how others are actively pursuing similar goals.

The chapter is composed of three sections. To provide reality perspectives about limitations and possibilities, the first section summarizes suggestions and insights offered by Lisbeth Schorr (1997), who has studied the efforts and outcomes of many community-based improvement initiatives. The second section provides examples of initiatives that are community wide, school based, community based, and some other initial efforts to improve the quality of their members' lives. It also offers ways of making contact and getting further information about these and similar initiatives. The third section is composed of a diverse sampling of books, compendiums, Web sites, and other resources that provide a rich array of approaches, ideas, and formats that can be employed as your community initiates and conducts improvement efforts.

A REALITY PERSPECTIVE

Schorr (1997) observed and analyzed some of the most ambitious efforts to improve communities. Her analysis led her to the conclusion that the most effective programs share seven basic attributes:

Successful programs

1. are comprehensive, flexible, responsive and persevering . . .
2. see children in the context of their families . . . strong families are key to healthy children . . .
3. deal with families as parts of neighborhoods and communities . . .
4. have a long-term, preventive orientation, a clear mission, and continue to evolve over time . . .
5. are well managed by competent and committed individuals with clearly identifiable skills . . .
6. Staffs . . . are trained and supported to provide high-quality, responsive services . . .
7. operate in settings that encourage practitioners to build strong relation-ships based on mutual trust and respect (pp. 5–10).

In an earlier work, *Within Our Reach*, Schorr (1989) surveyed numerous programs that looked quite promising. However, in *Common Purpose* (Schorr, 1997), she reported that within five years of these observations, fully half of them were no longer in existence. It is important to assess reasons for the demise of so many good programs, particularly if we hope to improve our chances of successfully initiating and implementing school and community improvement efforts.

> A critical mass of Americans has come to understand that mere treatment of symptoms is not an adequate response to the diseases that plague us. We must fundamentally change the way we think.
>
> —*Marrianne Williamson*

Schorr's (1997) conclusion was that most of the time, the programs themselves were not deficient. Rather, it was "the failure to understand that the environment within which these programs have to operate, and which these programs depend on for long-term funding, skilled professionals, and public support, is profoundly out of sync with the key attributes of success. Scaling up effective services requires conditions that are still exceedingly rare" (p. 19).

So long as programs remain small and outside the mainstream of community power structures and government oversight, they have a good chance of persisting. However, the irony is that once they are recognized and valued, they become more involved with resource-granting centers, both public and private, that impose rules and other restrictions that tend to dilute their effectiveness and may eventually lead to their collapse. In short, they are more likely to persist if they stay small and free of entanglements with the very systems that they are trying to influence.

To get past this pervasive dilemma, initiatives that are attempting to positively affect the resiliency of communi-ties must become more effective in dealing with the systems they want to change. If they are to persist past the "hothouse" stage, Schorr (1997) said that they will need to do these things:

> We must reform if we would conserve.
>
> —*Franklin Delano Roosevelt*

1. Actively seek information about what seems to be working elsewhere so that they gain from these experiences and avoid making unnecessary mistakes.
2. Seek "nontechnical," noncategorized assistance from providers who get up close and personal and are present and available over the long haul to help initiate, implement, and institutionalize improvement efforts.
3. Develop political influence to affect decisions about neighborhoods and communities and mobilize community support for improvement initiatives.
4. Challenge the conditions under which they receive funding (i.e., away from narrow, categorical funding and reporting and toward funding that is more holistic, reflecting the complex goals and priorities that are being pursued).
5. Make a successful case for obtaining more funds from resource providers because the magnitude of the task is well beyond the current resources being set aside for community renewal.
6. Make it clear that failure to provide sufficient support now will likely lead to failures of improvement efforts and thus will increase the need for much larger funding support later (e.g., for police, prisons, court systems, public health systems, etc.).

Schorr's (1997) list of considerations for successful improvement programs may appear quite daunting. Certainly, it leaves the clear message that such programs need to be thought through carefully and that long-term, broad-based support to be obtained if goals are going to have a chance to be institutionalized.

> We do pretty much whatever we want to. Why can't we live in good cities?
> —Philip Johnson

The good news is that community improvement champions are becoming much more knowledgeable about what it takes to launch, sustain, and institutionalize change efforts because of the experiences that have been accumulated through earlier efforts. In fact, there are more sustaining efforts being launched than ever before. The increase is due, at least in part, to increasing awareness and readiness on the part of more people in many communities to get involved. Also many efforts have shifted the focus because of the mandates from government. Much can be learned from these efforts. We encourage you and others to study these efforts as your community gears up for its resiliency improvement initiatives.

> Nothing ever succeeds which exuberant spirits have not helped produce.
> —Frederick Nietzsche

COMMUNITIES ON THE FOREFRONT OF IMPROVEMENT

We know that, with sufficient motivation, communities can be mobilized to engage in improvement efforts. We have seen communities, individuals, and nations join together to help victims of the tsunami in 2004 in the Indian Ocean. Nearly 300,000 people were killed in that tragedy. Instant communities were formed to assist with the emergency, to clean up, and to plan for rebuilding. People joined together for a common cause. This reflects what Wheatley and Kellner-Rogers (1998b)

> We need more mass experience, not less. We need more civilized contact with our neighbors, not less.
> —James A. Michener

noted about community-wide efforts being initially seen as a problem for private and public organizations to solve and subsequently being recognized as everyone's problem that had to be solved through collaborative, community-wide efforts. Entire communities must rally together to tackle the problem.

Community resiliency-building challenges may not be as sharply etched as the tsunami problem, but there is significant evidence that it is becoming a priority focus in many communities around the country. In our review of resiliency-building efforts in rural, small town, suburban, metropolitan, and urban communities, many examples were readily found. This section highlights a few of the efforts that are taking place. The examples we have found range from homegrown to national efforts to help schools and communities. They vary in scope from individual schools and their neighborhoods to large and complex metropolitan population centers. There are far too many community initiatives to attempt any sort of coherent inventory and that is not our intent. What we can do is offer a sampling so that readers can get a sense of the variety of initiatives being implemented. We have divided them into stories about community wide, school based, community based, and some other initial efforts being made. We begin with a description of a community we have worked with, Ashland, Oregon, as it launched a community resiliency effort.

> Our behavior is a function of our decisions, not our conditions. . . . We have the initiative and the responsibility to make things happen.
> —*Stephen Covey*

Community-wide Initiative

Ashland, Oregon

Ashland, Oregon, a community of approximately 20,000, is the home of Southern Oregon University and the Oregon Shakespeare Festival. Its diverse population includes blue-collar workers, crafts people, merchants, educators, and actors.

The process started in February 1997 with seventy people who came together at the university for a workshop with us. They explored ways in which the community and the schools could promote resiliency, not just for students but also for all community members. What occurred that day and through follow-up activities holds several lessons for those interested in promoting resiliency development through interagency collaboration, school and business partnerships, and school-community partnerships.

The activity was initiated by Dr. John Daggett, then the superintendent of Ashland Public Schools, who believed that the time was ripe to bring all segments of the community together to explore ways of working together to move toward greater community resiliency. As he phrased it in the school district's community newsletter,

> Ashland, like the rest of the Rogue Valley, has seen social changes that have the potential of undermining our very special community. Gangs, drugs, violence, teen crime and other compromising factors pose a continual threat to our quality of life as a community. Resiliency training offers a means by which the entire Ashland community—including school, business, church, and other civic entities—may join together to fortify our patrons, and especially our children and youth, against these factors" (Ashland School District, 1996, p. 5).

The people who came together at the university purposefully represented a cross-section of the community. They included representatives of the clergy, chamber of commerce, service organizations, social service agencies, city government (e.g., the mayor, police chief, and fire chief), university, treatment and health centers, students, and educators—teachers, counselors, and site-based administrators, as well as the superintendent and other central office administrators. The head of the local teachers' union, which provided major support for the event, also participated.

After the group learned about the six resiliency elements, they were asked to apply them to current efforts under way to respond to needs in the Ashland community. These community members were able to understand the basic meaning of resiliency and believed that, although Ashland already had a number of resiliency-related activities going on, there was still plenty of room for better coordination. They also came to an agreement about the existence of gaps in current efforts and the need to consider implementing additional initiatives. In addition, they expressed concern about the need to broaden the base of support and involvement beyond that of the people in the room.

Equally important, they quickly grasped the importance of shifting the focus from at risk, which can potentially lead to self-fulfilling prophecies of failure, to a focus on resiliency, which emphasizes supporting everyone's potential for success, whether one is referring to students, educators, or other adult community members.

> None of us is as smart as all of us.
> —Ken Blanchard

They then came to agreement about a commonly held vision of community resiliency that enabled them to overcome their initial differences. With some facilitation, they were able to visualize what a resilient community might look like in Ashland and identified a number of creative activities that they were willing to commit their time and resources to in pursuit of this vision (e.g., annual celebrations, community potlucks, multimedia dissemination of resiliency concepts and activities, community fairs, town meetings, and awareness and training in safety issues). Last, they recognized the need to institutionalize resiliency initiatives through such activities as ongoing training, stronger focus on prevention, community consensus building, and pursuit of partnerships.

The next day, a smaller group, representing the diverse elements in attendance at the first day's activities, met to develop goals and plans to support making Ashland a more resilient community. Outcomes of this initiative included a commitment to pursue community-based activities that promote resiliency as well as an agreement from the school district's central office and several of the district's schools to focus on resiliency for students and educators. The group also finalized and disseminated its own definition of a resilient com-

> And in today already walks tomorrow.
> —Samuel Taylor Coleridge

munity to guide future actions: "A resilient community is comprised of people who bond together, support one another, take responsibility for their actions, are proactive about preparing for the future, and spring back from adversity."

They also decided to establish an ongoing group, open to community membership, to keep the momentum going and to guide planning for continuing resiliency development initiatives. A title was created, "Building a Resilient Community" (BARC), and in short order, a mission statement was developed: "To build a safer and healthier community." After some discussion, four goals were also established:

1. Increase the community's knowledge about resiliency.

2. Increase the number of opportunities for participation in intergenerational activities.

3. Strengthen ties within neighborhoods.

4. Expand the use of the school as a community resource center.

These goals helped BARC focus its attention on obtaining necessary resources. They also set a direction for priority activities, clarified expected outcomes, and helped the group identify and differentiate strategies to implement for individuals, families, schools, work sites, and the community in support of these goals.

As BARC initiated its activities, it soon discovered that, in addition to energy and goodwill, it needed to learn skills to communicate its vision and facilitate community dialogue. To help build confidence and skill levels, BARC sponsored a "Mentor Training" day a year after their efforts began in April 1998. At that session, forty-seven community members—varying from high school students to working adults and retired persons, from age sixteen to age ninety-two—learned basic facilitation skills, including how to set goals, develop plans, make presentations, run meetings, and manage conflicts. They also learned how to monitor and evaluate their efforts so they could keep on track as they continued to promote resiliency in the community.

> It is a man's destiny to ponder on the riddle of existence and, as a by-product of his wonderment, to create a new life on the earth.
>
> —*Charles F. Kettering*

BARC's membership, which was a good cross-representation of the community, continued to provide the leadership for community resiliency-building initiatives in Ashland. In fact, it expanded in membership and took on an ever-broader set of activities. As an example of the scope of its initiatives, BARC made presentations utilizing every form of communication available in the community. They posted their goals and activities to keep members of the community informed. They showed relevant videotapes to stimulate thinking and discussion, facilitated workshops and meetings, and provided rewards at the local ski resort.

In the first years of its existence, BARC's priorities were to clarify its mission and goals, develop the knowledge and skills necessary to meet them, and increase community awareness, understanding, and involvement in resiliency enhancement activities. With this foundation in place, BARC moved on to actualizing its long-term mission and goals. Within the first five years with Dr. Daggett at the helm, resiliency became increasingly more a part of the lives of all members of the community. The concept spread to many other districts within the state.

> It's amazing what ordinary people can do if they set out without preconceived notions.
>
> —*Charles F. Kettering*

In the last few years, the community and the state have had financial difficulties as well as new leadership. Currently, the focus has turned to specific problems such as bullying and harassment, positive behavior support, nutrition, and academic challenges. Their Web site is http://www.ashland.k12.or.us.

Communities in Schools in Charlotte, North Carolina

Communities in Schools (CIS), which provides support to over 200 communities across the nation, has been operating in Charlotte since 1985. It is touted to be the nation's largest and most effective program of its kind. CIS works closely with the schools to ensure their continued success.

The mission of CIS is to develop partnerships that connect appropriate services with at-risk youth in specifically identified areas. Unlike many programs, CIS brings assistance to young people instead of requiring them to seek these services. The focus of the Charlotte initiative has been on recruiting caring people and local organizations to help youngsters and their parents. The goals are to prevent dropping out and improving self-esteem. Rather than just focusing on crisis intervention, a broad range of services is made available. The approach is holistic, addressing the emotional, academic, and physical needs of children and their families through tutoring and mentoring, health care and counseling, parent involvement workshops, cultural and volunteer service activities, and college and post-secondary education and career services.

CIS in Charlotte boasts over 2,000 students receiving services annually. Charlotte has school-based site coordinators in seven elementary, eight middle, and ten high schools and involves over seventy agencies in the efforts. Cornerstones of the program include early involvement of key stakeholders and recognizing the need to deal comprehensively with the problems of young people and their families. Sustainability has been promoted through community-based ownership, accessibility, and flexibility, which are realized through individualized plans for children and families, key stakeholder involvement and support, and a vision of a healthy community (National Network for Family Resiliency, 1997). For more information, visit the Charlotte CIS Web site at www.cischarlotte.org.

Schoolwide Initiatives: Three Short Stories

Next will be a look at some school wide efforts to build resiliency. We will briefly describe three different school communities—one each from a primary level, middle school level, and high school level—with which we have worked. The reasons these schools chose to promote resiliency varies. Each, for its own reasons, concluded that it was ready to engage in resiliency improvement efforts and each made its own unique choice about the approach that was most appropriate. One felt a couple of workshops would shift the school to be more resilient. Another took a more ongoing approach, while the third chose a highly intensified approach.

> We know what we are, but know not what we may be.
>
> —*William Shakespeare*

The Workshop Approach: Nelson Central School, Nelson, New Zealand

Nelson Central School is located in the heart of Nelson, New Zealand—a town of approximately 42,000 residents on the South Island of New Zealand. Nelson Central School, built in 1878, is the oldest New Zealand school functioning on its original unitary site. Approximately 440 children ages five to eleven attend the school. The school has a diverse population, with the language of instruction in both English and Māori.

The principal, Dr. Paul Potaka, and his management team felt that resiliency would add to their already positive environment. They clearly understood what they needed to be healthy and viewed resiliency as the boost to achieve a new level of awareness. When a baseline assessment was conducted with the entire staff, many positive activities were identified as currently in place and recognition for these efforts was made. Dr. Potaka believed that building resiliency could strengthen the students and staff and, hopefully, the community.

Some of the comments from teachers after learning more about resiliency were that they saw their students differently. They have a more balanced image of their children. Instead of trying to "fix" them, they recognize their strengths and areas to improve. They also said that this positive shift in perceptions has made them realize the impact they have as individuals and collectively as a school. Resiliency serves as a lens for how they interact with others, particularly students, staff, parents, and the wider community. Learn more about the school at http://www.nelsoncentral.school.nz.

Planned Efforts Over the Course of Two Years: Broadgreen Intermediate School, Stoke, New Zealand

Broadgreen Intermediate School, housing approximately 570 students ages twelve to fourteen, is in a community of 41,000 residents on the South Island of New Zealand. The school has been undergoing transformation for a number of years. One of the first major changes was the physical structure of the building. A local artist, Princess Hart, began working with the school to bring more life and harmony to very conservative looking buildings. She brought other local artists to work with the school to achieve the environment that was necessary for a healthy school. The school was divided into six houses, each having its own color and theme.

The principal, Rodger Brodie, and his management team felt the health and well-being of the school was the next step toward being more effective. We worked with the full staff approximately once a term for about three hours each session over the course of nearly two years. First, we focused on the concept of resiliency and the relevance it has to everyone. Next, we examined how students could be more resilient and what educators could do to help them along their journey. Given the age of middle school students, it is challenging, even during the best of times. The rest of the time was spent on educator resilience. After looking at what they do well with kids and themselves, the lens was broadening to look holistically at the school. Most of the teachers felt they worked well in their classroom but felt the need to work better as a team for overall well-being at the school level. Several areas were identified to modify that would move them into a healthier place.

As the sessions unfolded, adjustments were made to strengthen the skills needed to make the change. Educators took on different roles to incorporate resiliency into their lives. As they learned about and experimented with resiliency, most of them concluded that resiliency is the basis for living healthy and being able to be positive role models for their students. Resiliency continues to be the agreed-upon approach to move the school forward. Learn more about Broadgreen Intermediate School at http://www.broadgreen.school.nz.

Highly Intensified Resiliency Efforts: Robertson High School, Las Vegas, New Mexico

Robertson High School serves grades nine through twelve in a community of approximately 14,000 residents. It is one of two high schools in the town. Of the 700 students, 87 percent are Hispanic. From 1989 to 2001 the school had high leadership turnover with twelve principals coming and going.

The high school was also undergoing renovations that took longer than expected. The result was that the school had to be closed for ten school days. The New Mexico State Department of Education did not require the students to make up the missed days but the educators were expected to do so. There were also many state mandated reforms under way and a new leader each year. The community freely voiced their opinions about the high school and they ranked it below level in academic performance. Staff morale was not good.

The superintendent at the time was Hank Dominguez. He was committed to improving the school. One of the teachers at the school thought he could make a difference as principal and his peers were supportive of him taking on this role.

In short order, we were contacted to help the staff move forward. The first year, because of the state's requirement that educators make up lost days, six of these days were used to bring the staff together to explore resiliency while the rest of the school district was on school vacation. During these days, the staff worked through what it meant to be a resilient school, shared their concerns, and decided that they had a choice about what happens at the school. Skill development was recognized as essential. At the last session in April 2000, the staff decided that having the extra time to focus on professional development as a school was worth the effort they had put into it. School improvement plans were made and committees were empowered to move ahead. The superintendent supported these efforts by arranging to have students to start late once a term the following year so the entire staff could focus on building resiliency. Also during the year, a steering committee met fortnightly to review what had been accomplished, what some of the glitches were, and what support was needed to move the plans forward. By the end of the first year, the total staff had met for six full days, committees met weekly, and the steering committee met every fortnight to guide the efforts.

The following year a new principal was selected. His agenda did not match the emerging resiliency focus of the school. Efforts were slowed down but not stopped because the staff, realizing the value of becoming healthier and stronger, continued to press for the resiliency plan they had developed. Committees continued to work but not meeting as frequently. Two workshops were held with the staff the second year with the steering committee pressing for continuing fortnightly meetings. The principal left at the end of the academic year and the assistant principal, Richard Lopez, was appointed principal.

Mr. Lopez had been an assistant principal since the start of resiliency building in 1999. He believed that strengthening the staff provided stronger role models for the students. During the third year, he had facilitated the initiative, carried by the staff, to build a sturdy resiliency foundation for everyone at the school. The students' academic level improved, exceeding standards toward the top ranking of excellence. The staff made a commitment to becoming stronger and healthier as a life choice. Learn more about the school at http://www.greatschools.net.

Community-Wide Initiatives

Many communities around the country are identifying ways in which to become more resilient. Although methods differ considerably among them, the intended outcomes are similar: to improve the health and well-being of community members.

Tucson Resiliency Initiative

The Tucson (Arizona) Mayor's School District Action Task Force formed in 1998 was the crucible for the formation of the *Tucson Resiliency Initiative* (TRI). Their approach is to provide a framework that schools and communities can use to build resiliency attitudes, policies, and strategies. Their reach is throughout the community, but especially with schools, to build resilient youth. They work with partner schools to create an environment that promotes healthy youth development and prevents violence and substance abuse. TRI is a support for the schools to assess and identify their needs, shape their focus, and create unique strategies to build resiliency among their students. TRI also serves as a source of the latest resiliency research and scientifically proven practices and programs. They use the six resiliency elements described in this book as the basis for their model and they provide training, support, information, and evaluation services for the partner schools. A training of trainers' model is employed with the schools. In return, the schools commit to developing and implementing school-wide plans that promote resiliency. Learn more at http://www.tucsonresiliency.org.

Nampa, Idaho

Nampa, a town of more than 30,000 people near Boise, has experienced rapid population growth. The residential base ranges from families whose breadwinners are employed in local high-tech industries to those who are migrant workers. An impetus to look at the community and at how its quality of life could be improved has been accelerated because of its unprecedented growth.

Local leaders decided to take a proactive approach to the escalating demands being placed on their community, especially on the schools. They began with a community meeting that attracted "people representing pivotal spheres of influence," which, in turn, led to the decision to start "off with a bold project that could unify the entire community" (Tyler, 1996, p. 9). The Search Institute, whose efforts have been described in Chapters 3 and 6, surveyed the community and found that, similar to findings in many other communities, Nampa's youth were engaging in risky behaviors. Participants asked tough questions, created a vision for the community, and developed a plan to accomplish it. As a result of about fifteen years of work, extensive energy and resources have been marshaled to improve the situation for young people and for the community as a whole. The focus has been on building trust, listening, reaching out, and developing partnerships. The shared belief is that healthy relationships improve the likelihood that children will make healthier choices. Building a healthier community has centered on strengthening the family unit as a key building block (Tyler, 1996). For more information, visit the Nampa Web site at http://www.healthyfamiliesnampa.org.

A Sampling of Other Initiatives

There are many other examples of schools and communities that are making the choice to promote resiliency as an important strategy toward health, well-being, and success. Many of them, either intuitively or purposefully, have set improvement efforts into motion that focus on one or more of the six elements in the resiliency wheel that have been explored in the book. While it is important to consider each of the six resiliency elements when school and community improvement efforts are launched, some initiatives emphasize certain resiliency elements more than others do. This can be appropriate, depending upon the growth areas that have been identified. A few examples follow.

Positive Connections

Mt. Tabor Middle School students in Oregon average fifteen points higher on their test scores than other middle school students in the state. They attribute the improvement to dividing themselves into three smaller schools, creating close ties between students and teachers. This nurtures students to keep on track through the adolescent years (Carter, 2007).

Clear, Consistent, and Appropriate Boundaries

There are many efforts being initiated to diminish the problem of bullying. For example, the United Kingdom has organized strategies to help youth combat bullying (Bindel, 2006), and in South Australia, the police are asking parents to supervise their children's Internet use ("Kids keep online threats," 2006).

Life-Guiding Skills

Bell Multicultural Senior High School in Washington, DC provides opportunities for free, career-oriented college programs to dropouts or students on the verge of quitting school. During the week, they attend classes that give them a jump start toward advanced coursework while completing their high school diplomas (Chandler, 2006).

Briarcliff Middle School in New York realized that the emotional and social growth of their students promoted higher achievement. Even though the school is in an affluent area, they had seen a drop in academic achievement. The school strives to develop critical thinking skills and organizational skills. They have adopted Costa and Kallick's *Habits of the Mind* to instill social and moral values and have seen an increase in the overall well-being of their students (Hu, 2007).

Nurture and Support

Carver High School in Atlanta, Georgia is a model for the school district. The school experienced low morale and a drop in attendance three years ago. They restructured the school into smaller communities with 400 students and autonomous principals and faculties. Each school had the power to determine its own academic themes. The attendance rate is now as high as 98 percent. With the $10.5 million received from the Bill and Melinda Gates Foundation, the district is preparing to transform all of its traditional high schools into smaller learning communities (Atlanta Journal & Constitution, 2007).

Purposes and Expectations

Chana High School in Auburn, California has achieved a 100 percent pass rate with their students on the California High School Exit Exam. They are one of thirteen model continuation high school programs identified in California. The high school serves students who are in trouble or on the verge of dropping out of other schools. The school offers five vocational programs and partners with local community and technical colleges so students can earn college credits while in high school (Lofing, 2007).

All middle school students in Detroit will be required to take a college level life skills class at Wayne County Community College beginning next year. District officials believe this will build excitement and a desire to complete high school (Mrozowski, 2007).

Meaningful Participation

Smyth and McInerney (2007) described how students who were given owner-ship and voice in their learning an Australian school engaged them to stay in school. The school wanted to tackle its dropout problem and found that this is a key indicator for their school reform.

ADDITIONAL RESOURCES FOR COMMUNITY IMPROVEMENT INITIATIVES

There are many resources for community improvement—some that describe projects working diligently to make a difference and others that provide helpful ideas, strategies, and techniques. The following list provides brief summaries about them and about how they can be accessed (sites and addresses) for your community's efforts; several excellent resource publications are also included.

- America's Promise, 909 N. Washington Street, Alexandria, VA 22314—A national initiative based on five resources: ongoing relationship with an adult, healthy start, safe places and structured activities, marketable skills, and opportunities to serve
- *At Home in Our Schools: A Guide to School-Wide Activities that Build Community*, Child Development Project, 2000 Embarcadero, Suite 305, Oakland, CA 94606—A book of ideas and strategies aimed at parents, teachers, and administrators for implementing school-wide activities
- *Building Communities from the Inside Out: A Path Toward Finding and Mobilizing a Community's Assets* (Kretzmann & McKnight, 1993)
- The Asset-Based Community Development Institute, Institute for Policy Research, Northwestern University, 2040 Sheridan Road, Evanston, IL 60208-4100—A guide for communities and schools to use to locate assets, skills, capacities of citizens, associations, and organizations
- Center for Community Partnerships, Dr. Ira Harkavy, 133 South 36th Street, Suite 519, Philadelphia, PA 19104-3246—More than a dozen comprehensive community schools have been created in West Philadelphia by the Center
- *Common Purpose: Strengthening Families and Neighborhoods to Rebuild America* (Schorr, 1997)—A book that we refer to regularly about building communities; many community improvement projects described
- Communities in Schools (CIS), J. Neil Shorthouse, President, 1252 West Peachtree Street, Suite 430, Atlanta, GA 30309—A program that brings community resources together to increase literacy, reduce tardiness and absences, and prevent dropouts
- Community Collaboration for Children and Youth, National Association of Counties, 440 First Street, NW, Washington, DC 20001-2080—A compendium of awards for excellence in community collaboration for children and youth projects throughout the country; outstanding projects selected each year
- *Connecting the Dots: Progress Toward the Integration of School Reform, School-Linked Services, Parent Involvement and Community Schools* (Lawson & Briar-Lawson, 1997)
- Educational Renewal, McGuffey Hall, Miami University, Oxford, OH 45056—Resource includes a model, "The Family-Supportive Community School," with ten strategies for community improvement

- *Community Update*, U.S. Department of Education, Washington, DC 20202-0498—Free national newsletter that focuses on community involvement
- Compact for Learning and Citizenship, 707 17th Street, Suite 2700, Denver, CO 80202-3427—Goals: to engage students in service learning and to maximize community volunteer efforts; sponsored by the Education Commission of the States, focuses on helping schools with service and volunteerism
- *Employers, Families, and Education*, Partnership for Family Involvement in Education, 600 Independence Avenue, SW, Washington, DC 20202-8173—Strategies published by U.S. Department of Education; focuses on partnerships for family involvement in education through employers, families, and schools
- *Everybody's House—The Schoolhouse: Best Techniques for Connecting Home, School and Community* (Warner, 1997)—Strategies for schools to use to involve the community
- First Day of School Holiday (First Day Foundation, annually), First Day Foundation, PO Box 10, Bennington, VT 05201-0010—Strategies for helping schools, teachers, employers, parents, and students enhance parents' positive involvement with their children's education through newsletter and booklet
- *Keeping Schools Open As Community Learning Centers: Extending Learning in a Safe, Drug-Free Environment Before and After School*, Partnership for Family Involvement in Education, copies and further information can be obtained through 1-800-USA-LEARN—A booklet of strategies for school and community to use school facilities in ways that extend the educational program for students, jointly sponsored by the National Community Education Association, U.S. Department of Education, Policy Studies Associates, and American Bar Association Division of Education
- *Learn and Live* (The George Lucas Educational Foundation, 1997), The George Lucas Educational Foundation, Patty Burness, Executive Director, PO Box 3494, San Rafael, CA 94912—Information about pioneering improvement efforts; includes a book and a video with ideas, strategies, stories, and resources; geared for community or school use or both
- National Center for Community Education, 1017 Avon Street, Flint, Michigan 48503—A compendium of community-school partnerships that are making a difference across the country, including comprehensive information about these communities and their programs
- National Center for Schools and Communities, Joy G. Dryfoos, Fordham University, 33 West 60th Street, 8th Floor, New York, NY 10023—A resource for information about different initiatives occurring nationwide
- *Positive Actions for Living: A Guide for Learning Parent, Family, Community, and Personal Positive Actions*, Carol Gerber Allred, President/Developer, 321 Eastland Drive, Twin Falls, ID 83301—A model for comprehensive school reform that was accepted by the U.S. Department of Education Title I office for the Catalog of School Reform Models; comprehensive approach for involving the community with the school
- Project Change: Educational Equity in Albuquerque, NM, 505-242-9536—Focuses on creating equity for students of color through a community-based approach
- *Promising Initiatives to Improve Education in Your Community*, Education Publications Center, U.S. Department of Education, PO Box 1398, Jessup, MD 20794-1398—A minicatalog of programs and free publications published by U.S. Department of Education

- *Promoting Your School: Going Beyond PR* (Warner, 1994)—A guide for schools to use to develop effective public relations with the community
- *Reaching All Families: Creating Family-Friendly Schools* (Moles, 1996), Office of Educational Research and Improvement, U.S. Department of Education, 600 Independence Avenue SW, Washington, DC 20202-8173—Strategies and resources for school administrators and teachers to involve parents and families as active participants in children's education
- *School, Family, and Community Partnerships: Your Handbook for Action* (Epstein, Coates, Salinas, Sanders, & Simon, 1997)—A comprehensive framework for developing and implementing school, family, and community partnerships; useful for community or school planning or both
- *Show Me the Evidence! Proven and Promising Programs for America's Schools* (Slavin & Fashola, 1998)—Reviews major reform efforts at the elementary and secondary school levels for their effectiveness in terms of student achievement and district-level strategies for introducing proven programs
- *Study Circles Resource Center*, PO Box 203, 697 Pomfret Street Pomfret, CT 06258—Education kit and guide for involving the community in initiating participatory discussion on education through study circles; communities and schools can find good uses for these materials

WEB SITES

Building a Collective Vision—http://www.ncrel.org/sdrs/areas/issues/educatrs/ leadrshp/lel00.htm (A North Central Educational Laboratories Web site about resiliency)

Building Communities of Support for Families—http://www.hec.ohio-state.edu/famlife/

Child and Family Resiliency Research Programme—http://www.quasar.ualberta.ca/ cfrrp/cfrrp.html

Coalition for Healthier Cities and Communities—http://www.healthycommunities.org

Creative Partnerships for Prevention—http://www.cpprev.org/contents.htm

Family Resiliency Iowa—http://extension.iastate.edu/families/Resiliency/

Human Development and Family Life Bulletin—http://www.hec.ohio-state.edu/farnlife/ bulletin/bullmain.htm

iCONNECT—http://web.aces.uiuc.edu/~iconnect/

The Mid Kids: Riding the Waves from Childhood to Adulthood— http://www.agnr.umd.edu/users/nnfr/

National Network for Family Resiliency: Building Family Strengths— http://www.nnfr.org/

Project Resilience—http://projectresilience.com/index.htm

Search Institute—http://www.search-institute.org/

IN CLOSING

We have tried to capture a sense of the passion, dedication, and connections that are required to build resilient communities. Regardless of the size of the community, enhanced resiliency can help it to weather almost any storm. As Mayor Giuliani proved, even a community the size of New York City can be improved.

> In the long run men hit only what they aim at. Therefore they better aim at something high.
> —Henry David Thoreau

As unique as each community is, one belief we hold is that community improvement cannot be just another project. An appropriate analogy might be

> If the fish in a stream were dying, we would not assume that we could solve this problem by pulling the fish out of the stream and allowing them to swim in a clean fish tank for 30 minutes each day, returning them to the original system for the remainder of the day. We would begin a systematic search to find out what was causing the fish to die. Solutions might be a combination of cleaning up the stream, educating the users of the stream, and spending money differently to respond to the problem. If the health of the fish were important to us, we would do what was necessary to restore the health of the stream so the fish could thrive. (Taylor, 1995, p. 1)

Like the fish, if we want community members to thrive we need to link all available resources and recognize that the well-being of every community sector is intimately linked with the well-being of all other sectors of our communities. This calls for the development of sustainable partnerships that provide a clear sense of mutual benefit.

Resources

HANDOUTS

Handout 1: How Resilient Are You?
Handout 2: Internal and Environmental Protective Factors
Handout 3: On Any Given Day
Handout 4: Judgment Test
Handout 5: Judgment Test Answers
Handout 6: Improving Student Resiliency: A Contract
Handout 7: Educator Plateauing Survey
Handout 8: Educator Plateauing Survey Scoring Sheet
Handout 9: Barriers to Educator Resiliency
Handout 10: My School: Does It Deter or Support Resiliency Development?
Handout 11: Examples of a Community With Characteristics of Resiliency
Handout 12: Examples of a Community Needing Resiliency Improvement
Handout 13: Do You Know How Resilient Your Community Is? Score Sheet
Handout 14: School and Community: From Reactive to Proactive Relations
Handout 15: Building Resiliency in Our Community: Now and Tomorrow
Handout 16: The Sense of a Goose

HANDOUT 1

How Resilient Are You?

How resilient are you? Here's a little test to help you get a sense of your own resiliency. Circle the choice that is *most true* or *most typical* of you for each of the following questions:

1. When I have difficulties I am more likely to
    a. confront them by taking the initiative.
    b. avoid them in hopes they will pass.
2. Regarding leisure time,
    a. I enjoy reading, learning, and exploring.
    b. I fill the time by pondering my situation and worrying about my future.
3. When faced with challenges,
    a. I enjoy figuring out how to respond to them.
    b. I let others take the lead.
4. My work and home environments are
    a. supportive and energizing.
    b. stressful and exhausting.
5. I believe that
    a. good things are most likely to happen to me.
    b. bad things are most likely to happen to me.
6. I believe that the best years of my life are
    a. yet to come.
    b. behind me.
7. I
    a. have a sense of purpose about life.
    b. find myself drifting from year to year without goals.
8. I am
    a. proud of my accomplishments and my abilities.
    b. not as capable as I could be when coping with challenging situations.
9. When going through life's inevitable transitions, I
    a. feel at ease with them.
    b. feel unsettled and need time to adjust.
10. I believe that I
    a. must earn whatever I get.
    b. am entitled to rewards that I want.

The more *a* responses you selected, the more likely it is that you exhibit resilient behaviors. These responses indicate that you probably feel good about yourself most of the time. You also probably view challenges that come your way as a part of life and try to respond to them effectively.

If you chose *b* responses more often than you chose *a* responses, you might want to consider making some changes:

- Focus on your attitudes and behaviors. Practice more positive self-talk, especially if you tend to be self-critical.
- Observe and talk with people who you think are highly resilient. See what you can learn from them.
- Read and think about resiliency-related areas such as self-esteem, career development, life stages, and dealing with transitions.
- In whatever ways possible, try to learn about and practice qualities and skills that promote resiliency.

Handout 2

Internal and Environmental Protective Factors

Internal Protective Factors
Characteristics of Individuals That Promote Resiliency

1. Gives of self in service to others or a cause or both
2. Uses life skills, including good decision making, assertiveness, impulse control, and problem solving
3. Is sociable and has ability to be a friend and form positive relationships
4. Has a sense of humor
5. Exhibits internal locus of control (i.e., belief in ability to influence one's environment)
6. Is autonomous, independent
7. Has positive view of personal future
8. Is flexible
9. Has spirituality (i.e., belief in a greater power)
10. Has capacity for connection to learning
11. Is self-motivated
12. Is "good at something," has personal competence
13. Has feelings of self-worth and self-confidence
14. Other:

Environmental Protective Factors
Characteristics of Families, Schools, Communities, and Peer Groups That Promote Resiliency

1. Promotes close bonds
2. Values and encourages education
3. Uses high warmth, low criticism style of interaction
4. Sets and enforces clear boundaries (rules, norms, and laws)
5. Encourages supportive relationships with many caring others
6. Promotes sharing of responsibilities, service to others, "required helpfulness"
7. Provides access to resources for meeting basic needs of housing, employment, health care, and recreation
8. Expresses high and realistic expectations for success
9. Encourages goal setting and mastery
10. Encourages prosocial development of values (such as altruism) and life skills (such as cooperation)
11. Provides leadership and opportunities for meaningful participation and decision making
12. Appreciates the unique talents of each individual
13. Other:

SOURCE: Adapted from Henderson and Milstein (1996).

HANDOUT 3

On Any Given Day

- 1 mother dies in childbirth;
- 4 children are killed by abuse or neglect;
- 5 children or teens commit suicide;
- 8 children or teens are killed by firearms;
- 77 babies die before their first birthdays;
- 177 children are arrested for violent crimes;
- 375 children are arrested for drug abuse;
- 390 babies are born to mothers who received late or no prenatal care;
- 860 babies are born at low birth weight;
- 1,186 babies are born to teen mothers;
- 1,900 public school students are corporally punished;
- 2,076 babies are born without health insurance;
- 2,341 babies are born to mothers who are not high school graduates;
- 2,385 babies are born into poverty;
- 2,482 children are confirmed abused or neglected;
- 2,756 high school students drop out;
- 3,742 babies are born to unmarried mothers;
- 4,262 children are arrested; and
- 16,964 public school students are suspended.

SOURCE: Children's Defense Fund (2005).

According to the Children's Defense Fund's (1990) Report Card, seventeen years ago, the outlook for children was that

- 6 teenagers commit suicide;
- 10 children die from guns;
- 30 children are wounded by guns;
- 211 children are arrested for drug abuse;
- 437 children are arrested for drinking or drunken driving;
- 623 teenagers get syphilis or gonorrhea;
- 1,512 teenagers drop out of school;
- 1,629 children are in adult jails;
- 1,849 children are abused or neglected;
- 2,556 children are born out of wedlock;
- 2,989 children see their parents divorced;
- 3,288 children run away from home;
- 7,742 teens become sexually active; and
- 135,000 children bring a gun to school.

HANDOUT 4

Judgment Test

1. This activity can be done individually, but it is best done with groups. Distribute copies of the case descriptions that follow.

Case A

A girl, age sixteen, was orphaned and willed to custody of her grandmother by her mother, who was separated from an alcoholic husband, now deceased. Her mother rejected the homely child, who had been proven to lie and steal sweets. She swallowed a penny to attract attention. Her father was fond of the child. The child lived in fantasy as the mistress of her father's household for years. The grandmother, who is widowed, cannot manage the girl's four young uncles and aunts in the household. The young uncle drinks and has left home without telling the grandmother his destination. The aunt, emotional over a love affair, locks herself in her room. The grandmother has resolved to be stricter with the granddaughter because she fears she has failed with her own children. She dresses the granddaughter oddly. She refuses to let her have playmates. She puts her in braces to keep her back straight. She was not sent to grade school. An aunt on the paternal side of family is crippled, and an uncle is asthmatic.

Case B

A boy, who is a senior in high school, has obtained a certificate from a physician stating that a nervous breakdown makes it necessary for him to leave school for six months. The boy is not a good all around student, he has no friends, teachers find him to be a problem, he developed speech late, he has poorly adjusted to school, and his father is ashamed of his son's lack of athletic ability. The boy has odd mannerisms, makes up his own religion, and chants hymns to himself—his parents regard him as "different."

Case C

A boy, age six, had a large head at birth. He was thought to have had brain fever (meningitis). His three siblings died before his birth. His mother does not agree with relatives and neighbors that the child is probably abnormal. The child is sent to school, and the teacher diagnoses him as mentally ill. The boy's mother is angry—she withdraws the child from school, saying she will teach him herself.

2. After reading the three cases, group members should discuss their predictions:
   - How will each of these young people function as they grow up?
   - Will they be gifted, average-normal, psychotic, neurotic, delinquent, or mentally deficient?
   - Will they excel or will they lead very difficult lives? Ask members why they have come to these conclusions.

3. Last, look at the additional information about these cases that Handout 5 in the Resource section provides and respond to the question posed there.

SOURCE: Unknown

HANDOUT 5

Judgment Test Answers

The three case studies, in the order presented, summarize the youthful years of three exceptional individuals: Eleanor Roosevelt, Thomas Edison, and Albert Einstein.

What would their lives have been like if, out of the best of intentions, they had been labeled "at risk" and channeled into narrow, limited educational tracks?

What adults say and do when making judgments about youngsters does indeed matter! In fact, too often, much of the coping that youngsters have to do is directly related to adult judgments or lack of support (or both).

HANDOUT 6

Improving Student Resiliency: A Contract

Resiliency Element	Strengths	Areas to Strengthen
Positive Connections		
Clear, Consistent, and Appropriate Boundaries		
Life-Guiding Skills		
Nurture and Support		
Purposes and Expectations		
Meaningful Participation		

Signed by: _____ Student   Date:_____

_____ Parent

_____ Teacher

Meeting Dates: _____

_____

_____

_____

HANDOUT 7

Educator Plateauing Survey

Select the response that best completes each item, using a scale from 1 to 5, with 1 indicating *strongly agree*, 2 indicating *agree*, 3 indicating *undecided*, 4 indicating *disagree*, and 5 indicating *strongly disagree*.

1. _____ The realities of my job come close to matching my initial expectations.
2. _____ I have high professional regard for those in leadership positions in my organization's structure.
3. _____ I feel trapped because I am unable to advance in my organization.
4. _____ My work is satisfying to me.
5. _____ I feel burdened with the many things I am responsible for in my life.
6. _____ I am bored in my current job.
7. _____ I usually start a new day with a sense of enthusiasm.
8. _____ To the extent that I am interested, I have opportunities to advance in my organization.
9. _____ Work is the most important thing in my life.
10. _____ My job is full of repetitive tasks.
11. _____ I feel like I have been passed over when advancement opportunities have occurred in my organization.
12. _____ I can usually find time to engage in leisure activities that I enjoy.
13. _____ I have little interest in advancing within my organization's structure.
14. _____ My life is too predictable.
15. _____ I participate in challenging and meaningful activities in my job.
16. _____ I believe I can achieve my career goals within my organization's structure.
17. _____ I have been in my job too long.
18. _____ I find myself being impatient too often with family and friends.
19. _____ I wish I had more opportunities to advance in my organization so I could do more meaningful work.
20. _____ I know my job too well.
21. _____ I rarely think of my life as boring.
22. _____ Although I would like to advance in my organization, given my abilities, my present position is the highest I can realistically attain in my organization.
23. _____ My job affords me little opportunity to learn new things.
24. _____ I am energized by the challenges and opportunities in my job.
25. _____ I consider myself a risk taker in my approach to life.
26. _____ Advancing further in my organization's structure would require that I give up many of the things I really like about my current position.
27. _____ I feel I perform successfully in my current job.
28. _____ My family and friends get irritated with me for being more involved with work than I am with other aspects of my life.
29. _____ My life is turning out as well as I hoped it would.
30. _____ I relate career success to promotion within my organization's structure.

Copyright © 1993 by Mike Milstein

HANDOUT 8

Educator Plateauing Survey Scoring Sheet

The numbers in categories A, B, and C correspond to the thirty statements in the Plateauing Survey. Transfer your responses to the blanks provided.

Note that those numbers followed by an asterisk (*) are reverse-scoring items. For these items, a score of one should be entered as five, two becomes four, three remains three, four becomes two, and five becomes one. Be sure to reverse these items as noted.

Category A	*Category B*	*Category C*
1. _____	2. _____	5.* _____
4. _____	3.* _____	7. _____
6.* _____	8. _____	9.* _____
10.* _____	11.* _____	12. _____
15. _____	13. _____	14.* _____
17.* _____	16. _____	18.* _____
20.* _____	19.* _____	21. _____
23.* _____	22.* _____	25. _____
24. _____	26. _____	28.* _____
27. _____	30.* _____	29. _____

Category Totals (add each column):

A = _____   Divide by 10 = _____

B = _____   Divide by 10 = _____

C = _____   Divide by 10 = _____

Total = _____   Divide by 30 = _____

Plateau Area:

Content (work has become routine)

Structure (organization does not offer opportunity for growth or promotion)

Life (life is too predictable or not fulfilling)

Overall plateauing

The higher the score is in each category and overall, the higher the level of plateauing is. This survey can be used to assess the need for resiliency building in any of the three plateauing categories or regarding overall plateauing.

Copyright © 1993 by Mike Milstein

HANDOUT 9

Barriers to Educator Resiliency

Positive Connections

Education is a lonely business. We work in isolation.
Performance evaluation is based on individual rather than team efforts.

Clear, Consistent, and Appropriate Boundaries

Rules and norms may be complex, unclear, unstated, nonexistent, or ever changing: for example, expected time to be at work, service expectations, discipline policies, and mandates.
Rules are not applied consistently and equitably.

Life-Guiding Skills

Preservice education is only minimally sufficient and is soon outdated.
The rate of change is rapid (e.g., knowledge development, technology, and societal changes).
Little time is allowed to learn new skills.

Nurture and Support

Little focus is given to regular, meaningful, and supportive feedback.
Little time is available for adults to share and support each other.

Purposes and Expectations

Reward systems do not recognize individual efforts.
The dominant message is to "maintain order and discipline" rather than "take risks" and "make things happen."
Group norms focus on minimal effort and output.

Meaningful Participation

Few career development opportunities exist for professional growth or becoming mentors to others.
Role definitions are narrow.
Little time is available to participate.

HANDOUT 10

My School: Does It Deter or Support Resiliency Development?

1. The six resiliency elements are listed in the following table. If definitions are needed, refer to Chapter 1.

2. To what extent does your school deter or support the development of the six resiliency elements among students, educators, and community members? Use the following five-point scale to record your judgment in each of the columns:

   Supports Resiliency   5   4   3   2   1   Deters Resiliency

3. Think about how the school does overall and record your judgment in the "Overall" column.

4. Add any comments you may want that support your judgments.

Resiliency Elements	Students	Educators	Community	Overall	Comments
Positive Connections					
Clear, Consistent, and Appropriate Boundaries					
Life-Guiding Skills					
Nurture and Support					
Purposes and Expectations					
Meaningful Participation					

HANDOUT 11

Examples of a Community With Characteristics of Resiliency

Increase Positive Connections	*Set Clear, Consistent, and Appropriate Boundaries*	*Teach Life-Guiding Skills*	*Provide Nurture and Support*	*Set and Communicate Purposes and Expectations*	*Provide Meaningful Opportunities to Participate*
Citizens engage in meaningful discourse	Norms for participation and decision making are established	Human services collaborations exist	Widespread collaboration on community projects exist	Community supports positive vision for the future	Many civic clubs exist with broad membership
An infrastructure exists that promotes cooperative efforts	Proactivity and acceptance are practiced	Lifelong learning opportunities are available	Respect for law and order is widespread	Quality of life is a high priority	Volunteerism is encouraged
Celebrations and rituals exist	Participatory governance exists	Intergenerational programs are operating	Intergenerational connections are made	High standards of acceptable behavior are set	Community vision is shared and pursued
Interorganizational activities are common	Emphasis is on community	Preventive programs that are proactive are widespread	Service to others is encouraged	Family and community spirit is prevalent	Leadership training is available and effective
Community symbols are evident	Regular and clear communications exist	Support groups are established		Recognition for efforts and achievements are common	
Meaningful partnerships are nurtured					
Past and current cultures are celebrated					

HANDOUT 12

Examples of a Community Needing Resiliency Improvement

Increase Positive Connections	Set Clear, Consistent, and Appropriate Boundaries	Teach Life-Guiding Skills	Provide Nurture and Support	Set and Communicate Purposes and Expectations	Provide Meaningful Opportunities to Participate
People are isolated	Laws, policies, and rules are applied inconsistently	There is denial of problems	Few community services are available	Status quo orientation is maintained	Apathy is evident
Streets are unsafe	Few opportunities for community input	Poor problem-identifying and problem-solving skills are apparent	There is need for much greater resources than are made available	A sense of hopelessness prevails	The focus is on differences
A culture of fear and discrimination exists	Tension exists among ethnic, racial, and other groups	There is little evidence of cooperation	Absence of partnerships is the rule	Widespread poor self-esteem/self-concept	Minimal infrastructure for citizen input
There is a lack of effective programs	Favoritism is the norm	Ineffective conflict management is common	Individuals feel anonymous	There is little evidence of mutual trust	There is little or no celebration of successes
Little effort to communicate is made	A sense of community is not shared	Teenage pregnancy and other risky behaviors are prevalent	There is an absence of community celebrations	There are few cooperative or cohesive efforts	Few if any community improvement initiatives are undertaken
Lack of trust is common		Bullying exists	Leadership is not visible	There is an absence of community vision	
Factions thrive within community			Leadership lacks vision		

HANDOUT 13

Do You Know How Resilient Your Community Is? (Score Sheet for Exercise 6.1)

Review the two examples of communities needing resiliency and communities with resiliency (Handouts 11 and 12). Think about your community and place an "X" in the column that you think rates its resiliency for each of the six elements. The last column, "Group Score," is a place to record the average scores your group gives each of the six resiliency elements. Please note additional thoughts in the space provided.

Resiliency Elements	(Low) 1	2	3	4	(High) 5	Score Group
Positive Connections						
Clear, Consistent, and Appropriate Boundries						
Life-Guiding Skills						
Nurture and Support						
Purposes and Expectations						
Meaningful Opportunities to Participate						

Comments:

HANDOUT 14:

School and Community: From Reactive to Proactive Relations

	Reactive	*Tolerance*	*Involvement*	*Connectivity*	*Outreach*
Beliefs	• Locked down mentality	• Grudging acceptance of legitimate, but limited, role of parents in school	• Community support for school sought and encouraged	• Active networking to develop community-wide, comprehensive, integrated programs	• Mutual support and partnerships
Expectations	• Minimal involvement of parents (controlled by school staff) • Limited time set aside for engagement	• Limited and formalized engagement in school affairs for parents and possibly others in community	• Parents and others actively involved • Social agencies encouraged to collaborate on youth-related activities	• Extensive open, flexible, and ongoing relationship between community and school	• All community elements represented • Equal access for initiation, involvement, and decision making
Governance structures	• Explicit and detailed policies or rules for parent involvement set by the school	• Advice sought from select group of parents (PTA or PTO) • PTAs or PTOs dominated by educators • School-dominated governance and decision making	• School sets parameters but seeks active involvement with parents and community	• Schools and other agencies focused on youth meet together regularly to set priorities and monitor activities	• Interagency councils • Nonbureaucratic and fluid structures that promote mutual influence
Communications	• Highly limited and one way, from school to parents	• Primarily one way, from school to parents and community	• School-initiated feedback encouraged from parents and community • Invitational and regular to parents and community	• Two way and formalized with youth-related agencies and other organizations	• Multichanneled • Two way • Frequent
Resources	• Minimal resources set aside for relationship purposes • Parents or community resources not pursued	• PTA/PTO fund raising for school priorities • Room Mothers or Fathers with limited roles • Focus limited to students and classroom needs	• Resources for the school identified and solicited	• School facilities made available for community use • Community facilities made available for school use	• School personnel and students engaged as community volunteers
Activities	• School calls on parents when student-related problems arise • Formal and limited parent committees	• Structured and limited parent committees • Principal apprises parents and others of school activities	• Students mentored by community members • Volunteers sought for school programs • Social service agencies function in the school	• Shared use of facilities (e.g., meeting rooms, libraries, and computers) • Summer programs developed cooperatively to meet community needs	• Agreed-upon joint initiatives that focus on community improvement • Service learning

HANDOUT 15

Building Resiliency in Our Community: Now and Tomorrow

	Increase Positive Connections	*Set Clear, Consistent, and Appropriate Boundaries*	*Teach Life-Guiding Skills*	*Provide Nurture and Support*	*Set and Communicate Purposes and Expectations*	*Provide Meaningful Opportunities to Participate*
Community as it currently exists						
Community of the future						

HANDOUT 16

The Sense of a Goose

In the fall when you see geese heading south for the winter flying along in "V" formation, you might be interested in knowing what science has discovered about why they fly that way. It has been learned that as each bird flaps its wings, it creates uplift for the bird immediately following. By flying in a "V" formation, the whole flock adds at least 71% greater flying range than if each bird flew on its own.

(People who share a common direction and sense of community can get where they are going quicker and easier because they are traveling on the thrust of one another.)

Whenever a goose falls out of formation, it suddenly feels the drag and resistance of trying to go it alone, and it quickly gets back into formation to take advantage of the lifting power of the bird immediately in front.

(If we have as much sense as a goose, we will stay in formation with those who are headed the same way we are going.)

When the lead goose gets tired, it rotates back in the wing and another goose flies point.

(It pays to take turns doing hard jobs—with people or with geese flying south.)

The geese honk from behind to encourage those up front to keep up their speed.

(What messages do we give when we honk from behind?)

Last, when a goose gets sick or is wounded by gun shot and falls out, two geese fall out of formation and follow it down to help and protect it. They stay with it until it is either able to fly or until it is dead, and then they launch out on their own or with another formation to catch up with their group.

If we have the sense of a goose, we will stand by each other like that.

References

Anthony, E. J., & Cohler, B. J. (Eds.). (1987). *The invulnerable child.* New York: Guilford Press.

Ashland School District. (1996). Resiliency skills: Building a healthier community. *Reflections, 1*(1), 5.

Ashland School District. (2007). *Ashland school district.* Retrieved April 30, 2007, from http://www.ashland.k12.or.us

Atlanta Journal and Constitution. (2007). Carver High School Model. *Atlanta Journal and Constitution.* Retrieved from http://www.ajc.com 13 May 2007.

Bardwick, J. (1986). *The plateauing trap.* New York: American Management Association.

Benard, B. (1991). *Fostering resiliency in kids.* Portland, OR: Western Regional Center for Drug-Free Schools and Communities, Northwest Educational Laboratory.

Benard, B. (2004). *Resiliency what we have learned.* San Francisco: WestEd.

Bennis, W. (1989). *Why leaders can't lead: The unconscious conspiracy continues.* San Francisco: Jossey-Bass.

Benson, P. L. (1997). *All kids are our kids: What communities must do to raise caring and responsible children and adolescents.* San Francisco: Jossey-Bass.

Benson, P. L., Galbraith, J., & Espeland, P. (1995). *What kids need to succeed.* Minneapolis, MN: Free Spirit.

Berman, P., & McLaughlin, M. (1978). *Federal programs supporting educational change: Vol. 8: Implementing and sustaining innovations.* Santa Monica, CA: RAND.

Bindel, J. (2006, November 21). Absent enemies. *The Guardian,* p 1.

Blum, D. (1998, May/June). Finding strength. *Psychology Today,* pp. 32–38, 66–70, 72–73.

Blum, R. W., & Rinehart, P. M. (1997). *Connections that make a difference in the lives of youth.* Minneapolis: University of Minnesota, Division of General Pediatrics and Adolescent Health.

Broadgreen Intermediate School. (2007). *Broadgreen Intermediate School.* Retrieved March 3, 2007, from http://www.broadgreen.school.nz

Brown, B. L. (1996). *Career resilience* (Digest No. 178). Columbus, OH: ERIC Clearinghouse.

Canfield, J., & Hansen, M. V. (1993). *Chicken soup for the soul.* Deerfield Beach, FL: Health Communications.

Carter, S. (2007, May 5). Mt. Tabor Middle School: Close ties bind kids to success. *The Oregonian.* Retrieved May 12, 2007, from http://www.oregonlive.com

Chandler, M. A. (2006, November 7). A new tack to help high schoolers at risk: College [Electronic version]. *The Washington Post,* p. A4.

Chapman, C. H. (Ed.). (1997). *Becoming a superintendent: Challenges of school district leadership.* Columbus, OH: Merrill/Prentice Hall.

Children's Defense Fund. (1990). *Children 1990: A report card, briefing book, and action primer.* Washington, DC: Author.

Children's Defense Fund. (2005). *The state of America's children.* Washington, DC: Author.

Communities in Schools. (2007). *Communities in Schools.* Retrieved May 12, 2007, from http://www.cischarlotte.org

Covey, S. R. (1989). *The 7 habits of highly effective people.* New York: Simon & Schuster.

Davis, E. (2006, June 13). *Children's Defense Fund gun report reveals 2,827 child and teen deaths by firearms in one year exceed total U.S. combat fatalities during three years in Iraq.* Retrieved May 12, 2007, from http://www.childrensdefense.org/gunrpt_revised06.pdf

Drucker, P. F. (1998). Introduction: Civilizing the city. In F. Hesselbein, M. Goldsmith, R. Beckhard, & R. F. Schubert (Eds.), *The community of the future* (pp. 3–19). San Francisco: Jossey-Bass.

Drury, S. (2006, December 1). Sink or swim. *This American Life.* Retrieved April 10, 2007, from http://www.thislife.org

Elder, G. H., Liker, K., & Cross, C. E. (1984). Parent-child behavior in the great depression: Life course and intergenerational influences. In T. B. Baltes & O.G. Brim, Jr. (Eds.), *Lifespan development and behavior* (Vol. 6, pp. 109–158). New York: Academic Press.

Epstein, J. L., Coates, L., Salinas, K. C., Sanders, M. G., & Simon, B. S. (1997). *School, family, and community partnerships.* Thousand Oaks, CA: Corwin.

Farrington, D. P. (1989). Long-term prediction of offending and other life outcomes. In H. Wegener, F. Loesel, & J. Haisch (Eds.), *Criminal behavior and the justice system* (pp. 26–39). New York: Springer-Verlag.

Fullan, M. (1985). Change process and strategies at the local level. *The Elementary School Journal, 84*(3), 391–420.

Fullan, M. (with S. Stiegelbauer). (1991). *The new meaning of educational change* (2nd ed.). New York: Teachers College Press.

Fullan, M. (1993). *Change forces: Probing the depths of educational reform.* London: Falmer.

Futernick, K. (2007). *A possible dream: retaining California teachers so all students learn.* Sacramento: California State University, Sacramento Centre for Teacher Quality.

Gardner, H. (1983). *Frames of mind: The theory of multiple intelligences.* New York: Basic Books.

Goleman, D. (1995). *Emotional intelligence.* New York: Bantam.

Harshman, C., & Phillips, S. (1996). *Team training.* New York: McGraw-Hill.

Hawkins, J. D., Catalano, R. F., & Miller, J. Y. (1992). Risk and protective factors for alcohol and other drug problems. *Psychological Bulletin, 112*(1), 64–105.

Healthy Families Nampa. (2007). Healthy families, healthy youth in Nampa. Retrieved May 12, 2007, from http://www.healthyfamiliesnampa.org

Henderson, N., & Milstein, M. M. (2002). *Resiliency in schools: Making it happen for students and educators,* (Updated Edition). Thousand Oaks, CA: Corwin Press.

Henry, D. A., & Milstein, M. M. (2004). Promoting resiliency in youth, educators, and communities. In H. C. Waxman, Y. N. Padron, & J. P. Gray (Eds.), *Educational resiliency.* Greenwich, CT: Information Age Publishing. pp. 247–263.

Higgins, G. O. (1994). *Resilient adults: Overcoming a cruel past.* San Francisco: Jossey-Bass.

Higgins, R. (1985). *Psychological resilience and the capacity for intimacy: How the wounded might "love well."* Unpublished doctoral dissertation, Harvard University, Cambridge, MA.

Hord, S. M., Rutherford, W. L., Huling-Austin, L., & Hall, G. E. (1987). *Taking charge of change.* Alexandria, VA: Association for Supervision and Curriculum Development.

Houston, P. D., Blankstein, A. M., & Cole, R. W. (2007). *Out-of-the-box leadership.* Thousand Oaks, CA: Corwin Press.

Hu, W. (2007, May 12). A model middle school. *New York Times,* p. 17. 12 May 2007.

Huberman, M., & Miles, M. (1984). *Innovation up close.* New York: Plenum.

Johnson, D. W., & Johnson, F. P. (1991). *Joining together* (4th ed.). Englewood Cliffs, NJ: Prentice Hall.

Kids keep online threats secret from parents. (2006, December 4). *The Australian.* Retrieved from http://www.theaustralian.news.com.au 4 February 2007.

Kretzmann, J. P., & McKnight, J. L. (1993). *Building communities from the inside out.* Chicago: ACTA.

Krovetz, M. L. (1999). *Fostering resiliency: Expecting all students to use their minds and hearts well.* Thousand Oaks, CA: Corwin Press.

Krueger, R. A. (1994). *Focus groups: A practical guide for applied research* (2nd ed.). Thousand Oaks, CA: SAGE.

Lawson, H., & Briar-Lawson, K. (1997). *Connecting the dots: Progress toward the integration of school reform, school-linked services, parent involvement and community schools.* Oxford, OH: Danforth Foundation and Institute of Educational Renewal at Miami University.

Leffert, N., Benson, P. L., & Roehlkepartain, J. L. (1997). *Starting out right: Developmental assets for children.* San Francisco: Jossey-Bass.

Lelchuk, I. (2007, Mar 17). School's bullies new turf—Internet. *San Francisco Chronicle,* p. A1.

Lickona, T. (1991). *Educating for character.* New York: Bantam.

Lofing, N. (2007, April 5). Chana named model school. *Sacramento Bee.* Retrieved April 28, 2007, from http://www.sacbee.com

Masters, B. A., & Shear, M. D. (1998). *As Suburbia Surges, Violence Tags Along.* The Washington Post. www.washingtonpost.com/wp-srv/local/longterm/library/crime1.htm

Mathews, J. (2007, May 7). Officials' silence puts parents at arm's length. *Washington Post,* p. B01.

McLaughlin, M. W., Irby, M. A., & Langman, J. (1994). *Urban sanctuaries.* San Francisco: Jossey-Bass.

Mehan, H., Hubbard, L., & Villanueva, I. (1994). Forming academic identities: Accommodation without assimilation. *Anthropology and Education Quarterly, 25,* 91–117.

Meier, D. (1995). *The power of their ideas.* Boston: Beacon Press.

Merriam Webster's collegiate dictionary (10th ed.). (1993). Springfield, MA: Merriam-Webster.

Miles, M. (1987, April). *Practical guidelines for school administrators: How to get there.* Paper presented at the Annual Meeting of American Educational Research Association.

Milstein, M. M. (1993). *Restructuring schools: Doing it right.* Newbury Park, CA: Corwin Press.

Milstein, M. M., & Bader, M. (1992). Impact of organizations and communities on educator plateauing. *Journal of Personnel Evaluation in Education, 6*(1), 23–30.

Moles, O. C. (Ed.) (1996 August). *Reaching all families: Creating family-friendly schools*. U. S. Department of Education, Washington, DC.

Mrozowski, J. (2007, February 2). College classes in middle school? *The Detroit News*. 4 Feburary 2007.

Mozes, A. (2007, April 13). Ninety percent of elementary school kids are bullied: Survey. *HealthDay News*. Retrieved April 18, 2007, from http://www.healthday.com

Mycek, S. (1998, October). Heritage of health: Charleston's lessons for the nation. *Trustee*, pp. 8–13.

Napier, R. W., & Gershenfeld, M. K. (1993). *Groups: Theory and experience* (5th ed.). Boston: Houghton Mifflin.

National Commission on Excellence in Education. (1983). *A nation at risk*. Washington, DC: Author.

National Network for Family Resiliency. (1997). *Communities in schools, Charlotte, NC*. Retrieved April 28, 2007, from http://www.exnet.iastate.edu/Pages?communications/Resiliency/cis.html

Nelson Central School. (2007). *Nelson central school Web site*. Retrieved March 6, 2007, from http://www.nelsoncentral.school.nz

New teacher roles. (2007, May 9). *Nelson Mail*, p. 3.

Owens, R. G. (1991). *Organizational behavior in education* (4th ed.). Englewood Cliffs, NJ: Prentice Hall.

Pascale, P. (1990). *Managing the edge*. New York: Touchstone.

Peters, T. J., & Waterman, R. H., Jr. (1982). *In search of excellence*. New York: Warner.

Pipher, M. (1996). *The shelter of each other: Rebuilding our families*. New York: Grosset/Putnam.

Reiss, K. (2007). *Leadership coaching for educators*. Thousand Oaks, CA: Corwin Press.

Richardson, G. E., Neiger, B. L., Jensen, S., & Krumpfer, K. L. (1990). The resiliency model. *Health Education, 21*(6), 33–39.

Robertson High School. (2007). *Great schools*. Retrieved April 28, 2007, from http://www.greatschools.net

Roehlkepartain, E. C., & Benson, P. L. (1996). *Healthy communities-healthy schools*. Minneapolis, MN: Search Institute.

Rutter, M. (1989). Pathways from childhood to adult life. *Journal of Child Psychology and Psychiatry, 30*, 23–51.

Sampson, H. (2007, May 4). Broward schools teachers' merit pay plan tied to teamwork. *Miami Herald*. Retrieved May 5, 2007, from http://www.miamiherald.com

Teacher collaboration key to award-winning schools, educators say. (2007, April 18). *San Diego Union-Tribune*.

Scales, P. C., Benson, P. L., Bartig, K., Streit, K., Moore, K. A., Lippman, L., et al. (2006). *Keeping America's promises to children and youth: A search institute-child trends report on the results of the America's promise national telephone polls of children, teenagers, and parents*. Minneapolis, MN: Search Institute.

Schmuck, R. A., & Runkel, P. J. (1994). *The handbook of organizational development in schools and colleges* (4th ed.). Prospect Heights, IL: Waveland Press.

Schorr, L. B. (1989). *Within our reach: Breaking the cycle of disadvantage.* New York: Anchor.

Schorr, L. B. (1997). *Common purpose: Strengthening families and neighborhoods to rebuild America.* New York: Doubleday.

Senge, P. (1990). *The fifth discipline.* New York: Doubleday.

Senge, P., Cambron-McCabe, N., Lucas, T., Smith, B., Dutton, J., & Kleiner, A. (2000). *Schools that learn.* New York: Doubleday/Currency.

Sergiovanni, T. J. (1990). *Value-added leadership.* San Diego, CA: Harcourt Brace Jovanovich.

Sergiovanni, T. J. (1995). *Leadership for the schoolhouse.* San Francisco, CA: Jossey-Bass.

Siebert, A. (2005). *The resiliency advantage.* San Francisco: Berrett-Koehler Publishers.

Silverstein, S. (1974). *Where the sidewalk ends.* New York: HarperCollins.

Slavin, R. E., & Fashola, O. S. (1998). *Show me the evidence! Proven and promising programs for America's schools.* Thousand Oaks, CA: Corwin Press.

Smith, B. (1943). *A tree grows in Brooklyn.* Pleasantville, NY: Reader's Digest.

Smyth, J., & McInerney, P. (2007). Living on the edge: A case of school reform working for disadvantaged young adolescents. *Teachers College Record, 109*(5), 1123–1170

Starratt, R. J. (1996). *Transforming educational administration: Meaning, community, and excellence.* New York: McGraw-Hill.

Tannenbaum, R., & Schmidt. W. H. (1958, March/April). How to choose a leadership pattern. *Harvard Business Review, 36,* 95–101.

Taylor, M. (1995, June). *Fish in a stream: A metaphor for systemic and systematic school improvement.* Paper presented at the Region E TAC/Region 5 RTAC Title 1 regional Coordinating Council Meeting, Breckenridge, CO.

Tuckman, B. W. (1965). Developmental sequence in small groups. *Psychological Bulletin, 63,* 384–399.

Tucson Resiliency Initiative. (2007). *Tucson resiliency initiative Web site.* Retrieved April 28, 2007, from http://www.tucsonresiliency.org

Tyler, K. (1996). Collaboration: One community's. *Assets Magazine (of Search Institute),* 8–11.

U.S. Department of Education. (2001). *No child left behind act. Public Law 107-110.* Washington, DC.

Warner, C. (1994). *Promoting your school.* Thousand Oaks, CA: Corwin Press.

Warner, C. (with M. Curry). (1997). *Everybody's house—the schoolhouse.* Thousand Oaks, CA: Corwin Press.

Waxman, H. C., Gray, J. P., & Padron, Y. N. (2004). Promoting educational resilience for students at-risk of failure. In H. C. Waxman, Y. N. Padron, & J. P. Gray (Eds.), *Educational resiliency: student, teacher and school perspectives* (pp. 37–62). Charlotte, NC: Information Age Publishing.

Weiner, A., Remer, R., & Remer, P. (1992). Career plateauing: Implications for career development specialists. *Journal of Career Development, 19*(1), 47–48.

Werner, E. E., & Smith, R. S. (1992). *Overcoming the odds: High risk children from birth to adulthood.* New York: Cornell University Press.

Wheatley, M. J., & Kellner-Roger, M. (1998a). The paradox and promise of community. In F. Hesselbein, M. Goldsmith, R. Beckhard, & R. F. Schubert (Eds.), *The community of the future*. San Francisco: Jossey-Bass.

Wheelan, S. A., & Kesselring, J. (2005). Link between faculty group development and elementary student performance on standardized tests. *Journal of Educational Research, 98*(6), 323–330.

Wolin, S. J., & Wolin, S. (1993). *The resilient self: How survivors of troubled families rise above adversity.* New York: Villard.

Yukl, G. (1998). *Leadership in organizations.* Upper Saddle River, NJ: Prentice Hall.

Index

CORWIN PRESS